Church and Sunday School
Hymnal

*A Collection of Hymns and Sacred Songs, appropriate
for Church Services, Sunday Schools, and
General Devotional Exercises*

COMPILED AND PUBLISHED UNDER THE DIRECTION OF A
COMMITTEE APPOINTED BY MENNONITE CONFERENCES

J. D. BRUNK, MUSICAL EDITOR

*" O come, let us sing unto the Lord ; let us make a joyful noise to the Rock of our
Salvation.   Serve the Lord with gladness : come before his presence with singing."*

Mennonite Publishing House

SCOTTDALE   **PENNA**

PREFACE

THE service of song claims a very important place in all our devotional exercises. The Lord has in all ages encouraged His people to rejoice and sing praises to His holy name. In singing the soul gives expression of its devotion to God, and makes known its deep struggles and great needs. The service of song also leads to spiritual development and unity among the believers. Among the pleasures and joys of heaven will be the glorious song service of the redeemed: "'And they sang a new song—saying with a loud voice, Worthy is the Lamb that was slain to receive power and riches and wisdom and strength and honor and glory and blessing." In order to be prepared to join in the songs of the redeemed, our hearts and souls need to be set in tune by the hand that sets in tune every vocal and spiritual chord in all the universe. This is effected by following the divine instruction to "teach and admonish one another in psalms and hymns and spiritual songs, singing with grace in our hearts unto the Lord."

In compiling the "Church and Sunday School Hymnal," the committees have endeavored to select and adopt only such hymns as tend to promote true devotion and a deeper work of grace in the hearts of all who engage in the service of song.

The hymns and songs selected cover a wide range of subject matter suitable for all occasions in religious worship, both in the church and home. All the best old hymns and tunes sung by our sainted fathers and mothers, and which have left their sacred memories and influence upon the present generation, have been retained; many newer hymns of unquestionable worth secured at considerable cost, also a number of valuable new hymns written especially for this work, constitute a collection of hymns and tunes peculiarly adapted to the needs of the various lines of church work.

Great care has been taken in selecting tunes to express the sentiment of the words, and such as are best suited to congregational singing. Care has also been exercised in classifying the hymns under heads appropriate for the various occasions of worship, and any class can be readily found by referring to the topical index.

The committees appointed to arrange and compile the new hymnal now submit to the church the result of their labors. The same is sent out with the fond hope that it will meet with the approval and acceptance of our beloved Brotherhood, and that it may unify our song service, young and old uniting their voices in song and prayer, worshipping the Lord our God "with the spirit and with the understanding also,"— thus bringing us nearer to God, and preparing us all to sing the songs of Moses and the Lamb over Yonder.

C. H. BRUNK
J. D. BRUNK
SAMUEL BRUNK
ELI BRUNK
NOAH BLOSSER
F. B. SHOWALTER
MARTIN A. LAYMAN
GABRIEL D. RHODES
} *Virginia Committee.*

JOHN M. SHENK
M. S. STEINER
N. O. BLOSSER
} *Ohio Committee.*

A. B. KOLB
C. Z. YODER
NOAH STAUFFER
} *Advisory Committee.*

ELI S. HALLMAN
D. D. MILLER
J. S. SHOEMAKER
} *Compiling Committee.*

EDITOR'S NOTES

In submitting the present volume of Church and Sunday School music, we invite you to note in particular, five points.

1st. In the old, old songs which have been sung so often without books, it is easy to see, how it is that we differ as to what is correct for even the same melody. In these cases we have endeavored to get the best setting of the songs, and now trust they may suit those who may wish to use the Hymnal. The harmony in many places has been changed—sometimes because it was poor and sometimes because it was incorrect. I feel that it would so much improve our Church Music if each congregation would adjust itself to, and adopt, the music as now set in Church and Sunday School Hymnal. Some songs are represented at a different pitch from what they were in the older books. This has been done either to suit the voices better, or to give the song a better effect. Leaders should use a tuning fork to start the pieces at the correct pitch, or else practice at home until their judgment is true in this matter. (The safest and best plan is, to quietly use a fork at the time you wish to start a tune. This can be done without any display.)

2d. Not a few of the songs which were formerly written in half-notes, now appear in quarter-notes. This does not mean that they should be sung twice as fast. At this point I wish to *urge very strongly* that every leader should sing just as fast or slow, just as loud or soft, just as joyful or sad as the *words* suggest. Sing to express the words, that they may edify, and not to make a meaningless noise or jingle simply to gratify some inconsistent feeling.

3d. The songs which have a Refrain are not listed in the Metrical Index, nor are any of the songs that are not of a general hymn-tune character. Where hymns appear on a page which has music set to other words, no meter mark has been set to those separate words, for they are in every case of the same meter as the tune above, and are intended to be sung to that tune.

4th. The music which has been written especially for the book has been selected, after written, with the greatest care. It is of course untried. I trust it may receive very careful study and practice. That which proves good—well; if any should be found not good, *discard it.*

5th. We have adapted the tunes to the hymns according to our best judgment and taste. Wherein this mating of hymns and tunes differs from that which leaders are used to, we sincerely trust that all will first use the songs as given in the Hymnal, and then if found that the tune and hymn do not suit together, the leader may make his own selection of tunes. But in selecting other tunes great care should be exercised, that the words may be strengthened and not weakened.

Since singing has such a tendency to fill us with praise and thanksgiving and adoration for our great Father, since others may be brought to the Light by our singing, since God has given us a voice—let us sing for the salvation of sinners, the edifying of saints, and the glory of God.

Church and S. S. Hymnal

1

Coronation C. M.

E. PERRONET

O. HOLDEN

1. All hail the pow'r of Je - sus' name! Let an - gels pros - trate fall;
2. Ye chos - en seed of Is - rael's race, A rem - nant weak and small,
3. Ye Gen - tile sin - ners, ne'er for - get The worm-wood and the gall;
4. Let ev - 'ry kin - dred, ev - 'ry tribe On this ter - res - trial ball,
5. O that, with yon - der sa - cred throng, We at his feet may fall,

Bring forth the roy - al di - a - dem, And crown him Lord of all;
Hail him who saves you by his grace, And crown him Lord of all;
Go, spread your tro - phies at his feet, And crown him Lord of all;
To him all maj - es - ty as - cribe, And crown him Lord of all;
We'll join the ev - er - last - ing song, And crown him Lord of all;

Bring forth the roy - al di - a - dem, And crown him Lord . . of all.
Hail him who saves you by his grace, And crown him Lord . . of all.
Go, spread your tro - phies at his feet, And crown him Lord . . of all.
To him all maj - es - ty as - cribe, And crown him Lord . . of all.
We'll join the ev - er - last - ing song, And crown him Lord . . of all.

2

Baca L. M.

S. Browne

Wm. B. Bradbury

1. Come, gra-cious Spir - it, heaven-ly Dove, With light and com-fort from a-bove; Be thou our guar-dian, thou our guide, O'er ev'ry thought and step pre-side, O'er ev-'ry thought and step pre-side.
2. The light of truth to us dis-play, And make us know and choose thy way; Plant ho-ly fear in ev-'ry heart, That we from God may ne'er de-part, That we from God may ne'er de-part.
3. Lead us to ho-li-ness—the road Which we must take to dwell with God; Lead us to Christ, the liv-ing way; Nor let us from His pas-tures stray, Nor let us from his pas-tures stray.
4. Lead us to God, our fi-nal rest, To be with him for ev-er blest; Lead us to heaven, its bliss to share—Ful-ness of joy for ev-er there, Ful-ness of joy for ev-er there.

3 *" Take heed, therefore, how ye hear."* Luke 8: 18

1 Thy presence, gracious God, afford;
Prepare us to receive thy word;
Now let thy voice engage our ear,
||:And faith be mix'd with what we hear.:||

2 Distracting thoughts and cares remove,
And fix our hearts and hopes above;
With food divine may we be fed,
||:And satisfied with living bread :||

3 To us thy sacred word apply,
With sov'reign pow'r and energy,
And may we in thy faith and fear
||:Reduce to practice what we hear.:||

4 Father, in us thy Son reveal;
Teach us to know and do thy will;
Thy saving pow'r and love display,
||:And guide us to the realms of day.:||

4 *" Gathered together in my name."* Matt. 18: 20

1 With thankful hearts we meet, O Lord,
To sing thy praise and hear thy word,
To seek thy face in earnest prayer,
||:To cast on thee each earthly care.:||

2 Dear Shepherd of thy chosen flock,
Thy people's shield, their shadowing rock,
Once more we meet to hear thy voice,
||:Once more before thee to rejoice.:||

3 Oh, may thy servants, by thy word,
Refresh each wearied heart, dear Lord,
Wearied of earth's vain strife and woe,
||:Wearied of sin and all below.:||

4 Thy presence, Saviour, now we seek,
Confirm the strong, sustain the weak;
Way-worn and tried, we hither come,
||:Give us a foretaste of our home.:||

5 Stephenson L. M. D.

J. S. S.

J. S. Shoemaker

Fine.

1. We now have met to worship thee, And glo-ri-fy thy name, dear Lord;
Help ev-'ry one at-ten-tive be, And heed the teach-ing of thy word.

2. As-sist thy ser-vant to proclaim The gos-pel mes-sage plain and pure,
That all who hear ac-cept the same, And make in thee sal-va-tion sure.

D.C. Help each to say, Lord, we are thine, And all we have to thee we bring.
That when our bod-ies turn to dust, Our souls in heav'n be glo-ri-fied

D.C.

Fill ev-'ry heart with love di-vine, Teach ev-'ry tongue thy praise to sing.
In thee a-lone help us to trust, And in thy love and laws a-bide,

6 Freeport C. M.

J. S. S.

J. S. Shoemaker

1. Fa-ther, we come in Je-sus' name, To wor-ship at this place;
2. We know not how to come a-right, Ex-cept thou be our guide;
3. Give grace to hear and sing thy praise, And grace for thee to live;
4. Mo-ment by mo-ment be thou near, And keep us in thy love;

Do thou with love our hearts in-flame, And give us peace and grace.
Fill thou our hearts with heav'nly light, And with us now a-bide,
Keep us, O Lord, in all thy ways, To us thy spir-it give.
And when our life is end-ed here, Take us to thee a-bove.

7 Solitude C. M.

" Create in me a clean heart." Psalm 51: 10

C. WESLEY

A. J. SHOWALTER

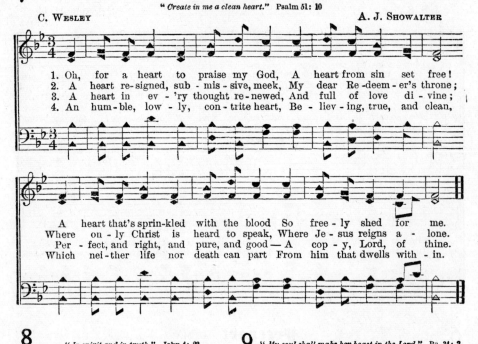

1. Oh, for a heart to praise my God, A heart from sin set free!
2. A heart re-signed, sub-mis-sive, meek, My dear Re-deem-er's throne;
3. A heart in ev-'ry thought re-newed, And full of love di-vine;
4. An hum-ble, low-ly, con-trite heart, Be-liev-ing, true, and clean,

A heart that's sprin-kled with the blood So free-ly shed for me.
Where on-ly Christ is heard to speak, Where Je-sus reigns a-lone.
Per-fect, and right, and pure, and good — A cop-y, Lord, of thine.
Which nei-ther life nor death can part From him that dwells with-in.

8

" In spirit and in truth." John 4: 23

1 Once more we come before our God,
Once more his blessing ask.
Oh, may not duty seem a load,
Nor worship prove a task.

2 Father, thy quickening Spirit send
On us in Jesus' name;
To make our waiting minds attend,
And put our souls in frame.

3 May we receive the word we hear,
Each in an honest heart;
Hoard up the precious treasure there,
And never with it part.

4 To seek thee all our hearts dispose,
To each thy blessings suit;
And let the seed thy servant sows,
Produce abundant fruit.

5 The thirsty bless with heavenly show-
The cold with warmth divine; [ers,
And as the benefit is ours,
Be all the glory thine.
JOSEPH HART

9

" My soul shall make her boast in the Lord." Ps. 34: 2

1 Long as I live I'll bless thy name,
My King, my God, my love;
My work and joy shall be the same
In the bright world above.

2 Great is the Lord; his power unknown;
And let his praise be great;
I'll sing the honors of thy throne,
Thy works of grace repeat.

3 Thy grace shall dwell upon my tongue,
And while my lips rejoice,
The men who hear my sacred song
Shall join their cheerful voice.

4 Fathers to sons, shall teach thy name,
And children learn thy ways;
Ages to come thy truth proclaim,
And nations sound thy praise.

5 The world is governed by thy hand;
The saints are ruled by love;
And thine eternal kingdom stand,
Though rocks, and hills remove.

W. H. CLARK

Arr. by WM. J. KIRKPATRICK

1. All praise to him who reigns a - bove, In ma - jes - ty su - preme,
2. His name a - bove all names shall stand, Ex - alt - ed more and more,
3. Re - deem - er, Sav - iour, Friend of man, Once ru - ined by the fall,
4. His name shall be the Coun - sel - lor, The might - y Prince of Peace,

Who gave his Son for man to die, That he might man re - deem.
At God the Fa - ther's own right hand, Where an - gel hosts a - dore.
Thou hast de - vised sal - va - tion's plan, For thou hast died for all.
Of all earth's king-doms con - quer - or, Whose reign shall nev - er cease.

REFRAIN.

Bless-ed be the name, bless-ed be the name, Blessed be the name of the Lord;

Bless - ed be the name, blessed be the name, Blessed be the name of the Lord.

5 The ransomed hosts to thee shall bring
  Their praise and homage meet;
With rapturous awe adore their King,
And worship at his feet.

6 Then shall we know as we are known,
  And in that world above
Forever sing around the throne
His everlasting love.

Evan C. M.

Arr. by HAVERGAL, 1849

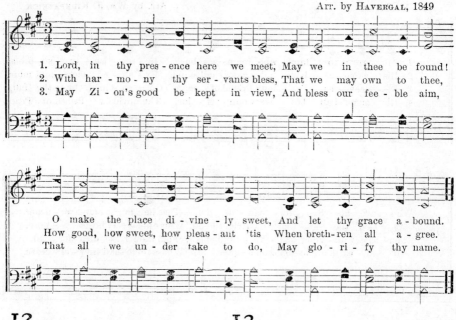

1. Lord, in thy pres-ence here we meet, May we in thee be found!
2. With har-mo-ny thy ser-vants bless, That we may own to thee,
3. May Zi-on's good be kept in view, And bless our fee-ble aim,

O make the place di-vine-ly sweet, And let thy grace a-bound.
How good, how sweet, how pleas-ant 'tis When breth-ren all a-gree.
That all we un-der-take to do, May glo-ri-fy thy name.

12

1 Salvation! oh, the joyful sound,
    What pleasure to our ears!
A sovereign balm for every wound,
    A cordial for our fears.

2 Buried in sorrow and in sin,
    On death's dark way we stray;
But we arise by grace divine,
    To see a heavenly day.

3 Salvation! let the echo fly
    The spacious earth around:
While all the armies of the sky
    Conspire to raise the sound!

4 Salvation! O thou bleeding Lamb,
    To thee the praise belongs;
Salvation shall inspire our hearts,
    And dwell upon our tongues.
                        ISAAC WATTS

13

1 Come, let us join our sacred songs,
    With angels round the throne;
Ten thousand thousand are their
    But all their joys are one [tongues,

2 "Worthy the Lamb that died," they cry,
    "To be exalted thus;"
"Worthy the Lamb," our lips reply,
    "For he was slain for us."

3 Jesus is worthy to receive
    Honor and power divine;
And blessings more than we can give
    Be, Lord, forever thine.

4 Let all that dwell above the sky
    And air and earth and seas
Conspire to raise thy glories high,
    And speak thine endless praise.

14

Nettleton 8s. 7s.

Robert Robinson, 1758

Asahel Nettleton, 1825

FINE

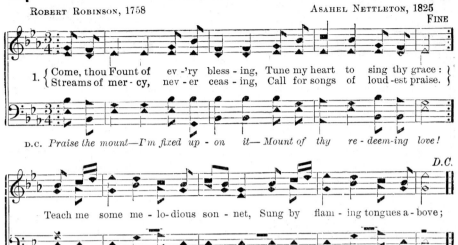

1. { Come, thou Fount of ev-'ry bless-ing, Tune my heart to sing thy grace :
{ Streams of mer-cy, nev-er ceas-ing, Call for songs of loud-est praise.

D.C. *Praise the mount—I'm fixed up - on it— Mount of thy re - deem-ing love!*

D.C.

Teach me some me - lo-dious son - net, Sung by flam - ing tongues a - bove;

2 Here I raise my Ebenezer,
  Hither by thine help I'm come;
And I hope, by thy good pleasure,
  Safely to arrive at home.
Jesus sought me when a stranger,
  Wandering from the fold of God,
He, to rescue me from danger,
  Interposed his precious blood.

3 Oh, to grace how great a debtor
  Daily I'm constrained to be!
Let that grace, now, like a fetter,
  Bind my wandering heart to thee.
Prone to wander, Lord, I feel it;
  Prone to leave the God I love—
Here's my heart, oh, take and seal it,
  Seal it from thy courts above.

15 *"Behold what manner of love."* 1 John 3: 1

1 Love divine, all love excelling,
  Joy of heaven, to earth come down !
Fix in us thy humble dwelling;
  All thy faithful mercies crown.
Jesus, thou art all compassion,
  Pure, unbounded love thou art;
Visit us with thy salvation ;
  Enter every trembling heart.

2 Breathe, oh, breathe thy loving Spirit
  Into every troubled breast !
Let us all in thee inherit,
  Let us find that second rest.
Take away our power of sinning ;
  Alpha and Omega be ;
End of faith, as its beginning,
  Set our hearts at liberty.

Wesley, 1757

16

1 Come, thou everlasting Spirit,
  Bring to every thankful mind
All the Savior's dying merit,
  All his sufferings for mankind.
True recorder of his passion,
  Now the living fire impart,
Now reveal his great salvation,
  Preach his gospel to his heart.

2 Come, thou Witness of his dying,
  Come, Remembrancer divine,
Let us feel thy power applying
  Christ to every soul and mine :
Let us groan thine inward groaning,
  Look on him we pierc'd and griev'd,
All receive the grace atoning,
  All the sprinkled blood receive.

Uxbridge L. M.

L. Mason

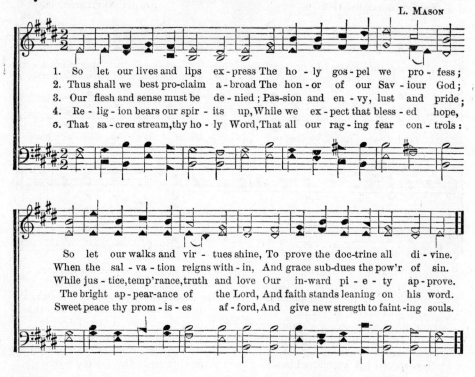

1. So let our lives and lips ex - press The ho - ly gos - pel we pro - fess;
2. Thus shall we best pro - claim a - broad The hon - or of our Sav - iour God;
3. Our flesh and sense must be de - nied; Pas - sion and en - vy, lust and pride,
4. Re - lig - ion bears our spir - its up, While we ex - pect that bless - ed hope,
5. That sa - cred stream, thy ho - ly Word, That all our rag - ing fear con - trols:

So let our walks and vir - tues shine, To prove the doc-trine all di - vine.
When the sal - va - tion reigns with - in, And grace sub-dues the pow'r of sin.
While jus - tice, temp'rance, truth and love Our in-ward pi - e - ty ap - prove.
The bright ap - pear-ance of the Lord, And faith stands leaning on his word.
Sweet peace thy prom - is - es af - ford, And give new strength to faint -ing souls.

18 *"Everything that hath breath praise the Lord."*
Psalm 150 : 6

1 From all that dwell below the skies,
Let the Creator's praise arise;
Let the Redeemer's name be sung
Through every land, by every tongue.

2 Eternal are thy mercies, Lord,
Eternal truth attends thy word;
Thy praise shall sound from shore to
shore,
Till suns shall rise and set no more.

3 Your lofty themes, ye mortals, bring,
In songs of praise divinely sing;
The great salvation loud proclaim,
And shout for joy the Saviour's name.

4 In every land begin the song,
To every land the strains belong;
In cheerful sound all voices raise,
And fill the world with loudest praise.

ISAAC WATTS

19 *"Bless the Lord, O my soul."* Psalm 103: 1

1 Bless, O my soul! the living God;
Call home thy thoughts that rove
abroad:
Let all the powers within me join
In work and worship so divine.

2 Bless, O my soul! the God of grace;
His favors claim thy highest praise;
Why should the wonders he hath
Be lost in silence, and forgot? [wrought

3 'Tis he, my soul, that sent his Son
To die for crimes which thou hast done;
He owns the ransom, and forgives
The hourly follies of our lives.

4 Let every land his power confess;
Let all the earth adore his grace:
My heart and tongue with rapture join
In work and worship so divine.

ISAAC WATTS. ab. 1719

Mrs. Barbauld

Asahel Abbott

1. Praise to God, im - mor - tal praise, For the love that crowns our days;
2. For the bless - ings of the field, For the stores the gar - dens yield,
3. Clouds that drop re - fresh - ing dews; Suns that ge - nial heat dif - fuse;
4. All that Spring with boun-teous hand, Scat - ters o'er the smil - ing land;
5. These, great God, to thee we owe, Source whence all our bless - ings flow;

Bounteous source of ev - 'ry joy, Let thy praise our tongues em - ploy.
For the joy which har - vests bring, Grate - ful prais - es now we sing.
Flocks that whit - en all the plain, Yel - low sheaves of rip - ened grain.
All that lib - 'ral Au - tumn pours From her o - ver - flow - ing stores;
And for these our souls shall raise Grate - ful vows and sol - emn praise.

21 **Ortonville** C. M.

John Newton, 1779

Dr. Thomas Hastings

1. How sweet the name of Je - sus sounds, In a be - liev - er's ear ! It soothes his
2. It makes the wounded spir - it whole, And calms the troubled breast; 'Tis man - na
3. Dear Name ! the rock on which I build, My shield and hid - ing place ; My nev - er -
4. Weak is the ef - fort of my heart, And cold my warm-est tho't; But when I
5. Till then I would thy love pro-claim With ev - 'ry fleet-ing breath; And may the

sor - rows, heals his wounds, And drives a - way his fear, And drives a - way his fear.
to the hun - gry soul, And to the wea - ry rest, And to the wea - ry rest.
fail - ing treas-ury filled With boundless stores of grace, With boundless stores of grace.
see thee as thou art, I'll praise thee as I ought, I'll praise thee as I ought.
mu - sic of thy name Re - fresh my soul in death, Re - fresh my soul in death !

Boylston S. M.

" Christ the great sacrifice." Heb. 7: 27

ISAAC WATTS, 1709

DR. MASON

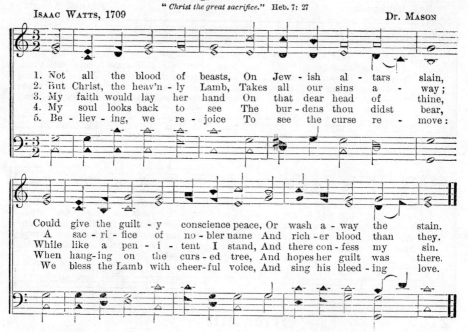

1. Not all the blood of beasts, On Jew-ish al-tars slain,
2. But Christ, the heav'n-ly Lamb, Takes all our sins a-way;
3. My faith would lay her hand On that dear head of thine,
4. My soul looks back to see The bur-dens thou didst bear,
5. Be-liev-ing, we re-joice To see the curse re-move:

Could give the guilt-y conscience peace, Or wash a-way the stain.
A sac-ri-fice of no-bler name And rich-er blood than they.
While like a pen-i-tent I stand, And there con-fess my sin.
When hang-ing on the curs-ed tree, And hopes her guilt was there.
We bless the Lamb with cheer-ful voice, And sing his bleed-ing love.

23 *" Bless the Lord, O my soul, and forget not all his benefits."* Ps. 103: 2

1 Oh, bless the Lord, my soul!
   Let all within me join,
And aid my tongue to bless his name
   Whose favors are divine.

2 Oh, bless the Lord, my soul!
   Nor let his mercies lie
Forgotten in unthankfulness,
   And without praises die.

3 'Tis he forgives thy sins;
   'Tis he relieves thy pain;
'Tis he that heals thy sicknesses,
   And gives thee strength again.

4 He crowns thy life with love,
   When rescued from the grave;
He, that redeemed our souls from death,
   Hath boundless power to save.

5 He fills the poor with good;
   He gives the suff'rers rest;
The Lord hath justice for the proud,
   And mercy for th' oppressed.

6 His wondrous works and ways
   He made by Moses known;
But sent the world his truth and grace
   By his beloved Son.

24 *" Behold, now is the accepted time."* 2 Cor. 6: 2

1 Now is th' accepted time,
   Now is the day of grace;
Now, sinners, come, without delay,
   And seek the Saviour's face.

2 Now is th' accepted time,
   The Saviour calls to-day;
To-morrow it may be too late,
   Then why should you delay?

3 Now is th' accepted time,
   The gospel bids you come;
And every promise in his word
   Declares there yet is room.

4 Now is th' accepted time,
   O sinners! why delay?
Come while the gospel trumpet sounds,
   Come in th' accepted day.

25

Nicholls L. M.

I. Watts

Chas. Edw. Pollock

1. My God, how end-less is thy love! Thy gifts are ev-'ry eve-ning new;
2. Thou spread'st the cur-tains of the night, Great Guardian of my sleep-ing hours;
3. I yield my pow'rs to thy command; To thee I con-se-crate my days;

And morn-ing mer-cies from a-bove Gent-ly dis-til like ear-ly dew.
Thy sov-'reign word re-stores the light, And quick-ens all my drow-sy powers.
Per-pet-ual bless-ings from thine hand De-mand per-pet-ual songs of praise.

26

Ohio 8s. 7s.

1. One there is a-bove all oth-ers, Well de-serves the name of Friend;
2. Which of all our friends, to save us, Could or would have shed his blood?
3. When he liv'd on earth a-bas-ed, Friend of sin-ners was his name;
4. Oh, for grace our hearts to soft-en! Teach us, Lord, at length to love;

His is love be-yond a broth-er's, Cost-ly, free, and knows no end.
But this Sav-iour died to have us Rec-on-ciled in him to God.
Now a-bove all glo-ry rais-ed, He re-joi-ces in the same.
We, a-las! for-get too oft-en, What a Friend we have a-bove.

27 Come, Thou Almighty King 6s. 4s

(ITALIAN HYMN)

CHARLES WESLEY   FELICE GIARDINI, 1769

1. Come, thou al - might-y King, Help us thy name to sing, Help us to praise;
2. Come, thou in - car - nate Word, Gird on thy might - y sword, Our pray'r at-tend;
3. Come, ho - ly Com-fort-er! Thy sa - cred wit - ness bear, In this glad hour;
4. To the great One in Three, The high-est prais - es be, Hence ev - er-more!

Fa-ther! all glo - ri - ous, O'er all vic - to - ri - ous, Come and reign o - ver us, Ancient of Days!
Come, and thy people bless, And give thy word success; Spir-it of ho - li-ness! On us de-scend.
Thou, who almight-y art, Now rule in ev-'ry heart, And ne'er from us depart, Spir-it of pow'r!
His sov'reign ma-jes-ty May we in glo-ry see, And to e - ter-ni-ty Love and a-dore!

28 Loving Kindness L. M.

SAMUEL MEDLEY   Western Melody

1. A -wake, my soul, to joy - ful lays, And sing thy great Redeemer's praise;
2. He saw me ru - ined in the fall, Yet loved me not - withstanding all;
3. Tho' num'rous hosts of might-y foes, Tho' earth and hell my way op-pose,
4. When trouble, like a gloom - y cloud, Has gath-er'd thick, and thunder'd loud,

He just - ly claims a song from me, His lov - ing- kind - ness, oh, how free!
He saved me from my lost es - tate, His lov - ing- kind - ness, oh, how great!
He safe - ly leads my soul a - long, His lov - ing- kind - ness, oh, how strong!
He near my soul has al - ways stood, His lov - ing- kind - ness, oh, how good!

Loving Kindness

Lov - ing - kind - ness, lov - ing - kind - ness, His lov - ing - kind - ness, oh, how free !
Lov - ing - kind - ness, lov - ing - kind - ness, His lov - ing - kind - ness, oh, how great !
Lov - ing - kind - ness, lov - ing - kind - ness, His lov - ing - kind - ness, oh, how strong!
Lov - ing - kind - ness, lov - ing - kind - ness, His lov - ing - kind - ness, oh, how good !

29   Ariel   C. P. M.

Samuel Medley, 1789

Arr. from Mozart, by Dr. L. Mason, 1836

1. Oh, could I speak the match-less worth, Oh, could I sound the glo - ries forth,
2. I'd sing the pre - cious blood he spilt, My ran - som from the dreadful guilt,
3. I'd sing the char - ac - ters he bears, And all the forms of love he wears,
4. Well—the de - light - ful day will come, When my dear Lord will bring me home,

Which in my Sav-iour shine! I'd soar and touch the heav'nly strings, And vie with Gabriel
Of sin, and wrath di - vine: I'd sing his glo-rious righteousness, In which all per-fect
Ex - alt - ed on his throne; In loftiest songs of sweetest praise I would to ev - er -
And I shall see his face ; Then with my Saviour, Brother, Friend, A blest e - ter - ni -

while he sings In tones al - most di - vine, In tones al - most di - vine.
heav'n-ly dress My soul shall ev - er shine, My soul shall ev - er shine.
last - ing days, Make all his glo - ries known, Make all his glo - ries known.
ty I'll spend, Tri - umph - ant in his grace, Tri - umph - ant in his grace.

Holy, Holy, Holy

REGINALD HEBER

J. B. DYKES

1. Ho - ly, ho - ly, ho - ly, Lord, God Al - might - y! Ear - ly in the
2. Ho - ly, ho - ly, ho - ly, all the saints a - dore thee. Cast-ing down their
3. Ho - ly, ho - ly, ho - ly, tho' the darkness hide thee, Tho' the eye of
4. Ho - ly, ho - ly, ho - ly, Lord, God Al - might - y! All thy works shall

morn - ing our song shall rise to thee; Ho - ly, ho - ly, ho - ly,
gold-en crowns a - round the glass - y sea; Cher - u - bim and ser - a - phim
sin - ful man thy glo - ry may not see; On - ly thou art ho - ly!
praise thy name. in earth, and sky, and sea; Ho - ly, ho - ly, ho - ly,

mer - ci - ful and might - y, God in Three Per - sons, bless- ed Trin - i - ty!
fall - ing down be - fore thee, Which wert, and art, and ev - er-more shalt be.
there is none be - side thee, Per - fect in pow - er, in love, in pur - i - ty.
mer - ci - ful and might - y, God in Three Per - sons, bless- ed Trin - i - ty!

31

Gloria Patri

Anon.

Glory be to the Father, and to the Son, And to the Ho - ly Ghost.
As it was in the beginning,
is now, and . . . . . . ev - er shall be, world with - out end. A - men.

Sweet Hour of Prayer L. M. D.

Rev. W. W. Walford

J. H. Hall

With expression.

1. Sweet hour of pray'r, sweet hour of pray'r, That calls me from a world of care,
2. Sweet hour of pray'r, sweet hour of pray'r, Thy wings shall my pe - ti - tion bear
3. Sweet hour of pray'r, sweet hour of pray'r, May I thy con so - la - tion share,

And bids me at my Fa-ther's throne Make all my wants and wish - es known.
To him whose truth and faith-ful - ness En - gage the wait - ing soul to bless.
Till from Mount Pisgah's loft - y height, I view my home and take my flight.

In sea - sons of dis - tress and grief, My soul has of - ten found re - lief,
And since he bids me seek his face, Be - lieve his word, and trust his grace,
This robe of flesh I'll drop, and rise, To seize the ev - er - last - ing prize,

And oft es - caped the temp-ter's snare, By thy re - turn, sweet hour of pray'r.
I'll cast on him my ev - 'ry care, And wait for thee, sweet hour of pray'r.
And shout, while pass-ing thro' the air, Fare-well, fare-well, sweet hour of pray'r

33 Huger 11s.

"Great and precious promise." 2 Pet. 1: 4

GEO. KEITH

ANNIE STEELE

1. How firm a foun-da-tion, ye saints of the Lord, Is laid for your
2. "Fear not, I am with thee, oh, be not dismayed; For I am thy
3. "When thro' the deep wa-ters I call thee to go, The riv-ers of
4. "The soul that on Je-sus hath leaned for re-pose I will not, I

faith in his ex-cel-lent word! What more can he say then to
God, I will still give thee aid; I'll strength-en thee, help thee, and
sor-row shall not o-ver-flow; For I will be with thee thy
will not, de-sert to his foes; That soul, though all hell should en-

you he hath said? Who un-to the Sav-iour for ref-uge have fled.
cause thee to stand, Up-held by my right-eous, om-nip-o-tent hand.
trou-bles to bless, And sanc-ti-fy to thee thy deep-est dis-tress.
deav-or to shake, I'll nev-er—no nev-er—no nev-er for-sake!"

34 God of Love

CHARLES WESLEY
Slow.

GEO. C. HUGG

1. God of love, who hear-est prayer, Kind-ly for thy peo-ple care,
2. Save us, in the pros-p'rous hour, From the flat-t'ring tempt-er's pow'r,
3. Save us from the great and wise, Till they sink in their own eyes,
4. Nev-er let the world break in, Fix a might-y gulf be-tween;
5. Let us still to thee look up, Thee, thy Is-rael's strength and hope,

God of Love

Who on thee a-lone de-pend: Love us, save us to the end.
From his un-sus-pect-ed wiles, From the world's per-ni-cious smiles.
Tame-ly to thy yoke sub-mit, Lay their hon-or at thy feet.
Keep us lit-tle and un-known, Prized and loved by God a-lone.
Noth-ing know, or seek, be-side Je-sus, and him cru-ci-fied.

35 Over the Ocean Wave

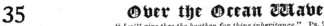

" I will give thee the heathen for thine inheritance." Ps. 2: 8

(MISSIONARY)

JULIA SAMPSON HASKELL

WM. B. BRADBURY, by per.

1. O-ver the o-cean wave, far, far a-way, There the poor
2. Here in this hap-py land we have the light Shin-ing from
3. Then, while the mis-sion ships glad tid-ings bring, List ! as that

REF. Pit-y them, pit-y them, Chris-tians at home, Haste with the

FINE.

hea-then live, wait-ing for day ; Grop-ing in ig-no-rance,
God's own word, free, pure, and bright ; Shall we not send to them
hea-then band joy-ful-ly sing, "O-ver the o-cean wave,

bread of life, has-ten and come.

D. C. Refrain.

dark as the night, No bless-ed Bi-ble to give them the light.
Bi-bles to read, Teach-ers, and preach-ers, and all that they need ?
oh, see them come, Bring-ing the bread of life, guid-ing us home."

Laban S. M.

GEORGE HEATH

DR. LOWELL MASON

1. My soul, be on thy guard; Ten thou-sand foes a-rise;
2. O watch, and fight, and pray; The bat-tle ne'er give o'er;
3. Ne'er think the vic-t'ry won, Nor lay thine ar-mor down;
4. Fight on, my soul, till death Shall bring thee to thy God;

The hosts of sin are press-ing hard To draw thee from the skies.
Re-new it bold-ly ev-'ry day, And help di-vine im-plore.
Thy ar-duous work will not be done, Till thou ob-tain thy crown.
He'll take thee, at thy part-ing breath, To his di-vine a-bode.

37 *" To seek and to save."* Luke 19: 10

1 Assist thy servant, Lord,
  The gospel to proclaim;
Let power and love attend thy word,
  And every breast inflame.

2 Bid unbelief depart;
  With love his soul inflame;
Take full possession of his heart,
  And glorify thy name.

3 May stubborn sinners bend
  To thy divine control;
Constrain the wandering to attend,
  And make the wounded whole.

4 Extend thy conquering arm,
  With banner wide unfurled,
Until thy glorious grace shall charm
  And harmonize the world.

38 *" Watch and pray."* Mark 14: 38

1 A charge to keep I have,
  A God to glorify;
A never-dying soul to save,
  And fit it for the sky.

2 To serve the present age,
  My calling to fulfil,—
Oh, may it all my powers engage
  To do my Master's will.

3 Arm me with jealous care,
  As in thy sight to live;
And oh, thy servant, Lord, prepare
  A strict account to give.

4 Help me to watch and pray,
  And on thyself rely;
Assured if I my trust betray,
  I shall forever die

39 Morrow's Hill C. M.

CHAS. EDW. POLLOCK

1. My God, I know, I feel thee mine, And will not quit my claim,
2. Oh, that in me the sa - cred fire Might now be - gin to glow!
3. Oh, that it now from heav'n might fall, And all my sins con-sume!
4. Re - fin - ing fire, go thro' my heart, Il - lu - mi - nate my soul;

Till all I have is lost in thine, And all re - newed I am.
Burn up the dross of base de - sire, And make the foun-tains flow!
Come, Ho - ly Ghost, for thee I call, Spir - it of burn - ing, come.
Scat - ter thy life through ev - 'ry part, And sanc - ti - fy the whole.

40 Shoemaker C. M.

D. C. PHILLIPS

CHAS. EDW. POLLOCK

1. To thee, O gra - cious Lord, we sing, To thee in faith we pray,
2. We glo - ry in thy bound-less love, We tri - umph by thy grace;
3. This bar - ren wil - der - ness is long, O, be thou with us, Lord,
4. Thy ho - ly love, O spread a - broad In these soiled hearts of ours,
5. When comes the time to fall a - sleep, Thou Morn-ing Star, we pray,

And all our sins to thee we bring; Lord, wash them all a - way.
When shall we come to heav'n a - bove, To see thee face to face?
And by thy Spir - it make us strong, And guide us by thy Word.
That we may con - se - crate to God Our bod - ies and our pow'rs,
Con-duct us safe a - cross the deep In thy own bless - ed way.

Azmon C. M.

Arr. from GLÄSER

1. Fa - ther, I stretch my hands to thee, No oth - er help I know;
2. What did thy on - ly Son en - dure, Be - fore I drew my breath!
3. O Je - sus, could I this be - lieve, I now should feel thy power;
4. Au - thor of faith, to thee I lift My wea - ry, long - ing eyes;

If thou with-draw thy - self from me, Ah, whith- er shall I go?
What pain, what la - bor to se - cure My soul from end - less death!
Now my poor soul thou would'st re-trieve, Nor let me wait one hour.
O may I now re - ceive that gift, My soul with-out it dies.

---

42 *"Order my steps in thy word: and let not any iniquity have dominion over me."* Psalm 119: 133.

1 Give me to know thy will, O God,
　And may I see to-day
A light from heaven upon my road
　To clearly point the way:

2 That I may know just what to do,
　And what to leave undone,
And be unto thy service true
　From dawn to setting sun:

3 That I may speak the timely word,
　And timely silence keep,—
By passion's hasty words unstirr'd
　That cause the soul to weep.

4 Lord Jesus! from thy holy place
　The Spirit on me breathe,
Open the mantle of thy grace
　And keep my soul beneath.

THOS. MACKELLAR, 1880

43 *"They shall talk of thy power"*

1 While thee I seek, protecting Power!
　Be my vain wishes stilled;
And may this consecrated hour
　With better hopes be filled.

2 Thy love the power of tho't bestowed;
　To thee my thoughts would soar;
Thy mercy o'er my life has flown;
　That mercy I adore.

3 In each event of life, how clear
　Thy ruling hand I see!
Each blessing to my soul more dear,
　Because conferred by thee.

4 My lifted eye, without a tear
　The gathering storm shall see;
My steadfast heart shall know no fear;
　That heart will rest on thee.

Miss WILLIAMS

More Like Thee

Frank M. Davis

J. Henry Showalter, by per.

1. More like thee, O Sav-iour, let me be, More like thee from day to day; Nev-er
2. More like thee, O Sav-iour, let me be, Pure with-out, and pure with-in; Keep me
3. More like thee, O Sav-iour, let me be, All my pil-grim jour-ney thro'; Meek and

let me from thy foot-steps stray, Keep me in the nar-row way.
ev-er from the ways of sin, I the crown of life would win.
low-ly, ev-er kind and true, Like thy-self in all I do.

REFRAIN.
More like thee,   More like thee,

More like thee, yes, more like thee, More like thee, yes, more like thee, More like thee, O Christ, like thee;

By thy grace, O let me day by day Grow more and more like thee.

45

I Do Believe C. M

"Lord, remember me." Luke 23: 47

RICHARD BURNHAM

1. Je - sus, thou art the sin - ner's Friend; As such I look to thee;
2. Re - mem - ber thy pure word of grace, Re - mem-ber Cal - va - ry;
3. Thou won-drous Ad - vo - cate with God! I yield my - self to thee;
4. I own I'm guilt - y, own I'm vile, Yet thy sal - va - tion's free;
5. How - e'er for - sak - en or dis-tressed, How - e'er op-pressed I be,

Now in the ful - ness of thy love, O Lord! re - mem - ber me.
Re - mem-ber all thy dy - ing groans, And then re - mem - ber me.
While thou art sit - ting on thy throne, O Lord! re - mem - ber me.
Then in thy all - a - bound-ing grace, O Lord! re - mem - ber me.
How - e'er af - flict - ed here on earth, Do thou re - mem - ber me.

46 *"The Father seeketh such to worship him."* John 4: 23

1 Prayer is the soul's sincere desire,
    Unuttered or expressed;
The motion of a hidden fire
    That trembles in the breast.

2 Prayer is the burden of a sigh,
    The falling of a tear;
The upward glancing of an eye,
    When none but God is near.

3 Prayer is the simplest form of speech
    That infant lips can try;
Prayer, the sublimest strains that reach
    The majesty on high.

4 Prayer is the contrite sinner's voice,
    Returning from his ways,
While angels in their songs rejoice,
    And say, "Behold, he prays!"

5 Prayer is the Christian's vital breath,
    The Christian's native air,
His watchword at the gate of death—
    He enters heaven with prayer.

47

1 There is a name I love to hear;
    I love to sing its worth;
It sounds like music in mine ear,
    The sweetest name on earth.

2 It tells me of a Saviour's love,
    Who died to set me free;
It tells me of his precious blood,
    The sinner's perfect plea.

3 It tells of One whose loving heart
    Can feel my smallest woe:
Who in each sorrow bears a part
    That none can bear below.

4 Jesus! the name I love so well,
    The name I love to hear!
No saint on earth its worth can tell,
    No heart conceive how dear.

5 This name shall shed its fragrance still
    Along this thorny road;
Shall sweetly smooth the rugged hill
    That leads me up to God.

48 More about Jesus

E. E. Hewitt   Jno. R. Sweney

1. More a-bout Je-sus would I know, More of his grace to oth-ers show;
2. More a-bout Je-sus let me learn, More of his ho-ly will dis-cern;
3. More a-bout Je-sus; in his word, Hold-ing commun-ion with my Lord;
4. More a-bout Je-sus; on his throne, Rich-es in glo-ry all his own;

More of his sav-ing ful-ness see, More of his love who died for me.
Spir-it of God, my teach-er be, Show-ing the things of Christ to me.
Hear-ing his voice in ev-'ry line, Mak-ing each faith-ful say-ing mine.
More of his kingdom's sure in-crease; More of his com-ing, Prince of Peace.

Refrain.

More, more a-bout Je-sus, More, more a-bout Je-sus;

More of his sav-ing ful-ness see, More of his love who died for me.

49

Dundee C. M.

" Thy mercy, C Lord, is in the heavens." Psalm 36: 5

Mrs. Price
Slowly.

Guil. Franc, 1545

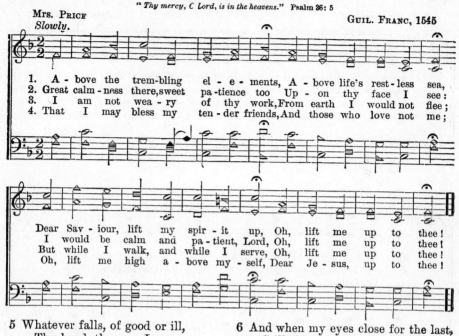

1. A - bove the trem-bling el - e - ments, A - bove life's rest-less sea,
2. Great calm - ness there, sweet pa - tience too Up - on thy face I see:
3. I am not wea - ry of thy work, From earth I would not flee;
4. That I may bless my ten - der friends, And those who love not me;

Dear Sav - iour, lift my spir - it up, Oh, lift me up to thee!
I would be calm and pa - tient, Lord, Oh, lift me up to thee!
But while I walk, and while I serve, Oh, lift me up to thee!
Oh, lift me high a - bove my - self, Dear Je - sus, up to thee!

5 Whatever falls, of good or ill,
 Thy hand, thy care I see,
And while these varied dealings pass,
 Oh, lift me up to thee!

6 And when my eyes close for the last,
 Still this my prayer shall be,—
Dear Saviour, lift my spirit up,
 And lift me up to thee.

50

" Unto him be glory "

1 O for a thousand tongues to sing
 My dear Redeemer's praise,
The glories of my God and King,
 The triumphs of his grace!

2 My gracious Master and my God,
 Assist me to proclaim,
To spread through all the earth abroad
 The honors of thy name.

3 Jesus! the name that calms our fears,
 That bids our sorrows cease—
'Tis music to my ravished ears,
 'Tis life, and health, and peace.

4 He breaks the power of reigning sin,
 He sets the prisoner free;
His blood can make the foulest clean :
 His blood availed for me!

51

1 The Saviour! oh, what endless charms
 Dwell in the blissful sound ?
Its influence every fear disarms,
 And spreads sweet peace around.

2 Here pardon, life, and joys divine,
 In rich effusion flow,
For guilty rebels, lost in sin,
 And doomed to endless woe.

3 Oh, the rich depths of love divine,
 Of bliss, a boundless store!
Dear Saviour, let me call thee mine:
 I cannot wish for more.

4 On thee alone my hope relies,
 Beneath thy cross I fall;
My Lord, my Life, my Sacrifice,
 My Saviour, and my all.

52 At the Golden Gate of Prayer

Mrs. C. L. SHACKLOCK

J. HENRY SHOWALTER. By per.

1. Would you know the love of Je - sus? Would you cast on him your care?
2. Oh! what peace the Sav-iour giv - eth To the souls that seek him there;
3. He will bless you, he will shield you, He will all your bur - dens bear,
4. Oh! the sweet fore - taste of heav - en, That with an - gels we may share,

Seek his help and bless - ed guid -ance, At the gold- en gate of prayer.
How they gain the full as - sur -ance, At the gold- en gate of prayer.
When in trust and hope you gath - er, At the gold- en gate of prayer.
When with God we hold com - mun -ion, At the gold- en gate of prayer.

REFRAIN.

At the gold - en gate, We will come with all our need;
At the gold-en, golden gate of pray'r, We will come with all our need, yes, all our need;

At the gold - en gate, We will come and humbly plead.
At the gold - en, gold -en gate of pray'r,

53 **Purity** 7s.

"We love him, because he first loved us." 1 John 4: 19

1. Sav - iour, teach me day by day Love's sweet les - son to o - bey;
2. With a child - like heart of love, At thy bid - ding may I move,
3. Love in lov - ing finds em - ploy— In o - be - dience all her joy;
4. Thus may I re - joice to show That I feel the love I owe;

Sweet - er les - son can - not be: Lov - ing him who first loved me.
Prompt to serve and fol - low thee— Lov - ing him who first loved me.
Ev - er new that joy will be: Lov - ing him who first loved me.
Sing - ing till thy face I see, Of his love who first loved me.

54 **Stover** 7s.

J. M. Bowman

Very slow.

1. Lord, we come be - fore thee now, At thy feet we hum - bly bow;
2. In thine own ap - point - ed way, Now we seek thee, here we stay;
3. Send some mes - sage from thy word, That may peace and joy af - ford;
4. Grant that all may seek and find Thee a gra - cious God and kind;

Oh ! do not our suit dis - dain, Shall we seek thee, Lord, in vain?
Lord, we know not how to go, Till a bless - ing thou be - stow.
Let thy spir - it now im - part Full sal - va - tion to each heart.
Heal the sick, the cap - tive free, Let us all re - joice in thee.

What a Friend We Have in Jesus

C. C. CONVERSE. By per.*

1. What a friend we have in Je - sus, All our sins and griefs to bear;
2. Have we tri - als and temp - ta - tions? Is there trou - ble a - ny-where?
3. Are we weak and hea - vy la - den, Cum - bered with a load of care?—

What a priv - i - lege to car - ry Ev - 'ry-thing to God in pray'r!
We should nev - er be dis - cour - aged, Take it to the Lord in pray'r!
Pre - cious Sav - iour, still our ref - uge,— Take it to the Lord in pray'r!

Oh, what peace we of - ten for - feit, Oh, what need-less pain we bear,
Can we find a friend so faith - ful, Who will all our sor - rows share?
Do thy friends de -spise, for-sake thee? Take it to the Lord in pray'r;

All be -cause we do not car - ry Ev - 'ry-thing to God in pray'r!
Je - sus knows our ev - 'ry weak - ness, Take it to the Lord in pray'r!
In his arms he'll take and shield thee, Thou wilt find a sol - ace there.

* New copyright, 1892

56

" Blessed are the meek." Matt. 5: 5

1 Let thy grace, Lord, make me lowly,
  Humble all my swelling pride;
Fallen, guilty, and unholy,
  Greatness from mine eyes I'll hide:
I'll forbid my vain aspiring,
  Nor at early honors aim,
No ambitious heights desiring,
  Far above my humble claim.

2 Weaned from earth's delusive pleasures,
  In thy love I'll seek for mine:
Placed in heav'n my nobler treasures,
  Earth I quietly resign:
Thus the transient world despising,
  On the Lord my hopes rely;
Thus my joys from him arising,
  Like himself shall never die.

57 Watchman's Call 11s.

JOSIAH HOPKINS

Slow.

Arr. by J. D. B.

" It is high time to awake." Rom. 13: 11

1. Why sleep ye, my breth-ren? come, let us a - rise; Oh, why should we
2. Oh, how can we slum-ber? the Mas-ter will come; He's call-ing on
3. Oh, how can we slum-ber? our foes are a-wake; To ru-in poor
4. Oh, how can we slum-ber? ye sin-ners, look round, Be-fore the last

slum-ber in sight of the prize? Sal - va-tion is near-er, our
sin-ners to seek them a home; The Spir-it and bride now in
souls ev-'ry ef-fort they make; T'ac-com-plish their ob-ject no
trum-pet your hearts shall con-found; Oh, fly to the Sav-iour! he

day is far spent, Oh, let us be ac-tive, a-wake, and re-pent.
con-cert u-nite, The wea-ry they wel-come, the care-less in-vite.
means are un-tried, The care-less they com-fort, the wake-ful mis-guide.
calls you to-day; While mer-cy is wait-ing, oh, make no de-lay!

58 Italian Hymn 6s. 4s.

CHARLES WESLEY

F. GIARDINI

1. The God of har-vest praise; In loud thanksgiv - ing raise Hand, heart, and voice;
2. The God of har-vest praise; Hearts, hands, and voi - ces raise, With sweet ac-cord;

Italian Hymn

The valleys smile and sing, Forests and mountains ring, The plains their tribute bring, The streams rejoice.
From field to gar-ner throng, Bearing your sheaves along, And in your har-vest song, Praise ye the Lord.

59 I Long to be There

S. J. S.

S. J. SMUCKER

1. I've read of a world of beauty Where there is no gloom-y night, While
2. I've read of its flow-ing river, That bursts from be-neath the throne, And
3. I long for that world of light, To breathe in its balm-y air, To

love is the mainspring of du - ty, And God is the foun-tain of light.
beau-ti - ful trees that ev - er Are found on its banks a - lone.
walk with the Lamb in white, And sing with the an - gels there.

REFRAIN.

I long, I long, I long to be there; I long, I long, I long to be there.

My Faith Looks up to Thee 6s. 4s.

"Looking unto Jesus"

RAY PALMER

Dr. LOWELL MASON

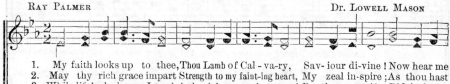

1. My faith looks up to thee, Thou Lamb of Cal-va-ry, Sav-iour di-vine! Now hear me
2. May thy rich grace impart Strength to my faint-ing heart, My zeal in-spire; As thou hast
3. While life's dark maze I tread, And griefs a-round me spread, Be thou my guide; Bid darkness
4. When ends life's transient dream, When death's cold, sullen stream Shall o'er me roll, Blest Sav-iour,

while I pray, Take all my guilt a-way; Oh, let me from this day Be whol-ly thine!
died for me, Oh, may my love to thee Pure, warm, and changeless be, A liv-ing fire!
turn to day, Wipe sorrow's tears a-way, Nor let me ev-er stray, From Thee a-side.
then, in love, Fear and dis-tress remove; Oh, bear me safe a-bove A ransomed soul!

61

Carrington 8s. 7s.

Anon.

CHAS. EDW. POLLOCK

1. Take my heart, O Fa-ther! take it; Make and keep it all thine own·
2. Fa-ther, make me pure and low-ly, Fond of peace and far from strife;
3. Ev-er let thy grace sur-round me, Strengthen me with pow'r di-vine,
4. May the blood of Je-sus heal me, And my sins be all for-giv'n;

Let thy Spir-it melt and break it— This proud heart of sin and stone.
Turn-ing from the paths un-ho-ly Of this vain and sin-ful life.
Till thy cords of love have bound me, Make me to be whol-ly thine.
Ho-ly Spir-it, take and seal me, Guide me in the path to heav'n.

Duane Street L. M. D.

Rev. Geo. Cole

1. Je - sus, from whom all bless-ings flow, Great build-er of thy church be-low;
2. O let them all thy mind ex-press, Stand forth thy cho-sen wit-ness-es;
3. Call them in - to thy won-drous light, Wor-thy to walk with thee in white;

If now thy spir - it move my breast, Hear, and ful - fil thine own re-quest.
Thy power un - to sal - va - tion show, And per - fect ho - li - ness be- low.
Make up thy jew - els, Lord, and show Thy glo - rious spot - less church be-low.

The few that tru - ly call thee Lord, And wait thy sanc - ti - fy - ing word,
In them let all man - kind be - hold How Christians lived in days of old;
From ev - 'ry sin - ful wrin - kle free, Redeemed from all in - i - qui - ty,

And thee their ut - most Sav - iour own,—U - nite and per - fect them in one.
Might - y their en - vious foes to move,—A prov-erb of re - proach and love.
The fel - low - ship of saints make known, And oh, my God, may I be one.

63

1 Be merciful, O God of grace,
  To us thy people; let thy face
  Beam on us that thy church may
    shine
  In this dark world with light divine.
  Reveal, O Lord, thy saving plan,
  To all the families of man;
  Let distant nations hear thy word,
  Let all the nations praise the Lord.

2 Let them with joy thy praises sing,
  Earth's righteous Judge and sovereign
    King;
  Illumined by thy holy word,
  Let all the nations praise the Lord.
  Then shall this barren world assume
  New beauty, and the desert bloom;
  Our God shall richly bless us then,
  And all men praise his name. Amen

64

Gorton 7s.

THOS. McKELLAR   "*My Father, thou art the guide of my youth.*" Jer. 3: 4   C. H. BRUNK

1. Fa - ther! in my life's young morning, May thy word di - rect my way;
2. Fa - ther! gen - tle is thy teach-ing; Be a doc - ile spir - it mine;
3. Fa - ther! let me nev - er cov - et Things of van - i - ty and pride;

Let me heed each gra - cious warn - ing, Lest my feet should go a - stray;
Ev - 'ry day thy grace be - seech-ing, Let thy lov - ing kind - ness shine.
Teach me truth, and may I love it Bet - ter than all else be - side.

Make me will - ing, make me will - ing, All its pre - cepts to o - bey;
Al - ways on me, al - ways on me, And my heart be whol - ly thine.
Bless - ed Bi - ble! bless - ed Bi - ble! May it be my heavenward guide.

Let me heed each gra - cious warn - ing, Lest my feet should go a - stray.
Ev - 'ry day thy grace be - seech-ing, Let thy lov - ing - kind - ness shine.
Teach me truth, and may I love it Bet - ter than all else be - side.

65

" Our Guide unto death "

1 Guide me, O thou great Jehovah,
   Pilgrim through this barren land;
D.S I am weak, but thou art mighty;
   Hold me with thy powerful hand:
   ‖: Bread of heaven! :‖
   Feed me till I want no more.

2 Open thou the crystal fountain,
   Whence the healing streams do flow;
D.S. Let the fiery, cloudy pillar
   Lead me all my journey through:

‖: Strong Deliverer! :‖ [shield.
Be thou still my strength and

3 When I tread the verge of Jordan,
   Bid my anxious fears subside;
D.S. Death of death and hell's de
   struction,
Land me safe on Cannaan's side:
   ‖: Songs of praises :‖
I will ever give to thee.

W. WILLIAMS

66 May the Christ=life Shine in Me

Rev. Johnson Oatman, Jr.

Geo. C. Hugg

With feeling.

1. In this world of sin and care, This shall ev - er be my pray'r:
2. Spot - less, pure, and un - de - filed, As be - com - eth, Lord, thy child,
3. May the pow'rs at my com-mand, Soul and bod - y, heart and hand,
4. May I find that in thy will, I my mis - sion can ful - fil;
5. May it shine in me each day, Till I leave this house of clay;

"Sav - iour, where-so - e'er I be, May the Christ - life shine in me."
Cloth'd in thy hu - mil - i - ty, May the Christ - life shine in me.
Ev - er con - se - cra - ted be, May the Christ - life shine in me.
Glo - ri - fy - ing on - ly thee, May the Christ - life shine in me.
Then thro' all e - ter - ni - ty, May the Christ - life shine in me.

REFRAIN.

Shine in me, yes, shine in me, May the Christ-life shine in me;

Ritard. . . . .

Sav - iour, where-so - e'er I be, May the Christ - life shine in me.

67 Purer in Heart

Mrs. A. L. Davison

J. H. Fillmore

1. Pur - er in heart, O God, Help me to be; May I de-
2. Pur - er in heart, O God, Help me to be; Teach me to
3. Pur - er in heart, O God, Help me to be; That I thy

vote my life Whol - ly to thee. Watch thou my way-ward feet,
do thy will Most lov - ing - ly. Be thou my Friend and Guide,
ho - ly face One day may see. Keep me from se - cret sin,

Guide me with coun - sel sweet; Pur - er in heart, Help me to be.
Let me with thee a - bide, Pur - er in heart, Help me to be.
Reign thou my soul with - in; Pur - er in heart, Help me to be.

By permission

68 I Need Thee Every Hour

Annie S. Hawks

Robert Lowry

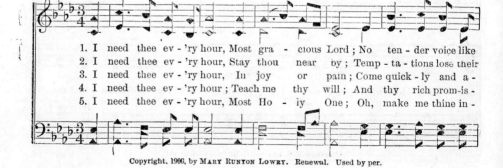

1. I need thee ev - 'ry hour, Most gra - cious Lord; No ten - der voice like
2. I need thee ev - 'ry hour, Stay thou near by; Temp - ta - tions lose their
3. I need thee ev - 'ry hour, In joy or pain; Come quick - ly and a -
4. I need thee ev - 'ry hour; Teach me thy will; And thy rich prom - is -
5. I need thee ev - 'ry hour, Most Ho - ly One; Oh, make me thine in -

I Need Thee Every Hour

REFRAIN

thine Can peace af - ford. I need thee, oh! I need thee; Ev 'ry hour I
pow'r When thou art nigh.
bide, Or life is vain.
es In me ful - fil.
deed, Thou bless - ed Son.

need thee; O bless me now, my Sav - iour! I come to thee.

69 Ever Will I Pray

A. Cummings

J. H. Tenney

1. Fa - ther, in the morn - ing Un - to thee I pray, Let thy lov - ing
2. At the bu - sy noon-tide, Press'd with work and care, Then I'll wait with
3. When the eve-ning shad-ows Chase a - way the light, Fa - ther, then I'll
4. Thus in life's glad morn-ing, In its bright noon - day, In the shad-owy

REFRAIN

kind-ness Keep me thro' this day. I will pray, I will pray,
Je - sus Till he hear my pray'r.
pray thee, Bless thy child to - night.
eve-ning, Ev - er will I pray. I will pray, I will pray.

Ev - er will . . I pray; Morn-ing, noon and evening Un - to thee I'll pray.
Ev - er will I pray; Un - to thee I'll pray.

By permission

70. Abide with Me. 10s.

EMMA G. DIETRICK   CHAS. EDW. POLLOCK, by per.

Slow.

1. A-bide with me, I need thee ev'ry day, To lead me safe thro' all the wea-ry way;
2. Be with me, Lord, where'er my path may lead, Ful-fil thy word, supply my ev-'ry need;
3. A-bide with me, my Lord, and when at last This earth and all its wea-ry cares are past,

When storms surround and on-ly clouds I see, Lord, be my comfort and a-bide with me!
Help me to live each day more close to thee, And oh, dear Lord, I pray, a-bide with me!
I'll pray no more that thou a-bide with me, For then, at last, I shall a-bide with thee!

71. Hide Me

F. J. CROSBY   W. H. DOANE

1. Hide me, O my Sav-iour, hide me In thy ho-ly place; Resting there beneath thy
2. Hide me, when the storm is rag-ing O'er life's troubled sea; Like a dove on o-cean's
3. Hide me, when my heart is breaking With its weight of woe; When in tears I seek the

REFRAIN.

glo-ry, O let me see thy face.   Hide me, hide me,
bil-lows, O let me fly to thee.
com-fort thou canst a-lone be-stow.   Hide me, hide me, safe-ly hide me,

O bless-ed Saviour, hide me; O Sav-iour, keep me Safe-ly, O Lord, with thee.
O my Sav-iour, keep thou me

72 Give Me a Foothold C. M. D.

"And the rock was Christ." 1 Cor. 10: 4

THOS. MACKELLAR   H. S. RUPP

1. Give me a foot-hold on the rock; The bil - lows round me roll;
2. Give me a foot-hold on the rock, O Sav - iour of the lost!
3. Give me a foot-hold on the rock, Till voi - ces 'yond the sea,

Let not their wild im - pet - uous shock O'er-whelm my trem - bling soul.
The world and sin my strug-gles mock, And I am tem - pest - tost.
Like eve - ning chim-ings of the clock, Bid wel - come home to me.

O thou that walk - est on the wave, Thou Rul - er of the sea,
I strive to reach an anchoring place: My God, give me a stay;
The day of toil and watch-ing o'er, The night of sor - row past,

Stretch forth thy might - y arm to save The soul that calls on thee.
Ex - tend to me thy hand of grace, Lest I be cast a - way.
I step up - on th'e - ter - nal shore, And rest in peace at last.

73

Webb 7s. 6s.

G. J. Webb

1. I need thee, precious Je - sus, For I am ver - y poor; A stran-ger and a pil-grim, I have no earth-ly store; I need the love of Je - sus To cheer me on my way, To guide my doubt-ing foot-steps, To be my strength and stay.

2. I need thee, precious Je - sus, I need a friend like thee; A friend to soothe and pit - y, A friend to care for me: I need the heart of Je - sus To feel each anx-ious care, To tell my ev - 'ry tri - al, And all my sor-rows share.

3. I need thee, precious Je - sus, I need thee day by day, To fill me with thy ful-ness, To lead me on my way; I need thy Ho - ly Spir - it To teach me what I am, To show me more of Je - sus, And point me to the Lamb.

74

1 Soon falls the evening twilight,
　　Fast fades the light away,
　And O, thou toiling pilgrim,
　　How didst thou spend thy day?
　Art thou oppressed and weary,
　　And sigh for quiet rest—
　And long to be with Jesus,
　　At home among the blest?

2 Or hast thou vainly struggled
　　To gain the world's applause,
　For honor, fame, or riches,
　　Which Christians count but loss?
　And heeded not, that evening
　　So quickly draweth nigh,
　And that the precious moments
　　Are swiftly passing by?

3 This world is not our mansion,
　　We seek a home more dear—
　The golden, heavenly city,
　　Where we shall know no fear.
　There naught shall mar our pleasures,
　　Nor cause one moment's woe,
　But sweet angelic music
　　In strains unceasing flow.

4 O come then, weary pilgrim,
　　Join in the happy band
　And seek the heavenly Canaan,
　　The glorious Beulah land.
　The evening now approaches,
　　Our labors soon will cease,
　And we shall meet up yonder,
　　And dwell with Christ in peace.

A. Metzler

75 Send Me Light

Horatius Bonar

Geo. C. Hugg

1. Lord, give me light to do thy work, For on - ly, Lord, from thee
2. The way is nar - row, of - ten dark, With lights and shad - ows strewn;
3. Oh, send me light to do thy work! More light, more wis - dom give;
4. The work is thine, not mine, O Lord; It is thy race we run;

Can come the light, by which these eyes The way of life can see.
I wan - der oft, and think it thine, When walk - ing in my own.
Then shall I work thy work in - deed, While on thine earth I live.
Give light! and then shall all I do Be well and tru - ly done.

REFRAIN.

Send me light! send me light! Light a - long the toil-some way!
Send me light! Send me light!

Send me light, dear Lord, that I may la - bor on, Till I rest in e - ter - nal day.

76 Keep Us Close to Thee

G. W. Lyon

J. Henry Showalter

Slow.

1. Sav - iour, keep us close to thee, As we jour - ney day by day,
2. Lead us with thy might - y hand, Help us trust thee more and more;
3. Pain and sick - ness may be - fall, Sin and sor - row o - ver - come,
4. While we toil and suf - fer here, Feed our souls with thy pure love;

Walk - ing near thy bless - ed side, We can nev - er lose the way.
There is nought that we need fear, If thou go - est on be - fore.
But with thee to cheer and bless, We will safe - ly reach our home.
Guide us sweet - ly on and on Till we reach thy throne a - bove.

Fine.

D.S. Ev - 'ry day and ev - 'ry hour, Draw us near - er with thy pow'r.

Refrain.

D.S.

Close to thee, close to thee, Sav - iour, keep us close to thee!
Close to thee, to thee, clos - er, Lord, to thee,

77 Pleading S. M.

C. U. L.

C. U. Link

1. O Lord, to thee I cry, Thou art my rock and trust;
2. O hear my ear - nest cry, Thy fa - vor I en - treat;
3. Oh, bless - ed be the Lord, He heard me when I cried.
4. From him I help ob - tained, And now my voice I raise;

Pleading

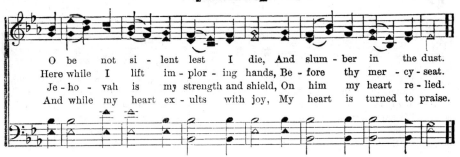

O be not silent lest I die, And slumber in the dust.
Here while I lift imploring hands, Before thy mercy-seat.
Jehovah is my strength and shield, On him my heart relied.
And while my heart exults with joy, My heart is turned to praise.

78 Huntingdon 6s. 4s.

"*Wash me thoroughly from mine iniquity.*" Psalm 51: 2

H. B. Beegle
Wm. Beery

1. Wash me, O Lamb of God, Wash me from sin; By thy atoning blood
2. Wash me, O Lamb of God, Wash me from sin; By faith thy cleansing blood
3. Wash me, O Lamb of God, Wash me from sin; Thou, while I trust in thee

Oh, make me clean; Purge me from ev'ry stain, Let me thine
Now makes me clean. So near thou art to me, So sweet my
Wilt keep me clean; Each day to thee I bring Heart, life, yea,

image gain, In love and mercy reign O'er all within.
rest in thee, O, blessed purity, Saved, saved from sin.
ev'rything; Saved, while to thee I cling, Saved from all sin.

Used by per. Brethren Pub. Co.

79

Watchman 8s. 7s. D.

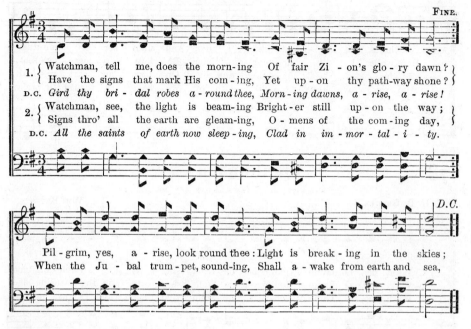

1. { Watchman, tell me, does the morn-ing Of fair Zi-on's glo-ry dawn?
{ Have the signs that mark His com-ing, Yet up-on thy path-way shone? }

D.C. Gird thy bri-dal robes a-round thee, Morn-ing dawns, a-rise, a-rise!

2. { Watchman, see, the light is beam-ing Bright-er still up-on the way;
{ Signs thro' all the earth are gleam-ing, O-mens of the com-ing day, }

D.C. All the saints of earth now sleep-ing, Clad in im-mor-tal-i-ty.

D.C.

Pil-grim, yes, a-rise, look round thee : Light is break-ing in the skies;
When the Ju-bal trum-pet, sound-ing, Shall a-wake from earth and sea,

80

1 Keep me, O my blessed Jesus,
  In the path that I should go ;
Grant that I may keep thy precepts,
  And thy perfect will may know.
Though a weak and mortal creature,
  Fain would I thy help implore,
Knowing 'tis through thee I conquer,
  Thee alone I will adore.

2 Often would I be discouraged,
  When reverses here I meet,
When temptations round me hover,
  When my toils are aught but sweet;
Then on thee my thoughts I center,
  Think of thy unbounded love,
Of thy sufferings to release us,
  Of thy bounteous stores above.

3 Though I never earned the blessing
  He is richly pouring down,
Nay, but rather am deserving
  For my deeds a righteous frown,
Yet on me he looked with pity,
  Offered free to make me whole;
I could do no more than trembling
  Say, Lord, take me, save my soul.

4 And I strengthened feel in weakness,
  When I know that God is nigh,
To prepare a mortal creature
  For a home beyond the sky.
Then my heart bounds with rejoicing,
  And my soul feels strong in thee;
Thus I labor in his service,
  Till I reach eternity.

A. METZLER

F. P. GRIFFITH

A. C. KOLB

Devotional.

1. Shine in my heart, Lord Je-sus, And lead me in-to light, .
2. Shine in my heart, Lord Je-sus, I need thee ev-'ry day, . .
3. In-crease my faith, Lord Je-sus, May thy dear pre-cious blood, . .
4. Come, Ho-ly Spir-it, fill me, Come show me all my need; .
5. And when the king of ter-rors Shall stand a-cross my way, . .

Dis - pel each cloud and shad - ow And chase a - way my night;
To help me keep thy stat - utes To walk the nar - row way;
Of sin com - plete - ly cleanse me And make me pure and good;
With heav'n's re - fresh - ing man - na My hun - gry spir - it feed;
Oh, help me to go for - ward, Re - gard - less of his sway;

Shine on my soul, O Je - sus, And warm me with thy love,
Oh, leave me not, my Sav - iour, Or else I faint, I fall;
In - crease my love O Je - sus, And bind my heart to thee,
And though the way is rug - ged, And though my path is drear,
Thy rod and staff to help me, My safe - ty will in - sure,

Oh, help me when I need thee, Thy faith - ful - ness to prove.
Come in thy might and help me When thou dost hear me call.
So when my days are num - bered Thy smile of love I'll see.
Thy pres - ence will sus - tain me, Give com - fort, hope, and cheer.
And with the Fa - ther's fa - vor I'll rest in love se - cure.

82

I Would Love Thee

8s. 7s

"I would love thee, O Lord, my strength"

Madame Guyon

1. I would love thee, God and Fa-ther! My Re-deem-er, and my King!
2. I would love thee; ev-'ry bless-ing Flows to me from out thy throne;
3. I would love thee; look up-on me, Ev-er guide me with thine eye:
4. I would love thee; I have vowed it; On thy love my heart is set;

I would love thee; for with-out thee Life is but a bit-ter thing.
I would love thee;—he who loves thee Nev-er feels him-self a-lone.
I would love thee; if not nour-ished By thy love, my soul would die.
While I love thee, I will nev-er My Re-deem-er's blood for-get.

83

Hendon

7s.

"The Lord is my Shepherd, I shall not want." Psa. 23: 1

James Merrick   Rev. Dr. Malan

1. To thy pas-tures fair and large, Heav'nly Shep-herd, lead thy charge; And my couch with
2. When I faint with summer's heat, Thou shalt guide my wea-ry feet To the streams, that,
3. Safe the drear-y vale I tread, By the shades of death o'erspread, With thy rod and
4. Constant to my lat-est end, Thou my foot-steps shalt at-tend; Thou shalt bid thy

tend'rest care, Midst the springing grass pre-pare, Midst the springing grass prepare.
still and slow, Thro' the ver-dant mead-ows flow, Thro' the ver-dant meadows flow.
staff sup-plied—This my guard, and that my guide, This my guard, and that my guide.
hallowed dome Yield me an e-ter-nal home. Yield me an e-ter-nal home.

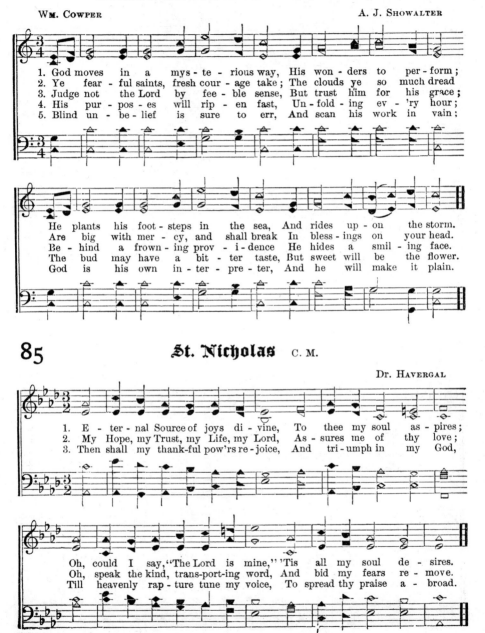

84

Dayton C. M.

O the depth of the riches both of the wisdom and knowledge of God. Rom. 11: 35

WM. COWPER   A. J. SHOWALTER

1. God moves in a mys - te - rious way, His won - ders to per - form;
2. Ye fear - ful saints, fresh cour - age take; The clouds ye so much dread
3. Judge not the Lord by fee - ble sense, But trust him for his grace;
4. His pur - pos - es will rip - en fast, Un - fold - ing ev - 'ry hour;
5. Blind un - be - lief is sure to err, And scan his work in vain;

He plants his foot - steps in the sea, And rides up - on the storm.
Are big with mer - cy, and shall break In bless - ings on your head.
Be - hind a frown - ing prov - i - dence He hides a smil - ing face.
The bud may have a bit - ter taste, But sweet will be the flower.
God is his own in - ter - pre - ter, And he will make it plain.

85

St. Nicholas C. M.

DR. HAVERGAL

1. E - ter - nal Source of joys di - vine, To thee my soul as - pires;
2. My Hope, my Trust, my Life, my Lord, As - sures me of thy love;
3. Then shall my thank-ful pow'rs re - joice, And tri - umph in my God,

Oh, could I say, "The Lord is mine," 'Tis all my soul de - sires.
Oh, speak the kind, trans-port - ing word, And bid my fears re - move.
Till heavenly rap - ture tune my voice, To spread thy praise a - broad.

86 Bethany 6s. 4s.

"*Draw nigh to God.*" James 4: 8

Mrs. Sarah F. Adams

Dr. Lowell Mason

1. Near-er, my God, to thee, Near-er to thee; E'en tho' it be a cross
2. Tho' like a wan-der-er, Day-light all gone, Dark-ness be o-ver me,
3. There let the way ap-pear, Steps up to heav'n; All that thou send-est me
4. Then with my wak-ing tho'ts Bright with thy praise, Out of my sto-ny griefs
5. Or if on joy-ful wing, Cleav-ing the sky, Caught up to meet my King,

FINE.

D.S. *Near-er, my God, to thee,*

D.S.

That rais-eth me; Still all my song shall be, Near-er, my God, to thee,
My rest a stone; Yet in my dreams I'd be, Near-er, my God, to thee,
In mer-cy giv'n; An-gels to beck-on me, Near-er, my God, to thee,
Beth-el I'll raise; So by my woes to be Near-er, my God, to thee,
Swift-ly I fly; Still all my song shall be Near-er, my God, to thee,

Near-er to thee.

87 Abide in Me

C. M. F.

Chas. M. Fillmore

1. A-bide in me, the true and liv-ing vine, A-bide in me, and
2. A-bide in me, each mo-ment day by day, A-bide in me, I'll
3. A-bide in me, my life thro' thee shall flow, A-bide in me, thus
4. A-bide in me, when death at last draws near A-bide in me, its

rest and peace are thine; Trust in my power, to keep thee each hour;
ev-er be thy stay; I will pro-vide, what-ev-er be-tide,
shalt thou live and grow; Much fruit and fair shalt thou rich-ly bear,
ter-rors do not fear; With thee I'll go, my com-fort be-stow,

Abide in Me

In full, con - fid - ing faith A - bide in me.
Cease all fore - bod - ing care, A - bide in me.
If thou un - ceas - ing - ly A - bide in me.
Vic - tor o'er death am I, A - bide in me.

88 Thou Thinkest, Lord, of Me

"The Lord thinkest upon me." Ps. 11: 17

E. D. MUND   E. S. LORENZ

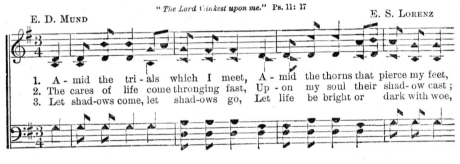

1. A - mid the tri - als which I meet, A - mid the thorns that pierce my feet,
2. The cares of life come thronging fast, Up - on my soul their shad - ow cast;
3. Let shad-ows come, let shad-ows go, Let life be bright or dark with woe,

Fine.

One thought re-mains su - preme-ly sweet, Thou think-est, Lord, of me !
Their gloom re-minds my heart at last, Thou think-est, Lord, of me !
I am con-tent for this I know, Thou think-est, Lord, of me !

D.S. *What need I fear since thou art near, And think - est, Lord, of me !*

REFRAIN.   *D.S.*

Thou think-est, Lord, of me,   Thou think-est, Lord, of me !
of me,   of me!

89 Shining Shore 8s. 7s.

Daniel Nelson, 1835

George F. Root

Slow.

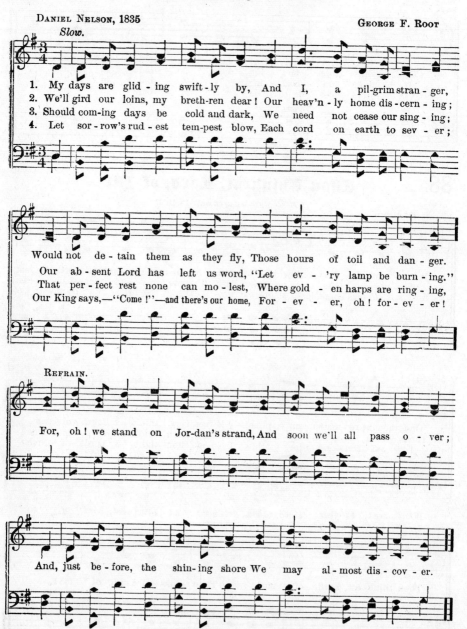

1. My days are glid-ing swift-ly by, And I, a pil-grim stran-ger,
2. We'll gird our loins, my breth-ren dear! Our heav'n-ly home dis-cern-ing;
3. Should com-ing days be cold and dark, We need not cease our sing-ing;
4. Let sor-row's rud-est tem-pest blow, Each cord on earth to sev-er;

Would not de-tain them as they fly, Those hours of toil and dan-ger.
Our ab-sent Lord has left us word, "Let ev-'ry lamp be burn-ing."
That per-fect rest none can mo-lest, Where gold-en harps are ring-ing,
Our King says,—"Come!"—and there's our home, For-ev-er, oh! for-ev-er!

REFRAIN.

For, oh! we stand on Jor-dan's strand, And soon we'll all pass o-ver;

And, just be-fore, the shin-ing shore We may al-most dis-cov-er.

Walk in the Light

J. Henry Showalter, by per.

1. Walk in the light, so shalt thou know The fel - low - ship of love;
2. Walk in the light, and thou shalt find Thy heart made tru - ly his,
3. Walk in the light, thy path shall be Peace - ful, se - rene and bright,

His spir - it on - ly can be - stow, Who reigns in light a - bove.
Who dwells in cloud - less light en-shrin'd, In whom no dark-ness is.
For God by grace shall dwell in thee, And God him - self is light.

Refrain.

Walk . . . in the light, . . . Walk . . . in the light, . . .
Walk in the light, yes, walk in the light, Walk in the light, yes, walk in the light,

Walk . . . in the light, . . The beau - ti - ful light of God.
Walk in the light, yes, walk in the light, The beau - ti - ful light of God.

91 Never Alone

Eben E. Rexford

Arr. by M. L. McPhail

1. How ma - ny times, dis - cour - aged, We sink be - side the way;
2. Oh, soul, hast thou for - got - ten The ten - der word and sweet
3. Take cour - age, way - worn pil - grim! Tho' mists and shad - ows hide

A - bout us all is dark - ness, We hard - ly dare to pray.
Of him who left be - hind him The print of bleed - ing feet?
The face of him thou lov - est, He's ev - er at thy side.

Then, thro' the mists and shad - ows, The sweet - est voice e'er known
"I nev - er will for - sake thee, Oh, child, so wea - ry grown;
Reach out thy hand and find him, And lo, the clouds have flown;

Says, "Child, am I not with thee, Nev - er to leave thee a - lone?"
Re - mem - ber, I have prom - ised Nev - er to leave thee a - lone."
He smiles on thee who prom - ised Nev - er to leave thee a - lone.

REFRAIN

No, nev - er a - lone, ... no, nev - er a - lone! He

Never Alone

prom - ised nev - er to leave me, Nev - er to leave me a - lone.

92 The Lord of Glory C. M.

Isaac Watts

T. B. Mosley

1. The Lord of glo - ry is my light, And my sal - va - tion too;
2. One priv - i - lege my heart de - sires, Oh, grant me an a - bode
3. There shall I of - fer my re - quests, And see thy beau - ty still;

FINE.

God is my strength ; nor will I fear What all my foes can do. . .
A - mong the church - es of thy saints, The tem - ples of my God !
Shall hear thy mes - sa - ges of love, And there in - quire thy will.

D.S. *God has a strong pa - vil - ion, where He makes my soul a - bide.* .

D.S.

REFRAIN.

When trou - bles rise and storms ap - pear, There may his chil - dren hide. .

93 Beneath Thy Shadow Hiding

J. E. Rankin, D.D.

J. H. Tenney

1. Be - neath thy shad - ow hid - ing, I sing my pil - grim song; Brief here is my a - bid - ing, My stay can - not be long; Thus far thy hand hath brought me, And I am far - ing on To where thy word has taught me, My Lord, him - self, is gone.

2. I'm naught, dear Lord, without thee, But fee - ble, falt - 'ring clay; Throw thy strong arms a - bout me, And cheer me on my way. What - ev - er lot be - tide me, This thing I sure - ly know: Sal - va - tion's stream be - side me Shall still un - fail - ing flow.

3. Thou hast my ran - som paid me, The wine-press for me trod, In faith's fair robe ar - rayed me, Now bring me home to God. While thou art there pre - par - ing For my poor soul a place, Thus heav'nward am I far - ing, To see thee face to face.

Refrain.

Be - neath thy shad - ow hid - ing, I sing my pil - grim song; My all to thee con - fid - ing, To whom I all be - long.

94 I am Trusting in my Saviour 8s. 7s.

G. W. LYON

T. B. MOSLEY

1. I am trust-ing in my Sav-iour, With a calm and stead-y light;
2. I am trust-ing in my Sav-iour, Oh, how sad my life would be,
3. I am trust-ing in my Sav-iour, Faith ex-ult-ant mounts a-bove
4. Oh, how sweet to trust my Sav-iour, Know-ing that he is a friend,

Hope is shin-ing on my path-way, Mak-ing all things fair and bright.
But for thy dear pres-ence, Sav-iour, And to know I'm led by thee.
This dark world and all its pas-sions To the realms of end-less love.
Who will cheer me thro' life's jour-ney, And be with me to the end.

REFRAIN.

I am trusting, trusting, trust-ing, . . . I am trusting day by day; . . .
whol-ly trusting, day by day;

I am trust-ing in my Sav-iour, . . . To go with me all the way.
bless-ed Sav-iour,

95 Trusting in Jesus

LAURA E. NEWELL   J. H. HALL

1. Walk - ing, Sav - iour, close to thee, (close to thee,) Trust - ing
2. Light the way our feet should go, (feet should go,) With the
3. Till shall close life's lat - est day, (lat - est day,) Keep us

1. Walk - ing, Sav - iour, Sav - iour, close to thee, Trust - ing
2. Light the way, the way our feet should go, With the
3. Till shall close, shall close life's lat - est day, Keep us

in thy love and grace; (love and grace;) Guide, oh, guide us ten - der -
sun-shine of thy love; (of thy love;) Gild life's path - way here be -
pure, oh, Sav - iour, Friend; (Sav-iour, Friend;) Nev - er, nev - er let us

trust - ing in thy love and grace; Guide, oh, guide us,
bless - ed sun-shine of thy love; Gild, oh, gild life's
pure and good, oh, Sav - iour, Friend; Nev - er, nev - er,

ly, (ten - der - ly,) Till we see thee face to face. (face to face.)
low, (here be - low,) Lead us to thy courts a - bove. (courts a - bove.)
stray, (nev - er stray,) Own and bless us to the end. (to the end.)

ev - er ten - der - ly, Till we see and know thee face to face.
path-way here be - low, Lead us, Sav - iour, to thy courts a - bove.
nev - er let us stray, Own and bless us, keep us to the end.

REFRAIN.

Sav - iour, Sav - iour, Keep us, Saviour, Thine a - lone, (Thine a - lone,)
Keep us thine a - lone, Keep us thine a-lone, Keep us,

Trusting in Jesus

Till the shadows all have flown, (all have flown,) And we meet beside thy throne, (great white throne.)
And we meet

96   Safe with Jesus

EDITH ROBINSON   CHAS. H. GABRIEL

1. Safe with-in the arms of Je - sus, There will I rest;
2. Safe with-in his arms I'll hide me, All thro' the way;
3. Safe with-in the arms of Je - sus Sweet peace is giv'n;

Safe with-in the arms of Je - sus, For he know-eth what is best.
And I know that he will guide me To the land of end - less day.
Bless-ings which on earth He giv - eth, And, at last, a home in heav'n.

REFRAIN.

Safe with-in the arms of Je - sus Till this life is past;

Then with him to dwell for - ev - er In my home at last.

97 I am Trusting in His Word

Mrs. Laura E. Newell   Robert M. Moon

1. I am trust - ing day by day in his word (bless - ed word); Oh, the
2. I'm re - joic - ing in a hope as I roam (as I roam), For I
3. Christ the faint - ing soul with love doth re - store (doth re - store); I will
4. Christ the an - chor of my soul still shall be (ev - er be), Tho' my

sweet-ness of his voice I have heard. Lov - ing - ly the Mas - ter called, "Come to
know each day I'm near - er my home. 'Tis the hand di - vine that's lead - ing me
mag - ni - fy his name and a - dore. Un - to him my heart's de-vo - tion I
barque is mad - ly toss'd on life's sea. O'er the waves I hear his words of com -

me" ("Come to me"), And my heart re - plied, "I'll come, Lord, to thee."
on (safe - ly on), And will guide me till the shad - ows are gone.
bring (glad - ly bring); All se - cured I safe - ly rest 'neath his wing.
mand (his command); E'en the tem - pest doth his voice un - der-stand.

REFRAIN

I am trust - - ing, I am trust - - ing, I am
Trust - ing in his word,   Trust - ing in his word,

trust-ing in my Lord and my King. I am trust - - ing, I am
and my King. I am trust-ing in his word.

I am Trusting in His Word

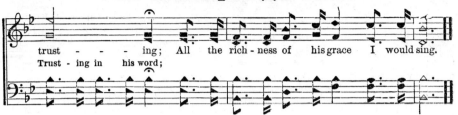

trust - - ing; All the rich-ness of his grace I would sing.

Trust - ing in his word;

98   'Tis so Sweet to Trust in Jesus

Mrs. Louisa M. R. Stead   Wm. J. Kirkpatrick

1. 'Tis so sweet to trust in Je - sus, Just to take him at his word;
2. Oh, how sweet to trust in Je - sus, Just to trust his cleans-ing blood;
3. Yes, 'tis sweet to trust in Je - sus, Just from sin and self to cease;
4. I'm so glad I learn'd to trust thee, Pre - cious Je - sus, Sav-iour, Friend;

Just to rest up-on his prom-ise; Just to know, "Thus saith the Lord."
Just in sim - ple faith to plunge me 'Neath the heal - ing, cleansing flood.
Just from Je - sus sim-ply tak-ing Life, and rest, and joy, and peace.
And I know that thou art with me, Wilt be with me to the end.

Refrain.

Je - sus, Je - sus, how I trust him; How I've prov'd him o'er and o'er.

p

Je - sus, Je - sus, Pre - cious Je - sus! O for grace to trust him more.

Smithville 8s. 7s.

Arr. by CHAUNCEY J. KING

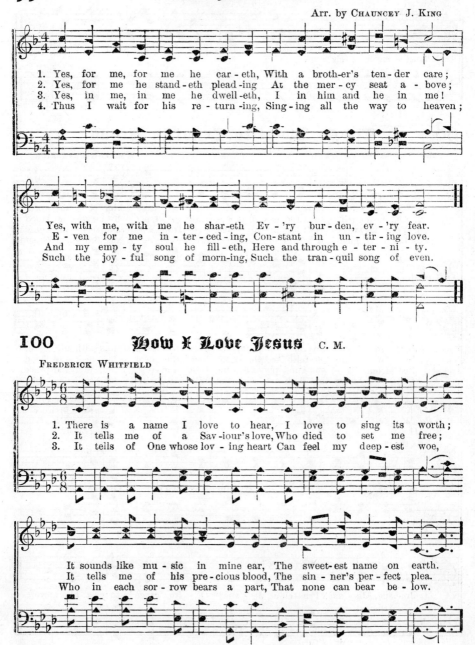

1. Yes, for me, for me he car - eth, With a broth-er's ten - der care;
2. Yes, for me he stand-eth plead-ing At the mer - cy seat a - bove;
3. Yes, in me, in me he dwell-eth, I in him and he in me!
4. Thus I wait for his re - turn-ing, Sing-ing all the way to heaven;

Yes, with me, with me he shar-eth Ev - 'ry bur - den, ev 'ry fear.
E - ven for me in - ter-ced-ing, Con-stant in un - tir-ing love.
And my emp - ty soul he fill-eth, Here and through e - ter - ni - ty.
Such the joy - ful song of morn-ing, Such the tran-quil song of even.

100 How I Love Jesus C. M.

FREDERICK WHITFIELD

1. There is a name I love to hear, I love to sing its worth;
2. It tells me of a Sav-iour's love, Who died to set me free;
3. It tells of One whose lov - ing heart Can feel my deep-est woe,

It sounds like mu-sic in mine ear, The sweet-est name on earth.
It tells me of his pre-cious blood, The sin - ner's per-fect plea.
Who in each sor - row bears a part, That none can bear be - low.

How I Love Jesus

REFRAIN.

Oh, how I love Je-sus! Oh, how I love Je-sus! (*Omit* . . . .)
Oh, how I love Je-sus! (*Omit* . . . . . .) Because he first loved me.

101   Trust in Jesus

" Let him trust in the name of the Lord." Isa. 50: 10

C. L. M.   C. L. MOORE

1. Oh, a - ny-where my Sav - iour leads, I'll put my trust in Je - sus; He
2. Tho' friends for-sake me here be - low, I'll put my trust in Je - sus; His
3. My way seems clear, I need not fear, I'll put my trust in Je - sus; For
4. O Je - sus, save me in thy love, I'll put my trust in Je - sus; At

will sup - ply my ev - 'ry need, I'll put my trust in Je - sus.
lov - ing grace he will be - stow, I'll put my trust in Je - sus.
he's a lov - ing friend so dear, I'll put my trust in Je - sus.
last I'll rest with him a - bove, I'll put my trust in Je - sus.

REFRAIN.

Trust him,   Trust him,

Trust him, trust him, yes, we'll trust him, Ev - er trust in Je - sus; His

prom - is - es He'll ev - er keep, I'll put my trust in Je - sus.

By per. the RUEBUSH KIEFFER Co., owners of copyright.

Only Trust Him

" Take my yoke upon you, and learn of me: and ye shall find rest unto your souls." Matt. 11: 29

Rev. J. H. S.

Rev. J. H. STOCKTON, by per.

1. Come, ev - 'ry soul by sin op-pressed, There's mer - cy with the Lord;
2. For Je - sus shed his pre - cious blood, Rich bless - ings to be - stow;
3. Yes, Je - sus is the Truth, the Way, That leads you in - to rest;
4. Come, then, and join this ho - ly band, And on to glo - ry go,

And he will sure - ly give you rest By trust - ing in his word.
Plunge now in - to the crim - son flood That wash - es white as snow.
Be - lieve in him with - out de - lay, And you are ful - ly blest.
To dwell in that ce - les - tial land, Where joys im - mor - tal flow.

REFRAIN.

On - ly trust him, on - ly trust him, On - ly trust him now;

He will save you, He will save you, He will save you now.

Used by per. of JOHN J. HOOD, owner

103 **I'll Live for Him**

R. E. HUDSON   C. R. DUNBAR

1. My life, my love I give to thee, Thou Lamb of God, who died for me;
2. I now be-lieve thou dost re-ceive, For thou hast died that I might live;
3. Oh, thou, who died on Cal-va-ry To save my soul and make me free,

REF. I'll live for him who died for me, How hap-py then my life shall be!

D.C. Refrain.

Oh, may I ev-er faith-ful be, My Sav-iour and my God!
And now hence-forth I'll trust in thee, My Sav-iour and my God!
I'll con-se-crate my life to thee, My Sav-iour and my God!

I'll live for him who died for me, My Sav-iour and my God!

Copyright, 1882, by R. E. Hudson. By per.

104 **Rittman** L. M.

S. J. S.   S. J. SMUCKER

1. O Lord, thy heav'n-ly grace im-part, And fix my frail, in-con-stant heart;
2. What-e'er pur-suits my time em-ploy, One tho't shall fill my soul with joy;
3. Thy glo-rious eye per-vad-eth space; Thy pres-ence, Lord, fills ev-'ry place;

Hence-forth my chief de-sire shall be, To ded-i-cate my-self to thee.
That si-lent, se-cret tho't shall be, That all my tho'ts are fixed on thee.
And wher-so-e'er my lot may be, Still shall my spir-it rest with thee.

105 Consecration

MARY BROWN

CARRIE E. ROUNSEFELL

Andante.

1. It may not be on the mountain's height, Or o - ver the storm - y sea; ..
2. Per-haps to - day there are lov - ing words Which Je - sus would have me speak —
3. There's sure - ly somewhere a low - ly place, In earth's har-vest fields so wide —

It may not be at the bat - tle's front My Lord will have need of me;
There may be now in the paths of sin Some wan - d'rer whom I should seek.
Where I may la - bor thro' life's short day For Je - sus the cru - ci - fied.

But if by a still small voice he calls To paths that I do not know,
O Sav - iour, if thou wilt be my guide, Tho' dark and rug - ged the way,
So trust - ing my all to thy ten - der care, And know - ing thou lov - est me,

I'll an - swer, dear Lord, with my hand in thine, I'll go where you want me to go.
My voice. shall ech - o thy mes - sage sweet, I'll say what you want me to say.
I'll do .. thy will with a heart sin - cere, I'll be what you want me to be.

REFRAIN.

I'll go where you want me to go, dear Lord, O - ver mountain, or plain, or sea;

Consecration

I'll say what you want me to say, dear Lord, I'll be what you want me to be...

106 Use Me, Saviour

Fred. Woodrow

Chas. H. Gabriel

1. Use me, O my gra - cious Sav - iour, Use me, Lord, as pleas - eth thee;
2. Be it noon or be it mid - night, Wea - ry watch or blaze of day,
3. Pride of will and lust of sta - tion, Lord, I would from all be free.

Noth - ing done for thee so low - ly But is great e - nough for me.
Shout - ing with the hap - py reap - ers, Toil - ing in the hid - den way.
And the on - ly hon - or seek - ing, Lord, to be of use to thee.

Refrain.

Use me, Use me,

Use me, O my Sav - iour, Use me, O my Sav - iour, Use me as it pleas - eth thee;

Use me, Use me,

Use me, O my Sav - iour, Use me, O my Sav - iour, Use me as it pleas - eth thee.

107 Sitting at the Feet of Jesus

8s. 7s. D.

J. H

Arr.

1. { Sit - ting at the feet of Je - sus, Oh, what words I hear him say!
   { Hap - py place! so near, so pre - cious! May it find me there each (*Omit.*) day.

2. { Sit - ting at the feet of Je - sus, Where can mor-tal be more blest?
   { There I lay my sins and sor - rows, And, when weary, find sweet (*Omit.*) rest.

3. { Bless me, O my Sav-iour, bless me, As I sit low at thy feet;
   { Oh, look down in love up - on me, Let me see thy face so (*Omit.*) sweet.

{ Sit - ing at the feet of Je - sus, I would look up - on the past:
{ For his love has been so gra - cious, It has won my heart at (*Omit.*) last.
{ Sit - ing at the feet of Je - sus, There I love to weep and pray,
{ While I from his ful - ness gath - er Grace and com-fort ev - 'ry (*Omit.*) day.
{ Give me, Lord, the mind of Je - sus, Make me ho - ly as he is;
{ May I prove I've been with Je - sus, Who is all my right-eous (*Omit.*) ness.

108 All for Jesus

8s. 7s. D.

Mary D. James

A. D. Lough

1. { All for Je - sus! All for Je - sus! All my be - ing's ransomed pow'rs,
   { All my tho'ts, and words, and do - ings, (*Omit.* . . . .)
   D.C. *All for Je - sus! All for Je - sus!* (*Omit.* . . . .)

2. { Let my hands per - form his bid - ding, Let my feet run in his ways,
   { Let my eyes see Je - sus on - ly, (*Omit.* . . . .)
   D.C. *All for Je - sus! All for Je - sus!* (*Omit.* . . . .)

2. Fine.

D.C.

All my days, and all my hours. All for Je-sus! all for Jesus! All my days, and all my hours.
All my days, and all my hours.
Let my lips speak forth his praise. All for Je-sus! all for Jesus! Let my lips speak forth his praise.
Let my lips speak forth his praise.

All for Jesus

3 Since my eyes were fixed on Jesus,
I've lost sight of all besides,
So enchained my spirit's vision,
Looking at the crucified;
‖:All for Jesus! all for Jesus!
Looking at the crucified.:‖

4 Oh, what wonder! how amazing!
Jesus, glorious King of kings,
Deigns to call me his beloved,
Lets me rest beneath his wings;
‖:All for Jesus! all for Jesus!
Resting now beneath his wings:‖

109 A Full Surrender

Rev. Johnson Oatman, Jr.　　　　　　　　　　　　Geo. C. Hugg

1. A full sur-ren-der I have made, I've giv-en all to Je-sus;
2. My hands, my feet, my head, my heart, I've giv-en all to Je-sus;
3. My loss or gain, my hopes and fears, I've giv-en all to Je-sus;
4. My mon-ey, la-bors, bur-dens, cares, I've giv-en all to Je-sus;
5. My life, my love, my fam-i-ly, I've giv-en all to Je-sus;

My all is on the al-tar laid, I've giv-en all to Je-sus.
I've not re-tained a sin-gle part, I've giv-en all to Je-sus.
My health and strength, my grief and tears, I've giv-en all to Je-sus.
My voice, my pen, my songs, my prayers, I've giv-en all to Je-sus.
For time, and for e-ter-ni-ty, I've giv-en all to Je-sus.

REFRAIN.

I've sur-ren-dered all, surrendered all, I've sur-ren-dered all; surrendered all;

Ev-'ry-thing is on the al-tar, I've sur-ren-dered all. . . . . sur-ren-dered all.

Christ is All

" Unto you therefore which believe he is precious." Pet. 11: 7

W. A. WILLIAMS, by per.

1. I en - tered once a home of care, For age and pen - u - ry were
2. I stood be - side a dy - ing bed, Where lay a child with ach - ing
3. I saw the mar - tyr at the stake, The flames could not his cour - age
4. I saw the gos - pel her - ald go To Af - ric's sand and Greenland's
5. I dreamed that hoar - ry time had fled, And earth and sea gave up their
6. Then come to Christ, oh ! come to - day, The Fa - ther, Son, and Spir - it

there, Yet peace and joy with - al ; I asked the lone - ly moth - er
head, Wait - ing for Je - sus' call ; I marked his smile, 'twas sweet as
shake, Nor death his soul ap - pall ; I asked him whence his strength was
snow, To save from Sa - tan's thrall ; Nor home nor life he count - ed
dead, A fire dis - solved this ball ; I saw the church - es ran - som'd
say ; The Bride re - peats the call ; For he will cleanse your guilt - y

whence Her help - less wid - ow-hood's de - fense : She said, "Oh, Christ is all."
May, And as his spir - it passed a - way, He whispered, "Christ is all."
giv'n, He look'd tri-umph - ant - ly to heav'n, And an-swered, "Christ is all."
dear, Midst wants and per - ils owned no fear ; He felt that "Christ is all."
throng, I heard the bur - den of their song, 'Twas " Christ is all in all."
stains, His love will sooth your wea - ry pains, For "Christ is all in all."

Christ is all, all in all, She said, " Oh, Christ is all."
Christ is all, all in all, He whis - pered, "Christ is all."
Christ is all, all in all, And an - swered, "Christ is all."
Christ is all, all in all, He felt that "Christ is all."
Christ is all, all in all, 'Twas "Christ is all in all."
Christ is all, all in all, For "Christ is all in all."

111 Take Time to be Holy

"Be ye holy: for I am the Lord your God." Lev. 20: 7

W. D. LONGSTAFF

GEO. C. STEBBINS

1. Take time to be ho - ly, Speak oft with thy Lord;
2. Take time to be ho - ly, The world rush - es on;
3. Take time to be ho - ly, Let him be thy Guide,
4. Take time to be ho - ly, Be calm in thy soul;

A - bide in him al - ways, And feed on his word;
Spend much time in se - cret With Je - sus a - lone;
And run not be - fore him, What - ev - er be - tide;
Each thought and each mo - tive Be - neath his con - trol;

Make friends of God's chil - dren, Help those who are weak,
By look - ing to Je - sus, Like him thou shalt be ;
In joy or in sor - row, Still fol - low thy Lord,
Thus led by his spir - it To foun - tains of love,

For - get - ing in noth - ing His bless - ing to seek.
Thy friends in thy con - duct His like - ness shall see.
And, look - ing to Je - sus, Still trust in his Word.
Thou soon shalt be fit - ted For ser - vice a - bove.

112   **Disciple**   8s. 7s. D.

Rev. H. F. LYTE   MOZART

1. Je - sus, I my cross have tak - en, All to leave and fol - low thee;
2. Let the world de - spise and leave me, They have left my Sav - iour too;
3. Man may trou - ble and dis - tress me, 'Twill but drive me to thy breast;

Na - ked, poor, de - spised, for - sak - en, Thou, from hence, my all shalt be.
D.S. *Yet, how rich is my con - di - tion! God and heav'n are still my own.*
Hu - man hearts and looks de - ceive me; Thou art not like them un - true.
D.S. *Foes may hate and friends may shun me, Show thy face and all is bright.*
Life with tri - als hard may press me, Heav'n will bring me sweet - er rest.
D.S. *Oh, 'twere not in joy to charm me, Were that joy un - mix'd with thee.*

                                                                      D.S.

Per - ish ev - 'ry fond am - bi - tion, All I've sought, or hop'd, or known;
And while thou shalt smile up - on me, God of wis - dom, love, and might,
Oh, 'tis not in grief to harm me, While thy love is left to me;

113   **Maitland**   C. M.

" Bear the cross after Jesus." Luke 23: 26

                                                      G. N. ALLEN

1. Must Je - sus bear the cross a - lone, And all the world go free?
2. Dis - owned on earth, 'mid griefs and cares, He led his toil - some way;
3. The con - se - crat - ed cross I'll bear, Till from the cross set free,

Maitland

No: there's a cross for ev-'ry-one, And there's a cross for me. .
But now in heaven a crown he wears, And reigns in end-less day. .
And then go home, my crown to wear, For there's a crown for me. .

114 Lead Me On

J. H. LESLIE.   CHAS. EDW. POLLOCK. By per.

1. Lead me safe-ly on by the nar-row way From the shores of time to the realms of day;
2. With a Shepherd's care thro' the night and day, Keep me close to thee lest I go a-stray;
3. Thro' the storms of life, 'mid the ocean's foam, Lead me safe-ly on to my heav'n-ly home;

By the cross of Christ may I ev-er stand, As I jour-ney on to the bet-ter land.
Lead me safe-ly on by thy ten-der love, Thro' this world of sin to my home a-bove.
At the fount of life on the oth-er shore, Let me free-ly drink till I thirst no more.

REFRAIN.

Lead me on, lead me on, By the straight and nar-row way;
Lead me on, lead me on,

Lead me on, lead me on, to the realms of end-less day.
Lead me on, lead me on,

115 Follow All the Way

Elisha A. Hoffman

Arr. by Ira Orwig Hoffman

TRIO.

1. I can hear my Sav - iour call-ing, In the tend'rest ac - cents call-ing;
2. Tho' the way be dark and drear - y, Tho' my feet be worn and wea - ry,
3. Je - sus, ev - er go be - fore me, Shin - ing heav-en's sun - light o'er me,
4. Thro' the val - ley safe - ly lead me, Heav'n-ly man - na dai - ly feed me;
5. In thy heart's af - fec - tion hold me, In thy arms of love en - fold me,

On my ear these words are fall - ing, "Take thy cross and dai - ly fol - low me."
Yet my heart keeps bright and cheery, As I fol - low, fol - low all the way.
And when weak by grace re - store me, As I fol - low, fol - low all the way.
Ev - 'ry hour, dear Lord, I need thee As I fol - low, fol - low all the way.
And with thine own grace up - hold me, As I fol - low, fol - low all the way.

CHORUS.

I will take my cross and fol - low, My dear Sav - iour I will fol - low;

Where he leads me I will fol - low, I'll go with him, with him all the way.

6 I will never leave thee, never;
Faithful I will be forever;
Help me in my weak endeavor
Thee to follow, follow all the way.

7 Thro' death's dark and gloomy portal,
Leaving there this body mortal,
Into yonder home immortal
I will follow, follow all the way.

116

Gerar S. M.

" Be at peace among yourselves." 1 Thess. 5: 13

Dr. LOWELL MASON

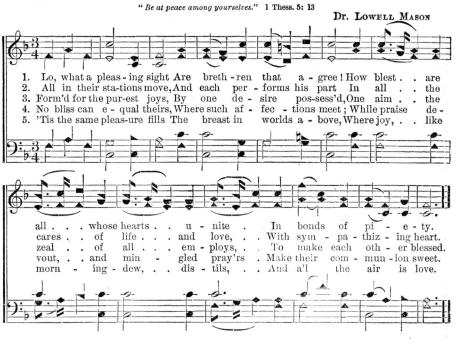

1. Lo, what a pleas-ing sight Are breth-ren that a-gree! How blest . . are
2. All in their sta-tions move, And each per-forms his part In all . . the
3. Form'd for the pur-est joys, By one de-sire pos-sess'd, One aim . . the
4. No bliss can e-qual theirs, Where such af-fec-tions meet; While praise de-
5. 'Tis the same pleas-ure fills The breast in worlds a-bove, Where joy, . . like

all . . . whose hearts . . u-nite . In bonds of pi-e-ty.
cares . . of life . . . and love, . . With sym-pa-thiz-ing heart.
zeal . . of all . . . em-ploys, . . To make each oth-er blessed.
vout, . . and min-gled pray'rs . Make their com-mun-ion sweet.
morn-ing-dew, . . dis-tils, . . And a'l the air is love.

117

Sweet Day S. M.

" The Lord is my shepherd, I shall not want." Psalm 23: 1

WATTS

B. C. UNSELD

1. The Lord my Shep-herd is; I shall be well sup-plied;
2. He leads me to the place Where heav'n-ly past-ure grows,
3. If e'er I go a-stray, He doth my soul re-claim,
4. While he af-fords his aid, I can-not yield to fear;

Since he is mine and I am his, What can I want be-side?
Where liv-ing wa-ters gen-tly pass, And full sal-va-tion flows.
And guides me in his own right way, For his most ho-ly name.
Tho' I should walk thro' death's dark shade, My Shep-herd's with me there.

118 He Knoweth the Way that I Take

"He knoweth the way that I take." Job 23: 10

Rev. Elisha A. Hoffman

Chas. Edw. Pollock

With expression.

1. He know-eth the way that I take, And nev-er his child will for-sake,
2. He know-eth the way that I take, He will not his cov-e-nant break;
3. He know-eth the way that I take, And hap-py my life he will make;

But he will be with me each day, And for me will light up the way.
His love will be faith-ful and true, And dai-ly its blessings re-new.
My side he is con-stant-ly near, To fill me with com-fort and cheer.

REFRAIN.

The way that I take he know-eth, And to me his love he show-eth; With-

in me his im-age grow-eth, And so I am hap-py al-way.

"Father, Lead Us"

ALICE JEAN CLEATOR

GEO. C. HUGG

With spirit.

1. O Fa - ther, lead us Gent - ly by the hand, Thro' sun and
2. When we would fal - ter Or when we would stray, O Fa - ther,

shad - ow Of the fu - ture land! Dim and un - trav - el'd
lead us All a - long our way! Help us to ev - er

Lies the way be - fore: O Fa - ther, lead us, Lead us ev - er - more!
Clos - er walk to thee, Thro' ways of dark - ness Where we can - not see!

CHORUS.

Fears oft af - fright us! Doubt - ings walk be - fore!

ff

O heav'n - ly Fa - ther, lead us, Now, and ev - er - more.

Jesus Leads

"And when he putteth forth his own sheep, he goeth before them, and the sheep follow him: for they know his voice." John x: 4

JOHN R. CLEMENTS   JNO. R. SWENEY

Andante.

1. Like a shep-herd, ten-der, true, Je-sus leads, .. Je-sus leads; ..
2. All a-long life's rug-ged road Je-sus leads, .. Je-sus leads, ..
3. Thro' the sun-lit ways of life Je-sus leads, .. Je-sus leads, ..

Je-sus leads,   Je-sus leads,

Dai-ly finds us pas-tures new, Je-sus leads, .. Je-sus leads; ..
Till we reach yon blest a-bode, Je-sus leads, .. Je-sus leads; ..
Thro' the war-rings and the strife Je-sus leads, .. Je-sus leads; ..

Je-sus leads;   Je-sus leads;

If thick mists .. are o'er the way, .. Or the flock .. 'mid dan-ger feeds,
All the way, .. be-fore he's trod, .. And he now .. the flock pre-cedes, ..
When we reach .. the Jordan's tide, .. Where life's boun-d'ry line re-cedes, ..

If thick mists are o'er the way,   Or the flock 'mid dan-ger feeds,

rit.

He will watch them lest they stray, Je-sus leads, .. Je-sus leads.
Safe in-to the fold of God Je-sus leads, .. Je-sus leads.
He will spread the waves a-side, Je-sus leads, .. Je-sus leads.

Je-sus leads,

F. M. Davis

Arranged from F. M. Davis, by A. J. S.

With expression.

1. Sav-iour, lead me lest I stray, lest I stray, Gen-tly lead me all the way, all the way;
2. Thou the ref-uge of my soul, of my soul, When life's stormy bil-lows roll, billows roll;
3. Sav-iour, lead me then at last, then at last, When the storm of life is past, life is past,

1. Sav-iour, lead me, lead me lest I stray, Gen-tly lead me, lead me all the way;
2. Thou the ref - uge, ref-uge of my soul, When life's storm-y, stormy billows roll;
3. Sav-iour, lead me, lead me then at last, When the storm, the storm of life is past,

I am safe when by thy side, by thy side, I would in thy love a - bide, love a-bide.
I am safe when thou art nigh, thou art nigh, All my hopes on thee re-ly, thee re-ly.
To the land of endless day, endless day, Where all tears are wiped a-way, wiped a-way.

I am safe, am safe when by thy side, I would in, would in thy love a-bide.
I am safe, am safe when thou art nigh, All my hopes, my hopes on thee re-ly.
To the land, the land of end-less day, Where all tears, all tears are wiped away.

REFRAIN.

Lead me, lead me, Sav - iour, lead me lest I stray, ...
Sav - iour, lead me lest I stray, lest I stray,

Gen - tly down the stream of time, Lead me, Saviour, all the way, all the way.
Gently down the stream of time, stream of time,

Battle Hymn

Rev. I. Watts, D.D.

Arr. by Wm. M. Blake

1. Am I a sol-dier of the cross, A fol-l'wer of the Lamb?
   And shall I fear to own his cause, Or blush to speak his name?
2. Must I be car-ried to the skies On flow-'ry beds of ease,
   While oth-ers fought to win the prize, And sail'd thro' blood-y seas?
3. Are there no foes for me to face? Must I not stem the flood?
   Is this vile world a friend to grace To help me on to God?
4. Sure I must fight if I would reign; In-crease my cour-age, Lord,
   I'll bear the toil, en-dure the pain, Sup-port-ed by thy word.

REFRAIN.

And when the bat-tle's o - ver we shall wear a crown! Yes, we shall wear a crown! Yes,

we shall wear a crown! And when the bat-tle's o - ver we shall wear a crown In the

FINE.

new Je-ru-sa-lem. Wear a crown, wear a crown, Wear a bright and shining crown.
Wear a crown, wear a crown,

D S

123 Just as Seemeth Good to Thee

Ida L. Reed

Geo. C. Hugg

Fervently.

1. Choose my path, O bless-ed Sav-iour, Let me, trust-ing, lean on thee;
2. Let thy wis-dom guide me ev-er, For I dare not trust my own;
3. Life is full of cares per-plex-ing, And a-lone, I lose the way;

Or-der thou life's joys and du-ties, Just as seem-eth good to thee.
Lead thou me in ten-der mer-cy, Leave me not to walk a-lone.
Keep me near to thee, dear Sav-iour, Choose for me the path, I pray.

REFRAIN.

Just as seem-eth good to thee, Just as seem-eth good to thee;

Or-der thou my steps, dear Sav-iour, Just as seem-eth good to thee.

124 The Promises of God

Lanta Wilson Smith   Wm. J. Kirkpatrick

1. I was wan-d'ring in a wil-der-ness ot deep de-spair and sin, And my
2. I was fol-low'd by the tempt-er, as he watch'd me day by day, While I
3. Aft-er days of joy-ful dream-ing came a time of grief and care, When I
4. So I pave the way be-fore me with the prom-is-es of God; They have

feet were grow-ing wea-ry of the road; But my sor-row, doubt and care Fled, when
sought the shin-ing path my Sav-iour trod; But with pan-o-ply and shield, And the
sank be-neath the heav-y chasten-ing rod; And the heart so torn by grief Found its
brightened ev-'ry step my feet have trod; And this shin-ing hap-py way Brightens

Je-sus met me there, And I learned to trust the prom-is-es of God.
Spir-it's sword to wield, I have con-quer'd thro' the prom-is-es of God.
com-fort and re-lief, On-ly thro' the bless-ed prom-is-es of God.
in-to per-fect day, Thro' the nev-er fail-ing prom-is-es of God.

REFRAIN.

I be-lieve the prom-is-es of God, I can trust his nev-er fail-ing word:

When earthly hopes shall fail, Or hosts of sin as-sail, I rest up-on the prom-is-es of God.

125 The Haven of Rest

H. L. GILMOUR

GEO. D. MOORE

1. My soul in sad ex - ile was out on life's sea, So
2. I yield - ed my - self to his ten - der em - brace, And
3. The song of my soul since the Lord made me whole Has
4. How pre - cious the thought that we all may re - cline, Like
5. Oh, come to the Sav - iour, he pa - tient - ly waits, To

burdened with sin and dis - trest, Till I heard a sweet voice say - ing,
faith tak - ing hold of the word, My . . fet - ters fell off, and I
been the old story so blest, Of Je - sus, who'll save who - so -
John the be - lov - ed and blest, On . . Je - sus' strong arm, where no
save by his pow'r di - vine; Come an - chor your soul in the

D.S. The . . tem - pest may sweep o'er the

FINE.

"Make me your choice;" And I en - tered the ha - ven of rest.
an - chored my soul; The ha - ven of rest is my Lord.
ev - er will have A . . home in the ha - ven of rest.
tem - pest can harm,— Se - cure in the ha - ven of rest.
ha - ven of rest, And say, "My Be - lov - ed is mine."

wild, storm - y deep, In . . Je - sus I'm safe ev - er - more.

REFRAIN.

D.S.

I've anchored my soul in the ha - ven of rest, I'll sail the wide seas no more;

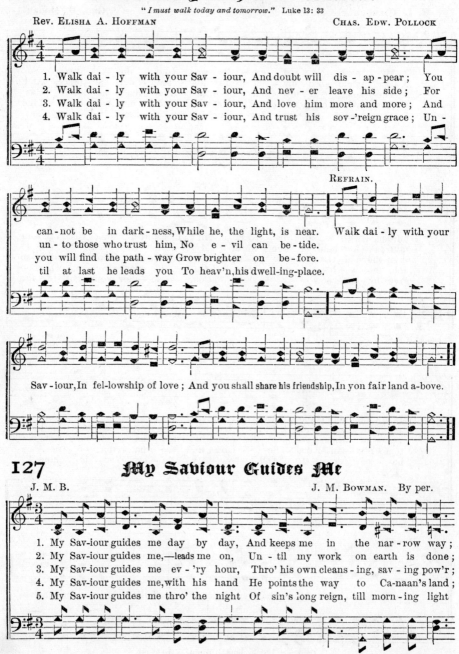

126 Walk Daily with Your Saviour

"I must walk today and tomorrow." Luke 13: 33

Rev. Elisha A. Hoffman

Chas. Edw. Pollock

1. Walk dai - ly with your Sav - iour, And doubt will dis - ap - pear; You
2. Walk dai - ly with your Sav - iour, And nev - er leave his side; For
3. Walk dai - ly with your Sav - iour, And love him more and more; And
4. Walk dai - ly with your Sav - iour, And trust his sov - 'reign grace; Un -

can - not be in dark - ness, While he, the light, is near.
un - to those who trust him, No e - vil can be - tide.
you will find the path - way Grow brighter on be - fore.
til at last he leads you To heav'n, his dwell - ing - place.

Refrain.

Walk dai - ly with your Sav - iour, In fel - low - ship of love; And you shall share his friendship, In yon fair land a - bove.

127 My Saviour Guides Me

J. M. B.

J. M. Bowman. By per.

1. My Sav - iour guides me day by day, And keeps me in the nar - row way;
2. My Sav - iour guides me,—leads me on, Un - til my work on earth is done;
3. My Sav - iour guides me ev - 'ry hour, Thro' his own cleans - ing, sav - ing pow'r;
4. My Sav - iour guides me, with his hand He points the way to Ca - naan's land;
5. My Sav - iour guides me thro' the night Of sin's long reign, till morn - ing light

My Saviour Guides Me

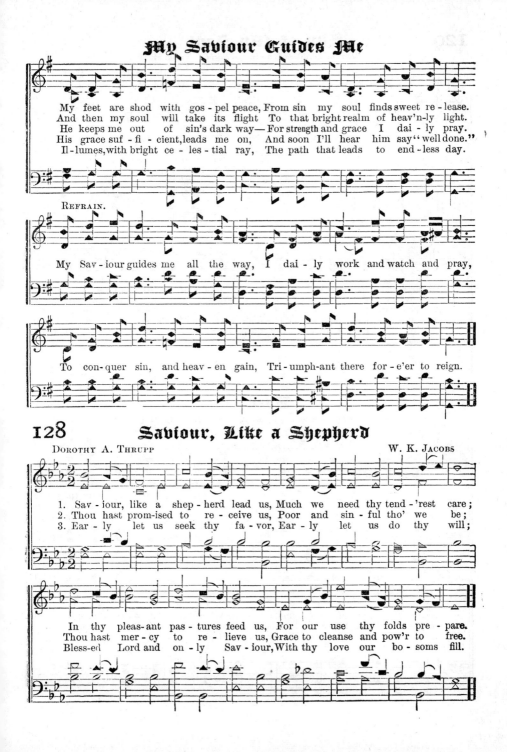

My feet are shod with gos-pel peace, From sin my soul finds sweet re-lease.
And then my soul will take its flight To that bright realm of heav'n-ly light.
He keeps me out of sin's dark way— For strength and grace I dai-ly pray.
His grace suf-fi-cient,leads me on, And soon I'll hear him say "well done."
Il-lumes,with bright ce-les-tial ray, The path that leads to end-less day.

REFRAIN.

My Sav-iour guides me all the way, I dai-ly work and watch and pray,

To con-quer sin, and heav-en gain, Tri-umph-ant there for-e'er to reign.

128 Saviour, Like a Shepherd

DOROTHY A. THRUPP

W. K. JACOBS

1. Sav-iour, like a shep-herd lead us, Much we need thy tend-'rest care;
2. Thou hast prom-ised to re-ceive us, Poor and sin-ful tho' we be;
3. Ear-ly let us seek thy fa-vor, Ear-ly let us do thy will;

In thy pleas-ant pas-tures feed us, For our use thy folds pre-pare.
Thou hast mer-cy to re-lieve us, Grace to cleanse and pow'r to free.
Bless-ed Lord and on-ly Sav-iour,With thy love our bo-soms fill.

129 **Sun of My Soul** L. M.

"For the Lord God is a sun and shield." Psalm 84: 11

Rev. JOHN KEBLE, 1827

PETER RITTER, 1792
Arr. by W. H. MONK, 1861

1. Sun of my soul, thou Sav-iour dear, It is not night if thou be near;
2. When the soft dews of kind-ly sleep My wea-ry eye-lids gen-tly steep,
3. A-bide with me from morn till eve, For with-out thee I can-not live;
4. Watch by the sick, en-rich the poor With bless-ings from thy boundless store;
5. Come near and bless us when we wake, Ere thro' the world our way we take;

Oh, may no earth-born cloud a-rise To hide thee from thy ser-vant's eyes.
Be my last tho't how sweet to rest For-ev-er on my Saviour's breast.
A-bide with me when night is nigh, For with-out thee I dare not die.
Be ev-'ry mourner's sleep to-night, Like in-fant's slum-bers, pure and light.
Till in the o-cean of thy love We lose our-selves in heaven a-bove.

130 **Eden** 8s. 7s.

"For we which have believed do enter into rest." Heb. 4: 3

J. S. C.
Slow.

Arr. by J. S. COFFMAN

1. Oh, the bliss of loved ones rest-ing By the crys-tal riv-er bright;
2. For this rest they longed and wait-ed, Heaven's glo-ry was their song;
3. May we not on earth sing with them, Ech-oing back their notes of praise?
4. Oh, the peace and rest in hea-ven! Oh, the bliss of loved ones there!

'Neath the shade of trees im-mor-tal, Where no shad-ows dim the light!
Liv-ing faith now bids us hear them Sing-ing with the blood-washed throng;
Yes, but bless-ed hope in-spires us Heaven's e-ter-nal songs to raise;
Love di-vine now bears us up-ward All their bless-ed-ness to share;

Eden

Refrain

Rest - ing, rest - ing, swee... - ly rest - ing, Where no shad-ows dim the light.
Rest - ing, rest - ing, sweet - ly rest - ing, Sing - ing with the blood-washed throng.
Rest - ing, rest - ing, sweet - ly rest - ing, Heav'n's e-ter - nal songs to raise.
Rest - ing, rest - ing, sweet - ly rest - ing, All their bless-ed - ness to share.

131 ## Bringing Home Our Sheaves 10s. 6s.

"He that goes forth weeping, bearing precious seed, shall come again rejoicing,
bringing his sheaves with him." Psalm 126: 6

Elizabeth Akers

H. S. Rupp

1. The time for toil is past, and night has come, The last and sad - dest
2. Few, light, and worth-less—yet their tri-fling weight Thro' all my frame a
3. Full well I know I have more tares than wheat, Bram-bles and flow'rs, dry
4. So do I gath - er hope and strength a-new; For well I know thy

of the har-vest eves; Worn out with la - bor long and wea-ri-some, Droop-ing and
wea - ry ach-ing leaves; For long I strug-gled with my hap-less fate, And staid and
stalks and withered leaves; Wherefore I blush and weep, as at thy feet I kneel down
pa-tient love per-ceives Not what I did, but what I strove to do— And though the

faint, the reapers hasten home, Each laden with his sheaves, Each laden with his sheaves.
toiled till it was dark and late, Yet these are all my sheaves, Yet these are all my sheaves.
rev - er - ent - ly, and re-peat, "Master, behold my sheaves," "Master, behold my sheaves."
full ripe ears be sad-ly few, Thou wilt accept my sheaves, Thou wilt accept my sheaves.

132 Deliverance Will Come

" We are journeying unto the place of which the Lord said, I will give it you." Num. 10: 29

J. B. M.

Rev. John B. Matthias, 1836

1. I saw a way-worn trav-'ler, In tat-tered garments clad, And struggling up the mountain; It seemed that he was sad. His back was la-den heav-y, His strength was al-most gone, Yet he shout-ed as he journeyed, "De-liv-er-ance will come."

2. The sum-mer sun was shin-ing, The sweat was on his brow, His gar-ments worn and dus-ty, His step seemed ver-y slow; But he kept pressing on-ward, For he was wending home; Still shout-ing as he journeyed, "De-liv-er-ance will come."

3. The song-sters in the ar-bor That stood be-side the way At-tract-ed his at-ten-tion, In-vit-ing his de-lay: His watchword be-ing "On-ward!" He stopped his ears and ran, Still shout-ing as he journeyed, "De-liv-er-ance will come."

4. I saw him in the eve-ning, The sun was bend-ing low, He'd o-ver-topped the mountain, And reached the vale below. He saw the gold-en cit-y,—His ev-er-last-ing home, And shout-ed loud, "Ho-san-na, De-liv-er-ance will come."

5. While gaz-ing on that cit-y, Just o'er the nar-row flood, A band of ho-ly an-gels Came from the throne of God; They bore him on their pin-ions Safe o'er the dashing foam; And joined him in his tri-umph, "De-liv-er-ance had come."

6. I heard the song of tri-umph They sang up-on that shore, Saying, Je-sus has redeemed us To suf-fer nev-er-more: Then, cast-ing his eyes backward On the race which he had run, He shout-ed loud, "Ho-san-na, De-liv-er-ance has come."

REFRAIN.

Then palms of vic-to-ry, crowns of glo-ry, Palms of vic-to-ry I shall wear.

133

Woodland C. M.

" There remaineth therefore a rest." Heb. 4: 9

W. B. TAPPAN

N. D. GOUNOD

1. There is an hour of peace-ful rest, To mourning wand'rers giv'n;There is a joy for
2. There is a soft and down-y bed,'Tis fair as breath of even; A couch for wea-ry
3. There is a home for wea-ry souls, By sin and sorrow driv'n, When toss'd on life's tem-
4. There faith lifts up her cheer-ful eye To brighter prospects giv'n, And views the tempest
5. There fragrant flow'rs immor-tal bloom, And joys supreme are giv'n; There rays di-vine dis-

souls distressed, A balm for ev-'ry wound-ed breast, 'Tis found a-lone in heaven.
mor-tals spread, Where they may rest the ach-ing head, And find re-pose in heaven.
pestuous shoals, Where storms a-rise, and o-cean rolls, And all is drear but heaven.
pass-ing by; The eve-ning shad-ows quick-ly fly, And all's se-rene in heaven.
perse the gloom;Be-yond the con-fines of the tomb Ap-pears the dawn of heaven.

134

Manoah C. M.

" We spend our years as a tale that is told." Psalm 90: 9

F. J. HAYDN

1. Our life is ev-er on the wing, And death is ev-er nigh;
2. Yet, might-y God, our fleet-ing days Thy last-ing fav-ors share;
3. 'Tis sov-'reign mer-cy finds us food, And we are clothed with love;
4. His good-ness runs on end-less round, All glo-ry to the Lord!
5. Thus we be-gin the last-ing song, And when we close our eyes,

The mo-ment when our lives be-gin, We all be-gin to die.
Yet with the boun-ties of thy grace,Thou load'st the roll-ing year.
While grace stands pointing out the road That leads our souls a-bove.
His mer-cy nev-er knows a bound,And be his name a-dored!
Let fu-ture a-ges praise pro-long, Till time and na-ture dies.

Home of the Blest

"And the city had no need of the sun, for the Glory of God did lighten it." Rev. 21: 23

H. B. B.

H. E. BRENNEMAN

1. There's a beau-ti-ful, beau-ti-ful land,—'Tis the home of the blest;
2. In that land is the ci-ty of light, Bright and fair, we are told:
3. There's no need of the sun in that land, For the Lamb is its light;
4. Oh, how glo-rious and sweet it must be, In that peace-ful a-bode!

Where with Je-sus, a glo-ri-fied band, They for-ev-er shall rest.
All its mansions are daz-zling and white, And its street are of gold.
And he sits at his Fa-ther's right hand, Crowned with glo-ry and might.
Where from sin and from mis-er-y free, We shall dwell with our God.

REFRAIN.

Oh, that beau-ti-ful, beau-ti-ful land Is for you and for me!

ritard.

There to be with the glo-ri-fied band, Oh, how sweet it will be.

5 There we hope many loved ones to meet,
And in tender embrace
We in triumph each other shall greet,
In that beautiful place.

6 When we get to that Home of the Blest,
From all pain to be free,
And with Jesus forever to rest,
Oh, how sweet it will be.

136
That Heavenly Home

A. C. K.

A. C. Kolb

Slow.

1. Oh, when I think of that hea - ven-ly home, Where all earth's sorrows shall cease,
2. Sweet is the tho't of that won - der-ful home, Shown by our Fa - ther of love,
3. When I shall meet in that hea - ven-ly place Loved ones who've gone on be-fore,

Free from all care, where no trou-ble may come, Dwell - ing for - ev - er in peace;
Where all the wea - ry are wel-come to come And dwell in glo - ry a - bove.
We may re - joice in each oth - er's em-brace, Nev - er to part ev - er-more.

Where I may see the dear Saviour's sweet face, E'en in his like-ness to be,
There I shall sing with the glo - ri fi- ed throng, Hap - py and joy - ous and free,
There in the sun-light of hea - ven-ly bliss, Feast-ing on joys nev- er told,

I'm o - ver-come with the tho't of his grace, What a blest home that must be !
Hea - ven shall ring with re-demption's glad song, Oh, what a joy that will be !
I shall be rest - ing se - cure-ly in peace, Safe in that hea - ven-ly fold.

137 Dunbar S. M.

Mrs. Mary S. B. Dana, 1800   Rev. C. R. Dunbar

1. Oh! sing to me of heav'n, When I am called to die;
2. When cold and slug-gish drops Roll off my mar-ble brow,
3. When the last mo-ments come, Oh, watch my dy-ing face,
4. Then to my rap-tured ear Let one sweet song be giv'n;

Ref. There'll be no sor-row there, There'll be no sor-row there;

Sing songs of ho-ly ec-sta-sy, To waft my soul on high.
Break forth in songs of joy-ful-ness, Let heav'n be-gin be-low.
To catch the bright ser-aph-ic gleam, Which on each fea-ture plays.
Let mu-sic cheer me last on earth, And greet me first in heav'n.

In heav'n a-bove, where all is love, There'll be no sor-row there.

138

" For the same cause also do ye joy." Phil. 2: 18

1 Come, we that love the Lord,
  And let our joys be known;
Join in a song with sweet accord,
  And thus surround the throne.

2 Let those refuse to sing
  Who never knew their God;
But favorites of the heavenly King
  May speak their joys abroad.

3 The hill of Zion yields
  A thousand sacred sweets,
Before we reach the heavenly fields,
  Or walk the golden streets.

4 Then let our songs abound,
  And every tear be dry; [ground
We're marching through Immanuel's
  To fairer worlds on high.

Watts

139 Fast to Thine Arm

G. W. L.   G. W. Lyon

1. Je-sus my Saviour, Look thou on me, Here I but wander Far, far, from thee;
2. I'm but a stran-ger, Sad-ly I roam, Thro' a strange country, Far from my home;
3. Lead me, my Sav-iour, Show me the way, That I may nev-er Far from thee stray;

Fast to Thine Arm

I am so wea-ry, Sigh-ing for rest, Bless me, my Sav-iour, Come to my breast.
Pit - y my weakness, Strengthen my feet, That I may jour-ney To rest complete.
I fear no dan-ger, No rude a-larm, While I am clinging, Fast to thine arm.

140 Some Near, Near Day

" Until the day break and the shadows flee away." Cant. 2: 17

Rev. E. A. Hoffman   Chas. Edw. Pollock

1. Some day these con-flicts will be o'er, And sin and sense mo-lest no more; And
2. Some day this toil-ing will be o'er, And hands a-wea-ried grow no more; Then
3. Some day these long-ings will be o'er, And hearts grow sick and faint no more; And
4. Some day our journeyings will be o'er, And we will rest for-ev-er more; En-

you shall pass from earth be-low, To where the tree of life doth grow.
from the skies a call will come, To go to your e-ter-nal home.
in the Par-a-dise so wide, All will be blest and sat-is-fied.
robed in gar-ments pure and white, In yon-der pal-a-ces of light.

REFRAIN.

Some near, near day, not far a-way, A-long a bright and shin-ing way An

an-gel of God's love will come, To guide you to your heav'n-ly home.

141

Varina C. M. D.

"Thine eyes shall behold the land that is very far off." Isa. 33: 17

ISAAC WATTS

GEO. F. ROOT

1. There is a land of pure de-light, Where saints immor-tal reign; E - ter-nal day ex-
2. Sweet fields beyond the swelling flood Stand dress'd in living green; So to the Jews old
3. Oh, could we make our doubts remove, Those gloomy doubts that rise, And see the Ca-naan

cludes the night, And pleasures ban-ish pain. There ev - er-last - ing spring a-bides, And
Ca-naan stood, While Jor - dan rolled be - tween. But tim'rous mor-tals start and shrink To
that we love, With un - be-cloud-ed eyes! Could we but climb where Mo-ses stood, And

nev-er-with-'ring flow'rs; Death, like a nar - row sea, divides This heavenly land from ours.
cross the nar-row sea, And lin-ger shiv'ring on the brink, And fear to launch a - way
view the landscape o'er, Not Jordan's stream, nor death's cold flood, Should fright us from the shore.

142

"Prospect of heaven." Deut. 34: 5

1 On Jordan's stormy banks I stand,
　And cast a wishful eye
To Canaan's fair and happy land,
　Where my possessions lie.
Oh, the transporting rapt'rous scene,
　That rises to my sight!
Sweet fields array'd in living green,
　And rivers of delight.

2 There gen'rous fruits that never fail,
　On trees immortal grow:
There rocks and hills, and brooks vales
With milk and honey flow.

All o'er those wide extended plains
　Shines one eternal day;
There God the Sun forever reigns,
　And scatters night away.

3 No chilling winds, nor pois'nous breath
　Can reach that healthful shore;
Sickness and sorrow, pain and death
　Are felt and feared no more.
When shall I reach that happy place,
　And be forever blest?
When shall I see my Father's face,
　And in his bosom rest?

STENNETT

143

Canaan C. M.

"The holy city, New Jerusalem." Rev. 21: 2

MONTGOMERY

H. S. RUPP

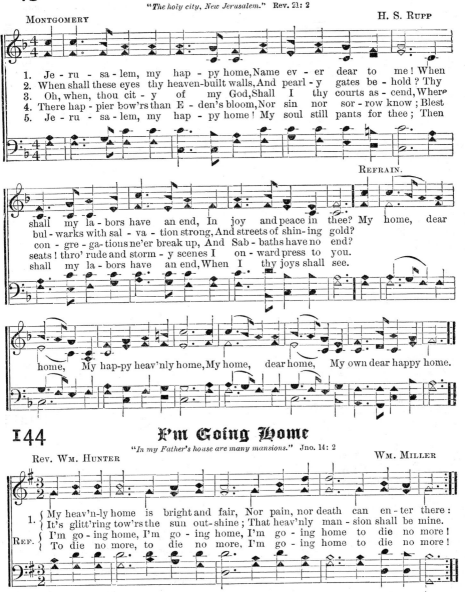

1. Je - ru - sa - lem, my hap - py home, Name ev - er dear to me! When
2. When shall these eyes thy heaven-built walls, And pearl - y gates be - hold? Thy
3. Oh, when, thou cit - y of my God, Shall I thy courts as - cend, Where
4. There hap - pier bow'rs than E - den's bloom, Nor sin nor sor - row know; Blest
5. Je - ru - sa - lem, my hap - py home! My soul still pants for thee; Then

REFRAIN.

shall my la - bors have an end, In joy and peace in thee? My home, dear
bul - warks with sal - va - tion strong, And streets of shin - ing gold?
con - gre - ga - tions ne'er break up, And Sab - baths have no end?
seats! thro' rude and storm - y scenes I on - ward press to you.
shall my la - bors have an end, When I thy joys shall see.

home, My hap-py heav'nly home, My home, dear home, My own dear happy home.

144

I'm Going Home

"In my Father's house are many mansions." Jno. 14: 2

Rev. WM. HUNTER

WM. MILLER

1. {My heav'n-ly home is bright and fair, Nor pain, nor death can en - ter there:
It's glitt'ring tow'rs the sun out-shine; That heav'nly man - sion shall be mine.

REF. {I'm go - ing home, I'm go - ing home, I'm go - ing home to die no more!
To die no more, to die no more, I'm go - ing home to die no more!

2 My Father's house is built on high,
Far, far above the starry sky;
When from this earthly prison free,
That heavenly mansion mine shall be.

3 Let others seek a home below,
Which flames devour, or waves o'er-
Be mine a happier lot to own   [flow;
A heavenly mansion near the throne.

Marching Home

J. Calvin Bushey

1. We are march-ing home-ward with the blest, (with the blest,) To
2. Je-sus stands and beck-ons to us now, (to us now,) When
3. Our dear Sav-iour has pre-pared the way, (the way,) Where

that bright world a-bove, Where our friends are gone and are at rest, (are at rest,)
fal-t'ring on the way; He will save us, if to him we bow, (him we bow,)
all who will may come; If we serve him tru-ly day by day, (day by day,)

In that world of light and love. Marching home, ... we're march-ing
He who rules both night and day.
He at last will bring us home.

March-ing home,

home, ... Hap-py home, ... of peace and love; March-ing
home, marching home, Hap-py home, peace and love;

home, ... we're marching home, To that bright land of love.
home, marching home, home, march-ing home,

Repeat refrain pp

146 Glory Gates

G. P. H.

Rev. G. P. Hott

1. I am look - ing for the cit-y built of God, Where the man-y man-sions be;
2. Thro' the val - ley of the shadow I may go, But his grace shall be my stay;
3. 'Tis the glo - ry now that fills and thrills my soul, As I walk the nar -row way;

I am walk-ing now the path that Je-sus trod, And his face I soon shall see.
Tho' the path be dark and dan-ger-ous, I know He will guide me all the way.
I am look-ing for the heav'nly light to dawn, That shall rise in end - less day.

REFRAIN.

Oh, the glo - ry gates are ev - er o-pen wide, In - vit - ing the world to come;

Oh, the glo - ry gates are ev - er o-pen wide, To wel-come the wea - ry home !

147 ♯ **Heaven is My Home** 6s. 4s.

Dr. L. Mason, 1834

1. I'm but a stranger here, Heav'n is my home; Earth is a des-ert drear, Heav'n is my home.
2. What tho' the tempest rage, Heav'n is my home; Short is my pilgrimage, Heav'n is my home.
3. There at my Sav-iour's side, Heav'n is my home ; I shall be glo - ri-fied, Heav'n is my home.

Dan-ger and sor-row stand Round me on ev-'ry hand. Heav'n is my fatherland, Heav'n is my home.
Time's cold and win-t'ry blast Shall soon be o - ver-past, I shall reach home at last, Heav'n is my home.
There are the good and blest, Those I love most and best, There, too, I soon shall rest, Heav'n is my home.

148 **Protection** C. M.

S. B. McManus
A. C. Kolb
Slow.

1. I would that I might walk, dear Lord, For - ev - er by thy
2. I would that thy dear lov - ing hand Might rest up - on my
3. Pro - tect me from all foes and snares; Di - rect my way - ward
4. Keep watch up - on my heart and life ; For - bid that I should
5. I need thy love and watch - ful care, To shield me ev - 'ry

side, That I might al - ways see thy face, And in thy love a - bide.
head, And lend me con - stant cour - age, Lord, As in thy path I tread.
feet In paths of right - eous - ness to walk, That lead to pas - tures sweet.
stray, And bid me by thy side in fear Walk clos - er ev - 'ry day.
hour; Oh, hide me, Lord, in thee I pray, Pro - tect me by thy power.

149 Rest by and by

W. F. Cosner   C. E. Pollock

1. Oft-en wea-ry and worn on the path-way below, When the burden is heav-y, my
2. You will not la-bor long for the Mas-ter be-low, Soon his call you will hear, your free
3. Then, dear Saviour, I would not in sad-ness repine, Nor would here on a bed of sweet

heart throbs with woe; Oh, there comes a sweet whis-per to quell ev-'ry sigh, "Do not
spir-it shall go To the light of his pres-ence in man-sions on high, Where the
ros-es re-cline; For a coun-try I seek where they nev-er-more die, And in

D.S. *Where the ran-somed shall live with the Sav-iour on high, In the*

Fine. Refrain.

faint 'neath the load, there is rest by and by." There is rest   by and
faith-ful re-pose, there is rest by and by.
Zi-on my home, there is rest by and by. There is rest by and by, there is

beau-ti-ful cit-y there is rest by and by.

D.S.

by,   In the beau-ti-ful cit-y there is rest by and by.
rest by and by,

The Unclouded Day

Rev. J. K. Alwood

J. F. Kinsey, by per

Moderato.

1. Oh, they tell me of a home far be-yond the skies, Oh, they tell me of a
2. Oh, they tell me of a home where my friends have gone, Oh, they tell me of a
3. Oh, they tell me of the King in his beau-ty there, And they tell me that mine
4. Oh, they tell me that he smiles on his chil-dren there, And his smile drives their

home far a-way; Oh, they tell me of a home where no storm-clouds rise,
land far a-way; Where the tree of . . life in e-ter-nal bloom
eyes shall be-hold Where he sits on the . . throne that is whit-er than snow,
sor-rows all a-way; And they tell me that no tears ev-er come a-gain,

Oh, they tell me of an un-cloud-ed day; Oh, the land of cloud-less day,
Sheds its fragrance thro' the un-cloud-ed day; Oh, the land of cloud-less day,
In the ci-ty that is made of . . gold; Oh, that land mine eyes shall see,
In that love-ly land of un-cloud-ed day; Oh, that land of love-ly smiles,

Oh, the land of an un-cloud-ed sky; Oh, they tell me of a home where no
Oh, the land of an un-cloud-ed sky; Oh, they tell me of my friends by the
Oh, the land of an un-cloud-ed sky; Oh, they tell me of the King on his
Oh, the smiles of his love-beam-ing eye; Oh, the King in his beau-ty in-

The Unclouded Day

storm - clouds rise, Oh, they tell me of an un - cloud - ed day.
tree of life, In the land .. of the un - cloud - ed day.
snow - white throne, In the land .. of the un - cloud - ed day.
vites us there, To the land .. of the un - cloud - ed day.

151   ## My Home Above

LOUSIA E.   CHAS. EDW. POLLOCK, by per.

1. I love to think of my home a - bove, In the glo-rious realms of light, Of the
2. I love to think of my home a - bove, Of that pure and ho - ly clime, Where the
3. I love to think of my home a - bove, Of the an - gel forms so bright, Of the

D.S. *In that*
FINE

pearl - y gates and the gold - en streets, In that land where there is no night.
sor - rows of earth can nev - er come, But e - ter - nal joys will be mine.
bless - ed ones there a-round the throne, In the land of pure de - light.

home a - bove, where all is love, And joy be - yond com - pare?

REFRAIN   D.S.

Home, sweet home! Hap-py home, sweet home! Oh! say will you meet me there,
Home,sweet home! Home,sweet home! Home,sweet home! Happy home,sweet home!

E. R. Latta   Geo. B. Holsinger, by per.

1. In the day of all days, when the world shall be judged, And the
2. But the wick - ed who will not re - pent and be - lieve, And will
3. We are jour - ney-ing on to e - ter - ni - ty now, On the
4. If our Shep - herd he is, and we fol - low his call, He will

chaff from the wheat shall be thor ough-ly fanned, Then the righteous shall shine as the
nev - er live up to the Mas-ter's command, Shall be placed on the left, as un -
bank of death's Jor-dan we sometime shall stand! Shall we fear to pass o - ver the
lead us safe home, to that beau - ti - ful land; And, with crowns on our brows, and with

stars in the sky, And their pla - ces shall be at the Sav-iour's right hand.
wor - thy to be With the chil - dren of God at the Sav-iour's right hand.
dark roll - ing flood, Lest our por - tion be not at the Sav-iour's right hand?
branch - es of palm, We shall ev - er a - bide at the Sav-iour's right hand.

Refrain.

Let me . . . . find a place . . with that . . . hap - py band, . .
Let me find a place with that hap-py band, Let me find a place with that hap-py band,

At the Saviour's Right Hand

Who shall ev - - - er a - bide, ... A - bide at the Saviour's right hand. ...
Who shall ev - er a - bide at the Saviour's right hand,
right hand.

153 THE CITY OF LIGHT

A. S. K.

A. S. KIEFFER

1. There's a cit - y of light 'mid the stars, we are told, Where they know not a
2. Broth - er dear, nev - er fear, we shall tri - umph at last If we trust in the
3. Let us walk in the light of the gos - pel di - vine, Let us ev - er keep

D.C. *For that home is so bright, and is al - most in sight, And I trust in my*
FINE.

sor - row or care; And the gates are of pearl and the streets are of gold,
word he has given; When our tri - als and toils, and our weep - ings are past,
near to the cross; Let us love, watch, and pray, in our pil - grim - age here,

heart you'll go there.

CHORUS.

And the build ing ex - ceed - ing - ly fair; Let us pray for each
We shall meet in that home up in heav'n.
Let us count all things else but as loss.

D.C.

oth - er, not faint by the way, In this sad world of sor - row and care.

154 The Open Gate

Mrs. Lizzie Underwood

S. C. Hanson

1. I've heard them sing a-gain and a-gain Of a gate that stands a-
2. A wel-come home at the o-pen gate, From a land of an-gels
3. The sin-ner's Friend, as he reach-es down, With a Sav-iour's won-drous

jar, . Of a sun-ny clime, and gold-en plain, And a sin-less land a-
bright, Do . these for the ran-som'd spir-its wait, As it gains the land of
love, Who pre-pares a man-sion, robe, and crown, In his shin-ing courts a-

far. . . But when I have past the chil-ly tide, And en-ter my home a-
light? We may not know of the joy un-told, The bliss of the oth-er
bove, . Will gath-er his flock in-to the fold, To the fold be-yond the

bove, I be-lieve the gate will o-pen wide, On its gold-en hinge of love.
side, But . when I come to the gate of gold, I be-lieve 'twill o-pen wide.
tide, As they near the gate, the gate of gold, I be-lieve 'twill o-pen wide.

REFRAIN.

It will o-pen wide, yes, o-pen wide, I'll pass thro' its por-tals free, And

The Open Gate

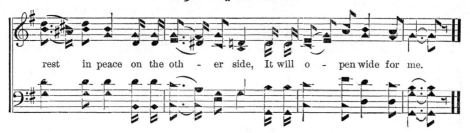

rest in peace on the oth - er side, It will o - pen wide for me.

155 Messiah 7s. D.

"Where I am, there ye may be also." John 14: 3

L. J. F. HEROLD, 1830
ARR. by GEORGE KINGSLEY, 1838

1. High in yon - der realm of light, Dwell the rap - tured saints a - bove,
2. Oft - en the un - bid - den tear, Steal - ing down the furrowed cheek,
3. All is tran - quil and se - rene, Calm and un - dis - turbed re - pose;

FINE.

Far be - yond our fee - ble sight, Hap - py in Im - man - uel's love.
Told in el - o - quence sin - cere Tales of woe they could not speak;
There no cloud can in - ter - vene, There no an - gry tem - pest blows;

D.S. *Tor - tur - ing pain and heavy woe, Gloom - y doubts, dis - tress - ing fears.*
D.S. *They shall feel dis - tress no more—Nev - er, nev - er weep a - gain.*
D.S. *Night is lost in end - less day, Sor - row—in e - ter - nal rest.*

D.S.

Once they knew, like us be - low, Pil - grims in this vale of tears,
But these days of weep - ing o'er, Past this scene of toil and pain,
Ev - 'ry tear is wiped a - way, Sighs no more shall heave the breast,

150 Shall We Know Each Other There

J. Henry Showalter, by per.

1. When we hear the mu-sic ring-ing In the bright ce-les-tial dome—
2. When the ho-ly an-gels meet us, As we go to join their band,
3. Yes, my earth worn soul re-joi-ces And my wea-ry heart grows light
4. Oh, ye wea-ry, sad, and tossed ones, Droop not, faint not by the way!

When sweet an-gels' voi-ces sing-ing Glad-ly bid us wel-come home
Shall we know the friends that greet us In that glo-rious spir-it land?
For the thrill-ing an-gels' voi-ces And the an-gel fa-ces bright
Ye shall join the loved and just ones In that land of per-fect day.

To the land of an-cient sto-ry, Where the spir-it knows no care,
Shall we see the same eyes shin-ing On us as in days of yore?
That shall wel-come us in heav-en, Our blest home of long a-go.
Harp-strings, touched by an-gel fin-gers, Mur-mured in my rapt-urous ear,

In that land of life and glo-ry— Shall we know each oth-er there?
Shall we feel the dear arms twin-ing Fond-ly round us as be-fore?
For to them 'tis kind-ly giv-en Thus their mor-tal friends to know.
Ev-er-more their sweet song lin-gers—"We shall know each oth-er there."

157 The Righteous Marching Home

Rev. W. P. Rivers

Arr. by R. M. McIntosh

1. As Zi - on's pil - grims in ac - cord, The sol - diers of our King,
2. In fel - low - ship of joys and woes, We'll bear the com - mon strife,
3. With faith and pray'r we'll urge the fray, Nor will we fear or fly;
4. Then while the Spir - it leads us on, Our march we'll still pur - sue,
5. Tho' worn with bat - tle-wounds and scars, Yet true to Christ in love,

In cov - 'nant bands we'll serve the Lord, And all his prais - es sing.
And on - ward press, thro' all our foes, And win e - ter - nal life.
For vic - t'ry waits us on the way, And crowns a - bove the sky.
Un - til the heav'n - ly goal is won, And we our king shall view.
We'll dwell with God be - yond the stars At home, in heav'n a - bove.

REFRAIN.

See the right - eous march - ing on! .. And the an - gels bid them come;
D.S. *To wel - come trav - 'lers home, To wel - come trav - 'lers home;*

D.S.

And the Sav - iour stands a - wait - ing To wel - come trav - 'lers home.
And the Sav - iour stands a - wait - ing To wel - come trav - 'lers home.

158 Sweet Rest in Heaven

Sarah C. Leatherman

M. Janie Leatherman

1. Some days are dark and drear-y, And some are warm and bright;
2. Some-times our hearts are lone-ly, Oft-times the way seems hard,
3. Yes, when this life is o-ver, When comes the time of rest,
4. We'll nev-er then grow wea-ry, Our toil will all be o'er;
5. Yes, there we'll meet to-geth-er, With loved ones gone be-fore;

And oft we feel so wea-ry, We're glad when comes the night.
But rest comes to us on-ly When we de-serve re-ward.
Our souls will rest for-ev-er In man-sions of the blest.
These days that are so drear-y Will trou-ble us no more.
We'll rest and sing for-ev-er On that ce-les-tial shore.

Refrain.

Our rest will soon be giv-en By him who has con-trol;

There's rest, sweet rest, in heav-en, Rest for the wea-ry soul.

159 Beautiful Land on High

J. Nicholson   C. A. Haven

1. There's a beau - ti - ful land on high, To its glo - ries I
2. There's a beau - ti - ful land on high, I shall en - ter it
3. There's a beau - ti - ful land on high, Then why should I
4. There's a beau - ti - ful land on high, And my kin - dred its

fain would fly; . . When by sor - rows pressed down, I long for my crown
by and by; . . There with friends hand in hand, I'll walk on the strand,
fear to die? . . When death is the way to the realms of the day
bliss en - joy; . . Me - thinks I now see how they're wait - ing for me

rit. REFRAIN.

In that beau - ti - ful land on high. . . In that beau - ti - ful land I'll
on high.

be, . . . From earth and its cares set free; . . My Je - sus is there,
I'll be,   set free;

He's gone to pre - pare A place in that land for me, (for me.)

Home of the Soul

(NEW)

A. S. D.

A. S. DOUGHTY

1. Soon tri-als and conflicts of life will be o'er, And we shall have crossed the dark main ;
2. Faith's raptu-rous vis-ion may sometimes be-hold An out-line of hea-ven-ly scene ;
3. That ci - ty of jew-els, and mansions un-told, And walls made of jas-per sub-lime ;
4. A land that's so pure and so free from all sin, Where pain never ut-tered a cry ;
5. When we with the saints and the glo - ri-fied throng As-sem-ble up - on that blest shore,

Earth's pleasures for- sak - en we'll nev - er de-plore, If heaven's blest portal we gain.
As Mo - ses be - held the fair Ca - naan of old, Far off, with a Jor-dan be - tween.
Re - ful-gent with lus - tre, like trans-par-ent gold, And nev - er cor - rod-ed by time.
Where sick-ness and death cannot en - ter therein, And nothing that maketh a lie.
With harps and with voices we'll chant the new song, With heaven's redeemed ever - more.

REFRAIN.

We're nearing the shore of that beau - ti-ful land, That far - a- way home of the soul ; . .

And soon we will stand on that glit - ter-ing strand, And chant while the a - ges shall roll.

"There shall be no night there." Rev. 22: 5

C. K. HOSTETLER   Arr. by A. B. KOLB

1. Shad - ows nev - er dark - en heav - en, End - less day shall ban - ish night;
2. In that land of gold - en sun - light, We shall meet those gone be - fore,
3. Nei - ther pain nor death nor sor - row E'er shall reach that land on high,

Dark-ness ne'er can cross its por - tals, For the Lamb shall be the light.
And shall join in that glad cho - rus, Prais - ing God for ev - er - more.
And the ran - somed shall be gath - ered To that home be - yond the sky.

REFRAIN.

There shall be no night in heav - en, There shall be no dark - ness there;

Glo - ry, glo - ry, be to Je - sus For his sun-shine ev - 'ry-where.

Nearing the Port

Rev. W. T. Dale

Chas. Edw. Pollock, by per.

Duet.

1. "I am near - ing the port," I will soon be at home, And the voy - age of life will be o'er; And be - neath the high arch - es of heav - en's bright dome I shall dwell with my friends gone be - fore. .

2. "I am near - ing the port," I will soon be at rest, I will an - chor in peace on the strand; I will stand on that shore 'mid the throng of the blest, I will dwell in that beau - ti - ful land. .

3. "I am near - ing the port," for the land is in sight, And the moun - tains in gran - deur are seen; And the land-scape of E - den I hail with de - light, And the plains that are cov - ered with green.

4. "I am near - ing the port," see, the bless - ed have come, And are gath - 'ring a - long on the shore; Now they watch to re - ceive me and wel - come me home, Where we'll part nev - er, no, nev - er - more.

5. "I am an - chored in port," I have reached the bright strand, And the voy - age of life is now past; With my Sav - iour I'll dwell in that beau - ti - ful land, And with rap - ture I'll shout, "Home at last!"

Refrain.

I am near - ing, yes, near - ing, I am nearing, yes, near-ing the

I am near-ing, yes, near-ing, I am near-ing the port, I am near-ing, yes, near-ing, I am

164 Home of the Soul

" In my Father's house are many mansions." John 14: 2

Mrs. ELLEN H. GATES   CHAS. E. POLLOCK, by per.

1. I will sing you a song of that beau-ti-ful land, The far a-way home of the soul; Where no storms ev-er beat on that glit-ter-ing strand, While the years of e-ter-ni-ty roll.

2. Oh, that home of the soul in my vis-ions and dreams, Its bright jas-per walls I can see; Till I fan-cy but thin-ly the vale in-ter-venes Be-tween the fair cit-y and me.

3. That un-chang-a-ble home is for you and for me, Where Je-sus of Naz-a-reth stands; The King of all king-doms for-ev-er, is he, And he hold-eth our crowns in his hands.

4. Oh, how sweet it will be in that beau-ti-ful land, So free from all sor-row and pain; With songs on our lips and with harps in our hands To meet one an-oth-er a-gain.

REFRAIN.

While the years of e-ter-ni-ty roll. While the years of e-ter-ni-ty roll, Where no storms ev-er beat on that glit-ter-ing strand, While the years of e-ter-ni-ty roll.

Used by per. of THE BIGLOW & MAIN CO.

The Christian's Passport S. M. D.

Words and melody by L. J. HEATWOLE

1. The saint who en-ters heav'n, Who comes of roy-al birth, Or
2. Who shines in that bright world, Or wears the blood-washed robe, Finds
3. To those who en-ter heav'n, And rest in tran-quil ease, On

dwells with all the sanc-ti-fied, Is first a saint on earth.
the first ray of bright-ness gleam, While yet in this a-bode.
earth first sought Christ's right-eous-ness, And found his prom-is-es.

To walk in heav'n's sun-light, . . To see its glo-ry there, And
Who joins the ju-bi-lee, . . . Or sings with the glad throng, Or
And when they reach the port, . The lan-guage all a-glow Stands

he who dwells with all the blest, First sees God's sun-light here.
shouts with all that hap-py choir, On earth first heard the song.
on the pass-port at the gate, "You first found heav'n be-low."

166

Avon C. M.

"Lord, make me to know mine end." Psalm 39: 4.

ISAAC WATTS

HUGH WILSON

1. Teach me the meas-ure of my days, Thou Ma - ker of my frame;
2. A span is all that we can boast; How short the fleet-ing time!
3. What should I wish, or wait for, then, From crea-tures—earth and dust?
4. Now I for - bid my car - nal hope, My fond de - sire re - call;

I would sur - vey life's nar - row space, And learn how frail I am.
Man is but van - i - ty and dust, In all his flower and prime.
They make our ex - pec - ta - tions vain, And dis - ap - point our trust.
I give my mor - tal in - terest up, And make my God my all.

167

1 How happy are these little ones
   Which Jesus Christ has blest;
 Come, let us praise him with our songs,
   For taking them to rest.

2 Yes, happy are these little lambs—
   Of such the kingdom is;
 The Lord our praise and thanks
     demands,
   Who made them heirs of bliss.

3 With his own blood he made them free
   From sin and every stain;
 For them he suffered on the tree—
   Yes, for them was he slain.

4 He takes them home, where pain and
     Will ne'er disturb them more; [woe
 Oh, let us all prepare to go
   And with them Christ adore.

5 However painful it may be,
   To know that they are gone,
 The thought is sweet that we may see
   Them in that heavenly home.

168

"Blessed is every one that feareth the Lord." Ps. 128: 1

1 Why do we mourn departing friends,
   Or shake at death's alarms?
 'Tis but the voice that Jesus sends
   To call them to his arms.

2 Are we not tending upward too,
   As fast as time can move?
 Nor should we wish the hours more
     slow,
   To keep us from our love.

3 The graves of all his saints he blest,
   And softened every bed;
 Where should the dying members
     rest,
   But with their dying Head?

4 Then let the last loud trumpet sound,
   And bid our kindred rise;
 Awake, ye nations under ground;
   Ye saints, ascend the skies.

ISAAC WATTS

Sleep till that Morning

B. F. Showalter

1. Peace-ful-ly lay her down to rest; Place the turf kind-ly o'er her breast;
2. Close to her lone and nar-row house, Graceful-ly wave, ye wil-low boughs;
3. Qui-et-ly sleep, be-lov-ed one, Rest from thy toil, thy la-bor's done;

Sweet be the slum-ber 'neath the sod, While the pure soul is rest-ing with God.
Flow'rs of the wild-wood, o-dors shed, O-ver the ho-ly, beau-ti-ful dead.
Rest till the trump from th'op-'ning skies, Bids thee from dust to glo-ry a-rise.

REFRAIN.

Peace - - - ful-ly sleep, . . . Sleep . . . till that
Peace-ful-ly, peace-ful-ly, sweet-ly sleep, Peace-ful-ly sleep till that

morn - ing, Yes, peace - - - - ful-ly sleep. . . . .
morn - ing, Yes, peace-ful-ly, peace-ful-ly, peace-ful-ly sleep.

By permission of J. Henry Showalter

Mount Vernon 8s. 7s.

L. Mason

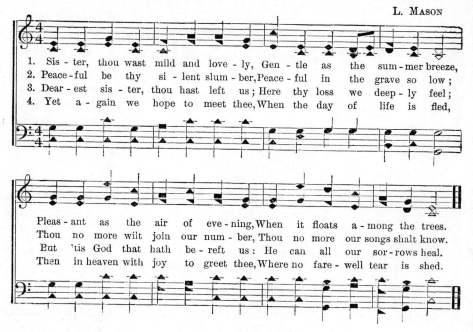

1. Sis - ter, thou wast mild and love - ly, Gen - tle as the sum - mer breeze,
2. Peace - ful be thy si - lent slum - ber, Peace - ful in the grave so low;
3. Dear - est sis - ter, thou hast left us; Here thy loss we deep - ly feel;
4. Yet a - gain we hope to meet thee, When the day of life is fled,

Pleas - ant as the air of eve - ning, When it floats a - mong the trees.
Thou no more wilt join our num - ber, Thou no more our songs shalt know.
But 'tis God that hath be - reft us: He can all our sor - rows heal.
Then in heaven with joy to greet thee, Where no fare - well tear is shed.

171 " *Blessed be the name of the Lord.* " Job 1 : 21

1 Jesus, while our hearts are bleeding
    O'er the spoils that death has won,
We would, at this solemn meeting,
    Calmly say, "Thy will be done."

2 Tho' cast down, we're not forsaken;
    Though afflicted, not alone:
Thou didst give, and thou hast taken:
    Blessed Lord, "Thy will be done."

3 Tho' to-day we're filled with mourning,
    Mercy still is on the throne;
With thy smiles of love returning,
    We can sing "Thy will be done."

4 By thy hands the boon was given;
    Thou hast taken but thine own:
Lord of earth, and God of heaven,
    Evermore, "Thy will be done."

THOMAS HASTINGS, 1850

172

1 Brother, thou hast left us lonely,
    Sorrow fills our hearts to-day;
But beyond this vale of sorrow
    Tears will all be wiped away.

2 Brother, thou art sweetly resting,
    Cold may be this earthly tomb,
But the angels sweetly whispered,
    " Come and live with us at home."

3 Brother, thou art sweetly resting
    On the lovely Saviour's breast,
Where the wicked cease from troubling,
    And the weary are at rest.

4 Brother, thou art sweetly resting,
    Here thy toils and cares are o'er;
Pain and sickness, death and sorrow,
    Never can distress thee more.

173 Safe in the Arms of Jesus

"Underneath are the everlasting arms." Deut. 33: 27

FANNY J. CROSBY

W. H. DOANE, by per.

1. Safe in the arms of Je - sus, Safe on his gen - tle breast,
2. Safe in the arms of Je - sus, Safe from cor - rod - ing care,
3. Je - sus, my heart's dear ref - uge, Je - sus has died for me;

REF. *Safe in the arms of Je - sus, Safe on his gen - tle breast,*

rit. FINE.

There by his love o'er - shad - ed, Sweetly my soul shall rest.
Safe from the world's temp - ta - tions, Sin can - not harm me there.
Firm on the rock of A - ges Ev - er my trust shall be.

There by his love o'er - shad - ed, Sweet-ly my soul shall rest.

Hark! 'tis the voice of an - gels, Borne in a song to me, . .
Free from the blight of sor - row, Free from my doubts and fears; .
Here let me wait with pa - tience, Wait till the night is o'er; .

D.C. REFRAIN.

O - ver the fields of glo - ry, O - ver the jas - per sea. . . . .
On - ly a few more tri - als, On - ly a few more tears! . . .
Wait till I see the morn - ing Break on the gold - en shore. . . .

174 Let Me Go 8s. 7s.

L. H.

L. HARTSOUGH

1. Let me go where saints are go - ing, To the man - sions of the blest;
2. Let me go where none are wea - ry, Where is raised no wail of woe;
3. Let me go, why should I tar - ry? What has earth to bind me here?

Let me go where my Re - deem - er Has pre - pared his peo - ple rest.
Let me go and bathe my spir - it In the rap - tures an - gels know.
What but cares, and toils, and sor - rows? What but death, and pain, and fear?

I would gain the realms of bright-ness, Where they dwell for - ev - er - more;
Let me go, for bliss e - ter - nal Lures my soul a - way, a - way,
Let me go, for hopes most cher-ished, Blast - ed round me oft - en lie;

I would join the friends that wait me O - ver on the oth - er shore.
And the vic - tor's song tri - um-phant Thrills my heart,— I can - not stay.
Oh! I've gath - ered bright-est flow - ers, But to see them fade and die.

Used by per. of The Biglow & Main Co.

175 Chelmsford C. M.

(On the Death of a Minister)

DODDRIDGE

A. CHAPIN, 1823

1. Now let our mourn-ing hearts re-vive, And all our tears be dry;
2. Tho' earth-ly shep-herds dwell in dust, The a-ged and the young,
3. Th'e-ter-nal Shep-herd still sur-vives, New com-fort to im-part;
4. "Lo, I am with you," saith the Lord, "My church shall safe a-bide;

Why should those eyes be drown'd in grief, Which view a Sav-iour nigh?
The watch-ful eye's in dark-ness closed, And mute th'in-struc-tive tongue.
His eye still guides us, and his voice Still an-i-mates our heart.
For I will ne'er for-sake my own, Whose souls in me con-fide."

176 Peaceful Rest 8s. 4s

L. O. EMERSON

1. There is a calm for those who weep, A rest for wea-ry
2. The storm that sweeps the win-t'ry sky No more dis-turbs their
3. There, trav-'ler in the vale of tears, To realms of ev-er-

_pp_

pil - grims found : They soft-ly lie, and sweetly sleep, Low in the ground.
deep re - pose, Than summer evening's la-test sigh, That shuts the rose.
last - ing light, Thro' time's dark wil-der-ness of years, Pur-sue thy flight.

177 **Burber** S. M

Softly

J. H. TENNEY

1. Go to thy rest, fair child! Go to thy dream - less bed,
2. Be - fore thy heart had learn'd In way - ward - ness to stray;
3. Ere sin had sear'd the breast, Or sor - row woke the tear;
4. Be - cause thy smile was fair, Thy lip and eye so bright,
5. Shall love, with weak em - brace, Thy up - ward wing de - tain?

While yet so gen - tle, un - de - filed, With bless - ings on thy head.
Be - fore thy feet had ev - er turn'd The dark and down - ward way;
Rise to thy throne of change - less rest, In yon ce - les - tial sphere!
Be - cause thy lov - ing cra - dle - care Was such a dear de - light;
No! gen - tle an - gel, seek thy place A - mid the cher - ub train.

178 **Dublin** C. M.

Arr. by J. D. B.

1. When bloom - ing youth is snatch'd a - way By death's re - sist - less hand,
2. While pit - y prompts the ris - ing sigh, O may this truth im - prest
3. Let this vain world en - gage no more; Be - hold the gap - ing tomb!
4. The voice of this a - larm - ing scene May ev - 'ry heart o - bey;

Our hearts the mourn - ful trib - ute pay, Which pit - y must de - mand.
With aw - ful pow'r — I too must die — Sink deep in ev - 'ry breast.
It bids us seize the pres - ent hour, To - mor - row death may come.
Nor be the heav'n - ly warn - ing vain, Which calls to watch and pray.

" Them also which sleep in Jesus will God bring with him." I THESS 4: Ǝ

Mrs. MACKAY   W. B. BRADBURY, 1843

1. A - sleep in Je - sus! bless-ed sleep, From which none ev - er wakes to weep;
2. A - sleep in Je - sus! oh, how sweet To be for such a slum-ber meet!
3. A - sleep in Je - sus! peace-ful rest! Whose wak-ing is su - preme-ly blest;
4. A - sleep in Je - sus! oh, for me May such a bliss-ful ref - uge be!

A calm and un - dis-turbed re - pose, Un - bro - ken by the last of foes.
With ho - ly con - fi - dence to sing That death has lost its ven-omed sting.
No fear, no woe shall dim that hour Which man - i - fests the Sav-iour's power.
Se - cure - ly shall my ash - es lie, And wait the sum-mons from on high.

180 **Retreat** L. M.

THOS. HASTINGS

1. In this lone hour of deep dis-tress, When hea - vy sor - rows round me press,
2. A hus - band lies in death's embrace, The grave is now his rest - ing place,
3. As - suage my grief, re - move my fears, Sup - press my mur-m'ring, dry my tears;

En - cour - aged by thy gra - cious word, I trust thee as the wid-ow's God.
Oh, as I pass be - neath thy rod, Re - veal thy - self the wid-ow's God.
Help me to own thee as my Lord, And bless thee as the wid-ow's God.

181

Death of a mother.

1 How many were the silent prayers
  My mother offered up for me!
  How many were the bitter cares
  She felt when none but God could see!

2 Well, she is gone, and now in heaven
  She sings his praise, who died for her,

And in her hand a harp is given,
And she's a heavenly worshipper.

3 And let me choose the path she chose,
  And her I soon again may see,
  Beyond this world of sin and woes
  With Jesus in eternity. __

182 **Liberty Hall** C. M.

Arranged

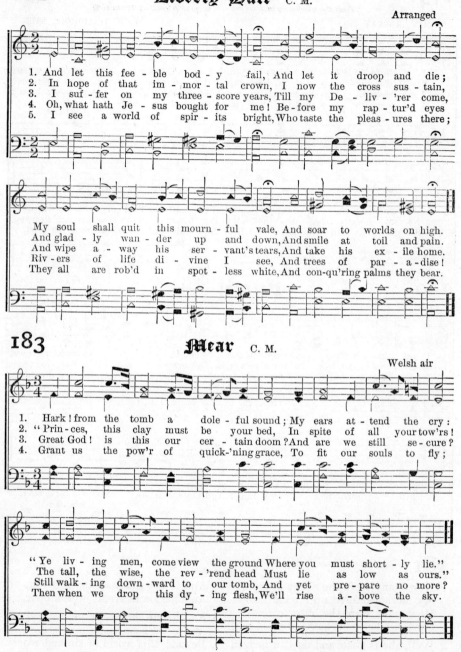

1. And let this fee - ble bod - y fail, And let it droop and die;
2. In hope of that im - mor - tal crown, I now the cross sus - tain,
3. I suf - fer on my three - score years, Till my De - liv - 'rer come,
4. Oh, what hath Je - sus bought for me! Be - fore my rap - tur'd eyes
5. I see a world of spir - its bright, Who taste the pleas - ures there;

My soul shall quit this mourn - ful vale, And soar to worlds on high.
And glad - ly wan - der up and down, And smile at toil and pain.
And wipe a - way his ser - vant's tears, And take his ex - ile home.
Riv - ers of life di - vine I see, And trees of par - a - dise!
They all are rob'd in spot - less white, And con - qu'ring palms they bear.

183 **Mear** C. M.

Welsh air

1. Hark! from the tomb a dole - ful sound; My ears at - tend the cry:
2. "Prin - ces, this clay must be your bed, In spite of all your tow'rs!
3. Great God! is this our cer - tain doom? And are we still se - cure?
4. Grant us the pow'r of quick-'ning grace, To fit our souls to fly;

"Ye liv - ing men, come view the ground Where you must short - ly lie."
The tall, the wise, the rev - 'rend head Must lie as low as ours.
Still walk - ing down - ward to our tomb, And yet pre - pare no more?
Then when we drop this dy - ing flesh, We'll rise a - bove the sky.

184 We'll Never Say Good=By

"*We shall never say 'good-by' in heaven.*" The words of a dying Christian woman

Mrs. F. W. Chapman   J. H. Tenney

1. Our friends on earth we meet with pleas-ure, While swift the mo-ments fly,
2. How joy-ful is the thought that lin-gers, When loved ones cross death's sea,
3. No part-ing words shall e'er be spo-ken In that bright land of flowers,

Yet ev-er comes the thought of sad-ness That we must say good-by.
That when our la-bors here are end-ed, With them we'll ev-er be.
But songs of joy, and peace, and glad-ness, Shall ev-er-more be ours.

REFRAIN.

We'll nev-er say good-by in heaven, We'll nev-er say good-by, . . .
good-by,

Repeat Refrain pp after last stanza.

For in that land of joy and song We'll nev-er say good-by.

185 We Shall Sleep, but not Forever

"Sown in corruption . . . . raised in incorruption." 1 Cor. 15: 42

Mrs. M. A. Kidder

S. J. Vail, by per.

1. We shall sleep, but not for-ev-er, There will be a glo-rious dawn;
2. When we see a pre-cious blos-som That we tend-ed with such care,
3. We shall sleep, but not for-ev-er, In the lone and si-lent grave;

We shall meet to part, no, nev-er, On the res-ur-rec-tion morn.
Rude-ly tak-en from our bo-som, How our ach-ing hearts de-spair!
Bless-ed be the Lord that tak-eth, Bless-ed be the Lord that gave.

From the deep-est caves of o-cean, From the des-ert and the plain,
Round its lit-tle grave we lin-ger, Till the set-ting sun is low,
In the bright e-ter-nal cit-y Death can nev-er, nev-er come!

From the val-ley and the moun-tain, Count-less throngs shall rise a-gain.
Feel-ing all our hopes have per-ished With the flow'r we cher-ished so.
In his own good time he'll call us From our rest, to home, sweet home.

Chorus. *cres.*

We shall sleep, but not for-ev-er, There will be a glo-rious dawn;

We Shall Sleep, but not Forever

We shall meet to part, no, nev - er, On the res - ur - rec - tion morn.

186 Silently Bury the Dead

C. E. Leslie

1. Si - lent-ly, si - lent-ly, they pass a-way, Si - lent-ly, si - lent-ly, short is their
2. Si - lent-ly, si - lent-ly, sweet is their sleep, Si - lent-ly, si - lent-ly, for them we
3. Si - lent-ly, si - lent-ly, bur - y the dead, Si - lent-ly, si - lent-ly, the soul has
4. Si - lent-ly, si - lent-ly, lay them to rest, Si - lent-ly, si - lent-ly, God tho't it

stay; From earth to hea - ven they've tak-en their flight, Far from all sor-row and pain and from
weep; Oh, how we mourn, and how sad are our hearts, When from the bod - y the spir - it de -
fied Up to our hea-ven-ly Father who gave, And thro' his great lov-ing kind-ness will
best A - loft in hea-ven their Saviour to meet, And all the sanc-ti-fied an-gels to

night, To their Sav-iour who is call-ing, Call-ing, come home, Call-ing, come home.
parts! But 'tis Je - sus who is call-ing, Call-ing, come home, Call-ing, come home.
save. For 'tis Je - sus who is call-ing, Call-ing, come home, Call-ing, come home.
greet. So 'tis Je - sus who is call-ing, Call-ing, come home, Call-ing, come home.

187 The Unseen City

(SOLO, QUARTET OR CHORUS)

EMMA TUTTLE   Arr. from CLARK, by W. E. M. HACKLEMAN

Very slowly

1. I think of a cit-y I have not seen Ex-cept in my hours of
2. I think of that cit-y, for oh, how oft My heart has been wrung at
3. That beau-ti-ful cit-y is home to me, My lov'd ones are go-ing

dream - ing; Where the feet of mor-tals have nev-er been To
part - ing; With friends all pale who with foot-fall soft To its
thith - er, And they who al-read-y have cross'd the sea Are

dark-en its soft, soft gleam-ing: A glim-mer of pearl, and a glint of
air - y heights were start-ing: I see them a-gain in their rai-ment
call-ing to me, "Come hith-er;" The ten-der eyes that I worshipped

gold, And a breath from the souls of ro-ses; And glo-ry and
white, In the blue, blue dis-tance dwell-ing; And I hear their
here, From the gold-en heights be-hold me; And their songs en -

The Unseen City

beau - ty all un - told, Steal o - ver my calm re - po - ses.
prais - es in calm de - light, Come down to the breez - es swell - ing.
trance my rap - tured ear When the wings of slum - ber fold me.

REFRAIN.

As I dream . . . . As I
As I dream of a cit - y I have not seen, As I

dream . . . . of a cit - y I have not seen,
dream of a cit - y I have not seen, As I dream, ...

As I dream . . . .
As I dream of a cit - y I have not seen, As I

dream . . . .
dream of a cit - y I have not seen, Of a cit - y I have not seen.

188 **In the Cross of Christ** 8s. 7s.

J. Bowring

I. Conkey

1. In the cross of Christ I glo - ry, Tow'ring o'er the wrecks of time ;
2. When the woes of life o'er-take me, Hopes de - ceive and fears an - noy,
3. When the sun of bliss is beam-ing Light and love up - on my way,
4. Bane and bless - ing, pain and pleas-ure, By the cross are sanc - ti - fied ;

All the light of sa - cred sto - ry Gath-ers round its head sub - lime.
Nev - er shall the cross for - sake me ; Lo ! it glows with peace and love.
From the cross the ra - diance stream-ing, Adds more lus - ter to the day.
Peace is there that knows no meas-ure, Joys that thro' all time a - bide.

189 **Antioch** C. M.

Isaac Watts

G. F. Handel

1. Joy to the world, the Lord is come ! Let earth re - ceive her King ;
2. Joy to the earth, the Sav - iour reigns ! Let men their songs em - ploy ;
3. He rules the world with truth and grace ; And makes the na - tions prove

Let ev - 'ry heart pre - pare him room, And heav'n and nature sing, And
While fields and floods, rocks, hills and plains, Re-peat the sounding joy, Re -
The glo - ries of his right-eous - ness, And wonders of his love, And

And heav'n and na-ture

Antioch

heav'n and na - ture sing, And heav'n, and heav'n and na - ture sing.
peat the sound-ing joy, Re - peat, re - peat the sound-ing joy.
won-ders of his love, And won - ders, won - ders of his love.
sing, And heav'n and na-ture sing, And heav'n and na - ture sing.

190 O Lord, within My Soul

E. A. H.   Rev. E. A. Hoffman

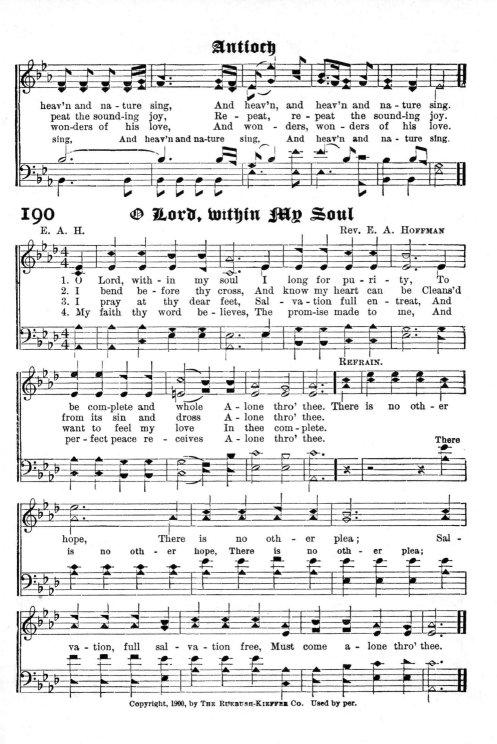

1. O Lord, with - in my soul I long for pu - ri - ty, To
2. I bend be - fore thy cross, And know my heart can be Cleans'd
3. I pray at thy dear feet, Sal - va - tion full en - treat, And
4. My faith thy word be - lieves, The prom-ise made to me, And

REFRAIN.

be com-plete and whole A - lone thro' thee. There is no oth - er
from its sin and dross A - lone thro' thee.
want to feel my love In thee com - plete.
per - fect peace re - ceives A - lone thro' thee.

There

hope, There is no oth - er plea; Sal -
is no oth - er hope, There is no oth - er plea;

va - tion, full sal - va - tion free, Must come a - lone thro' thee.

Rev. J. C. BURKETT

1. Death shall not de-stroy my com-fort,　Christ shall guide me thro' the gloom;
2. Jor-dan's streams shall not o'er-flow me　While my Sav-iour's by my side;
3. Smil-ing an-gels now sur-round me,　Troops re-splen-dent fill the skies;
4. Je-sus, clad in daz-zling splen-dor,　Now, me-thinks, ap-pears in view!

Down he'll send some an-gel con-voy　To con-vey my spir-it home.
Ca-naan, Ca-naan lies be-fore me,　Rise, and cross the swell-ing tide.
Glo-ry shin-ing all a-round me　While my hap-py spir-it flies.
Breth-ren, could you see my Je-sus,　You would love and serve him, too.

REFRAIN.

Soon with an-gels I'll be march-ing　With bright glo-ry on my brow;

Who will share my bliss-ful por-tion,　Who will love my Sav-iour now?

By permission

192 Rockingham L. M.

"He shall testify of me." John 15: 26

JOHN STEWART, 1803

Dr. LOWELL MASON

1. Come, Ho - ly Spir - it, calm my mind, And fit me to ap - proach my God;
2. Hast thou im - part - ed to my soul A liv - ing spark of ho - ly fire?
3. A bright - er faith and hope im - part, And let me now my Sav - iour see;

Re - move each vain, each world - ly tho't, And lead me to thy blest a - bode.
Oh, kin - dle now the sa - cred flame, And make me burn with pure de - sire.
Oh, soothe and cheer my bur - dened heart, And bid my spir - it rest in thee.

193 Sykes L. M.

"Gathered together in my name." Matt. 18: 20

SAMUEL STENNETT, 1787

J. H. HALL

1. "Where two or three, with sweet ac - cord, O - be - dient to their Sov - 'reign Lord,
2. "There," says the Sav - iour, "will I be, A - mid this lit - tle com - pa - ny;—
3. We meet at thy com - mand, dear Lord, Re - ly - ing on thy faith - ful word:

Meet to re - count his acts of grace, And of - fer sol - emn pray'r and praise:
To them un - veil my smil - ing face, And shed my glo - ries round the place."
Now send thy Spir - it from a - bove; Now fill our hearts with heav'n - ly love.

194 Fount of Glory

" O how love I thy law !" Psalm 119; 97

PHOEBE PALMER

A. L. LANDIS

1. { Bless - ed Bi - ble, how I love it! How it doth my bos - om cheer!
{ What hath earth like this to cov - et? Oh, what stores of wealth are here!
2. { Yes, I'll to my bos - om press thee, Pre - cious word! I'll hide thee here!
{ Sure my ver - y heart will bless thee, For thou ev - er say'st, "Good cheer!"
3. { Yes, sweet Bi - ble! I will hide thee Deep, yes, deep - er in this heart;
{ Thou thro' all my life wilt guide me, And in death we will not part.

Man was lost and doomed to sor - row, Not one ray of light or bliss
Speak, my heart, and tell my pond'rings, Tell how far thy rov - ings led,
Part in death! no, nev - er, nev - er! Thro' death's vale I'll lean on thee!

Could he from earth's treas - ures bor - row, Till his way was cheered by this.
When this book bro't back thy wand'rings, Speaking life as from the dead.
And in bright - er worlds, for - ev - er, Sweet - er far thy truths shall be.

195 My Jesus, I Love Thee

London Hymn Book

A. J. GORDON, by per.

1. My Je - sus, I love thee, I know thou art mine, For thee all the
2. I love thee be - cause thou hast first lov - ed me, And purchased my
3. I will love thee in life, I will love thee in death, And praise thee as
4. In man - sions of glo - ry and end - less de - light, I'll ev - er a-

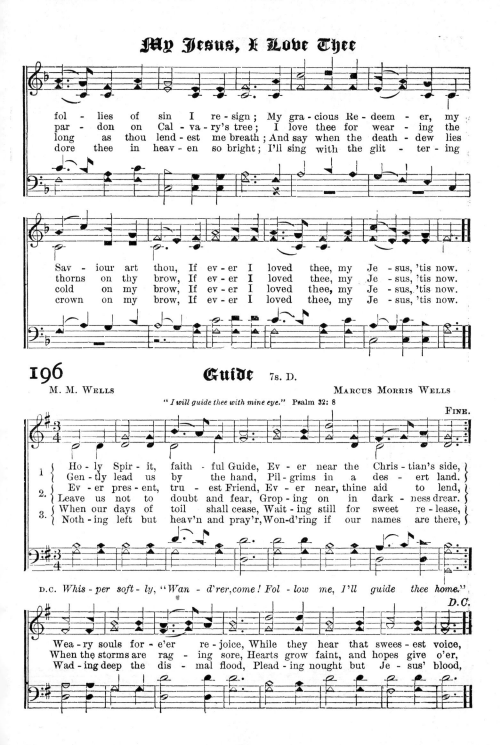

197 Only Thee 7s.

H. C. Blosser

Slowly.

1. Bless-ed Sav-iour, thee I love, All my oth-er joys a-bove;
2. Once a-gain be-side the cross, All my gain I count but loss;
3. From be-neath that thorn-y crown Tric-kle drops of cleansing down;
4. Bless-ed Sav-iour, thine am I, Thine to live, and thine to die;

All my hopes in thee a-bide, Thou my Hope, and nought be-side;
Earth-ly pleas-ures fade a-way; Clouds they are that hide my day;
Par-don from thy pierc-ed hand Now I take, while here I stand;
Height or depth, or earth-ly pow'r Ne'er shall hide my Sav-iour more:

DUET.

Ev-er let my glo-ry be, On-ly, on-ly, on-ly . . thee;
Hence, vain shad-ows! let me see Je-sus, cru-ci-fied for . me;
On-ly then I live to thee, When thy wounded side I . . see;
Ev-er shall my glo-ry be, On-ly, on-ly, on-ly . . thee!

Ev-er let . . my glo-ry be, On-ly, on-ly, on-ly thee.
Hence, vain shad-ows! let me see Je-sus, cru-ci-fied for me.
On-ly then . . I live to thee, When thy wounded side I see.
Ev-er shall . . my glo-ry be, On-ly, on-ly, on-ly thee!

198 Oh, I Love to Talk with Jesus

" Let me talk with thee." Jer. 12: 1

Words arr.

W. G. Fischer, by per.

1. Oh, I love to talk with Je - sus, for it smooths the rug - ged road;
2. Oft I tell him I am wea - ry, and I fain would be at rest;
3. Though the way is long and drear - y to that far - off, dis - tant clime,
4. So I'll wait a lit - tle lon - ger, till my Lord's ap - point - ed time,

And it seems to help me on - ward, when I faint be - neath my load;
That I'm dai - ly, hour - ly long - ing to re - pose up - on his breast;
Yet I know that my Re - deem - er jour - neys with me all the time;
And a - long the up - ward path - way still my pil - grim feet shall climb;

When my heart is crush'd with sor - row, and my eyes with tears are dim,
And he an - swers me so kind - ly, in the ten - d'rest tones of love,
And the more I come to know him, and his won - drous grace ex - plore,
Soon with - in my Fa - ther's dwell - ing, where the ma - ny man - sions be,

There is nought can yield me com - fort like a lit - tle talk with him.
"I am com - ing soon to take thee to my hap - py home a - bove."
How my long - ing grow - eth stron - ger still to know him more and more.
I shall see my bless - ed Sav - iour, and he then will talk with me.

199 Cross of Christ, O Sacred Tree

Daniel T. Taylor

Albert H. Grove

mf

1. Cross of Christ, O sa - cred tree, Hide my sins and shel - ter me;
2. Cross of Christ, O sa - cred tree, Let me to thy shad - ow flee;
3. Cross of Christ, O sa - cred tree, Type of love's deep mys - ter - y;
4. Cross of Christ, O sa - cred tree, This my boast shall ev - er be,

Claim or mer - it have I none, I am vile and all un - done;
Here they mocked the Cru - ci - fied, Here the roy - al suf - f'rer died;
'Twas my sins pro - voked this love, I this match - less pas - sion moved;
That thy blood for me was shed, That for me he groan'd and bled.

pp

I to thee for suc - cor fly— Give me ref - uge or I die.
Here was shed th'a - ton - ing blood, Here ex - pired the Son of God;
For my soul this love was stored, On my head the bless - ing poured.
Now I catch that gra - cious eye, Now I know I shall not die.

mf   *rit.*

Cross of Christ, O sa - cred tree, All my hopes are set on thee.
Cross of Christ, O sa - cred tree, Can the guilt - y trust in thee?
Cross of Christ, O sa - cred tree, Now I solve love's mys - ter - y.
Cross of Christ, O sa - cred tree, All my guilt is lost in thee.

I. N. McHose. Alt.

I. N. McHose

1. Oh, the great love the dear Sav - iour has shown To shame - ful - ly
2. Pal - a - ces, man - sions and inns had no room For Christ, who so
3. Man of great sor - rows and home - less was he, But yet my Re -

die on the tree, Leav - ing his scep - tre and beau - ti - ful throne
joy - ful - ly came Down from yon hea - ven our path to il - lume,
deem - er and Friend, Pour - ing in in - fi - nite streams up - on me

REFRAIN.

To res - cue a sin - ner like me! Oh, ... such
And save us from sin and from shame. Oh, such won - der - ful,
A love that can nev - er - more end.

won - der - ful love! Oh, ... such won - der - ful love! Je - sus, my
Oh, such won - der - ful

Sav - iour, left scep - tre and throne, To res - cue a sin - ner like me.

Used by per. of HENRY DATE, owner of copyright

201 Love Found Me

H. L. GILMOUR

Arr. by H. L. G.

1. When out in sin and dark-ness lost, Love found me; My
2. The Spir-it roused me from my sleep, Love found me; Con-
3. I'll praise him while he gives me breath, Love found me; For
4. And when I reach the gold-paved street, Love found me; I'll

faint-ing soul was tem-pest tossed, Love found me; I
vic-tion seized me strong and deep, Love found me; Al-
sav-ing from an end-less death, Love found me; Christ
sit a-dor-ing at his feet, Love found me; And

heard the Sav-iour's words so blest, Love found me, "Come, wea-ry, heav-y-
though I long withstood his grace, Love found me, He wooed me to his
is my ad-vo-cate a-bove, Love found me, I'm yoked to him in
sing ho-san-nas round the throne, Love found me, Where I shall know as

REFRAIN.

la-den, rest," Love found me. Oh, 'twas love, love,
kind em-brace, Love found me.
per-fect love, Love found me.
I am known, Love found me. Oh, 'twas love, 'twas won-drous love,

Love that moved the might-y God, Love, love, 'twas love found me.

I Want to Love Him more

Rev. F. L. Snyder   Howard E. Smith

1. There is a sto-ry ev-er new, I'll tell it o'er and o'er,
2. The Prince of life, yet as a babe, He came in days of yore,
3. The sto-ry ev-er sweet-er grows, How on the cross he bore
4. O, how he suf-fer'd on the tree, No love like that be-fore;

How Je-sus gave his life for me; I want to love him more.
To bring good-will and peace to men; I want to love him more.
My sins, and by his stripes I'm heal'd; I want to love him more.
I know and feel I love him, yet I want to love him more.

REFRAIN.

I want to love him more, I want to love him more;
love him more, love him more;

He did so ver-y much for me, I want to love him more.
love him more.

203

Spirit so Holy

"Lead me in thy truth, and teach me." Psalm 25: 5

D. W. WHITTLE

GEO. C. STEBBINS

1. Spir - it so ho - ly, Spir - it of love, Spir - it so
2. Spir - it of wis - dom, Spir - it of light, Spir - it of
3. Spir - it so hum - ble, Spir - it so meek, Spir - it so
4. Spir - it of pow - er, Spir - it of God, Spir - it of

gen - tle, Sent from a - bove; . Price - less pos - ses - sion,
knowl - edge, Show - ing the right; . Guide us and teach us,
kind - ly, Help - ing the weak; . Work in and through us,
burn - ing, Work through thy word; . Search us and sift us,

Pur - chase of blood, Good be - yond meas - ure, Gift of our Lord.
Ful - ly to know All that in Je - sus God would be - stow.
Make us to be Low - ly and lov - ing, Yield - ing to thee.
Spare not the dross, Show us that self life Ends at the cross.

204

Fill Me Now

Rev. E. H. STOKES, D.D.

JNO. R. SWENEY

1. Hov - er o'er me, Ho - ly Spir - it, Bathe my tremb - ling heart and brow;
2. Thou can'st fill me, gra - cious Spir - it, Tho' I can - not tell thee how;
3. I am weak - ness, full of weak - ness; At thy sa - cred feet I bow;
4. Cleanse and com - fort, bless and save me; Bathe, oh, bathe my heart and brow;

Fill Me Now

FINE.

Fill me with thy hal-low'd pres-ence, Come, oh, come and fill me now.
But I need thee, great-ly need thee, Come, oh, come and fill me now.
Blest, di-vine, e-ter-nal Spir-it, Fill with power, and fill me now.
Thou art com-fort-ing and sav-ing, Thou art sweet-ly fill-ing now.

D.S. *Fill me with thy hal-low'd pres-ence,—Come, oh, come and fill me now.*

D.S.

REFRAIN.

Fill me now, fill me now, Je-sus, come and fill me now;

---

205   O How Happy are They   12s. 9s.

1. Oh, how hap-py are they Who their Sav-iour o-bey, And have
2. 'Twas a hea-ven be-low My Re-deem-er to know, And the
3. Je-sus all the day long Was my joy and my song; Oh, that
4. Now my rem-nant of days Would I spend in his praise, Who has

laid up their treas-ures a-bove! Oh, what tongue can ex-press The sweet
an-gels could do noth-ing more, Than to fall at his feet, And the
more his sal-va-tion might see! He hath loved me, I cried; He hath
died, me from death to re-deem; Whether ma-ny or few, All my

com-fort and peace Of a soul in its ear-li-est love.
sto-ry re-peat, And the lov-er of sin-ners a-dore.
suf-fered and died, To re-deem such a re-bel as me!
days are his due—May they all be de-vot-ed to him.

206 The Comforter has Come!

" I will pray the Father, and he shall give you another Comforter, that he may abide with you forever." John 14: 16

Rev. F. Bottome, D.D.　　　　　　　　　　　　　　Wm. J. Kirkpatrick

1. Oh, spread the ti - dings round, wher - ev - er man is found, Wher-
2. The long, long night is past, the morn - ing breaks at last; And
3. Lo, the great King of kings, with heal - ing in his wings, To
4. O bound - less Love di - vine! how shall this tongue of mine To
5. Sing, till the ech - oes fly a - bove the vault - ed sky, And

ev - er hu - man hearts and hu - man woes a - bound; Let ev - 'ry Chris - tian
hush'd the dread - ful wail and fu - ry of the blast, As o'er the gold - en
ev - 'ry cap - tive soul a full de - liv - 'rance brings; And thro' the va - cant
won - d'ring mor - tals tell the match - less grace di - vine—That I, a child of
all the saints a - bove to all be - low re - ply, In strains of end - less

D.S. *Ho - ly Ghost from heav'n, The Fa - ther's promise giv'n; Oh, spread the tid - ings*

Fine.

tongue pro - claim the joy - ful sound : The Com - fort - er has come !
hills the day ad - van - ces fast ! The Com - fort - er has come !
cells the song of tri - umph rings : The Com - fort - er has come !
hell, should in his im - age shine ! The Com - fort - er has come !
love, the song that ne'er will die : The Com - fort - er has come !

round, Wher - ev - er man is found— The Com - fort - er has come !

Refrain.

D.S.

The Com - fort - er has come, The Com - fort - er has come ! The

207

Blessed Assurance

"He is faithful that promised." Heb. 10: 23

F. J. CROSBY   MRS. JOSEPH F. KNAPP

1. Bless-ed as-sur-ance, Je-sus is mine! Oh, what a fore-taste of
2. Per-fect sub-mis-sion, per-fect de-light, Vis-ions of rap-ture now
3. Per-fect sub-mis-sion, all is at rest, I in my Sav-iour am

glo-ry di-vine! Heir of sal-va-tion, pur-chase of God,
burst on my sight; An-gels de-scend-ing bring from a-bove
hap-py and blest; Watch-ing and wait-ing, look-ing a-bove,

REFRAIN.

Born of his spir-it, washed in his blood. This is my sto-ry,
Ech-oes of mer-cy, whis-pers of love.
Filled with his good-ness, lost in his love.

this is my song, Prais-ing my Sav-iour all the day long; This is my

sto-ry, this is my song, Prais-ing my Sav-iour all the day long.

208 May C. M.

Miss Ann Steele

Chas. Edw. Pollock, by per.

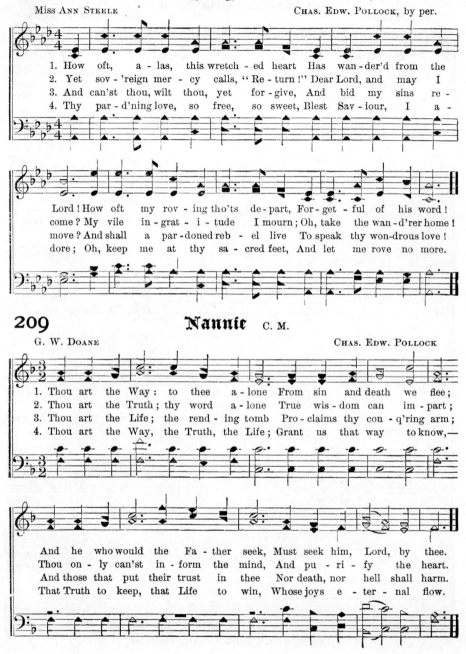

1. How oft, a - las, this wretch - ed heart Has wan - der'd from the
2. Yet sov - 'reign mer - cy calls, "Re - turn!" Dear Lord, and may I
3. And can'st thou, wilt thou, yet for - give, And bid my sins re -
4. Thy par - d'ning love, so free, so sweet, Blest Sav - iour, I a -

Lord! How oft my rov - ing tho'ts de - part, For - get - ful of his word!
come? My vile in - grat - i - tude I mourn; Oh, take the wan - d'rer home!
move? And shall a par - doned reb - el live To speak thy won - drous love!
dore; Oh, keep me at thy sa - cred feet, And let me rove no more.

209 Nannie C. M.

G. W. Doane

Chas. Edw. Pollock

1. Thou art the Way: to thee a - lone From sin and death we flee;
2. Thou art the Truth; thy word a - lone True wis - dom can im - part;
3. Thou art the Life; the rend - ing tomb Pro - claims thy con - q'ring arm;
4. Thou art the Way, the Truth, the Life; Grant us that way to know,—

And he who would the Fa - ther seek, Must seek him, Lord, by thee.
Thou on - ly can'st in - form the mind, And pu - ri - fy the heart.
And those that put their trust in thee Nor death, nor hell shall harm.
That Truth to keep, that Life to win, Whose joys e - ter - nal flow.

Saviour, We Come to Thee

Mrs. L. M. Evilsizer

S. J. Perry

1. Sav-iour, we come to thee In our hu-mil-i-ty, Lambs of thy
2. Sav-iour, we pray to thee, Heed thou our ear-nest plea, Help us to
3. Sav-iour, we trust in thee, In our sim-plic-i-ty, Know-ing thine

fold are we Seek-ing thy love; Grant us thy bless-ing now, While at thy
ev-er be Gen-tle and pure; As in the days of old, Keep us with-
eye doth see Wher-e'er we roam; And oh, 'tis sweet to know That where-so-

Refrain

feet we bow, O ten-der Shepherd, thou, Guide us a - bove. Sav-iour, O Sav-iour dear,
in thy fold; While we thy face be-hold, Rest we se - cure.
e'er we go Thou dost the pathway show, Leading us home.

To thee our hearts draw near; Hear thou our pray'r sin-cere, And meet with us here.

211 Weeping One of Bethany

Respectfully inscribed to "The Hall Quartet"

J. C. B.

J. Calvin Bushey

1. Je - sus wept! those tears are o - ver, But his love is still the same; . . Kins - man, friend, and eld - er broth - er, Is his ev - er - last - ing name. Weep-ing one,

2. Je - sus wept! and still in glo - ry He must mark the mourn - er's tear; . . Lov - ing still to trace the sto - ry Of the hearts he strengthened here. Weep-ing one,

3. Je - sus wept! that tear of sor - row If a leg - a - cy of love, . . . Yes - ter - day, to - day, to - mor - row, He the same doth ev - er prove. Weep-ing one,

REFRAIN.

weep-ing one, Sav - iour, who can love like thee? . . Weep-ing one, weep-ing one, weep-ing one, Weep-ing one of Beth - an - y.

212 **Hagerstown** L. M.

Psalm 63

I. WATTS

J. D. BRUNK, by per.

1. Great God, in-dulge my hum-ble claim, Thou art my hope, my joy, my rest;
2. Thou great and good, thou just and wise, Thou art my Fa-ther and my God!
3. With rea-dy feet I love t'ap-pear A-mong thy saints, and seek thy face;
4. I'll lift my hands, I'll raise my voice, While I have breath to pray or praise;

The glo-ries that com-pose thy name Stand all en-gaged to make me blest.
And I am thine by sa-cred ties, Thy son, thy ser-vant, bought with blood.
Oft have I seen thy glo-ry there, And felt the pow'r of sov-'reign grace.
This work shall make my heart re-joice, Throughout the rem-nant of my days.

213 **Woodworth** L. M.

"*Behold the Lamb of God.*" John 1: 29

CHARLOTTE ELLIOT

WM. B. BRADBURY

1. Just as I am, with-out one plea, But that thy blood was shed for me,
2. Just as I am, and wait-ing not To rid my soul of one dark blot,
3. Just as I am, tho' toss'd a-bout With ma-ny a con-flict, ma-ny a doubt,
4. Just as I am, poor, wretch-ed, blind, Sight, rich-es, heal-ing of the mind,

And that thou bid'st me come to thee, O Lamb of God, I come, I come!
To thee whose blood can cleanse each spot, O Lamb of God, I come, I come!
Fightings and fears with-in, with-out, O Lamb of God, I come, I come!
Yea, all I need in thee to find, O Lamb of God, I come, I come!

5 Just as I am, thou wilt receive,
Wilt welcome, pardon, cleanse, relieve;
Because thy promise I believe,
O Lamb of God, I come, I come!

6 Just as I am, thy love unknown
Hath broken every barrier down;
Now, to be thine, yea, thine alone,
O Lamb of God, I come, I come!

214 Come Just as You Are

Rev. A. Elisha Hoffman   J. Henry Showalter

1. Shall I come just as I am, Come with all my guilt and sin? If I
2. Shall I come vile as I am, And bend low at Je - sus' feet? Shall I
3. Shall I come with all my fear, Lest my sins have been too great? Shall I
4. Shall I come, tho' far a - way From the lov - ing Shepherd's fold? Will he

REFRAIN.

o - pen wide my heart, Will he en - ter in? As you are, just as you are
plead his pard'ning grace, And his love en - treat?
break thro' all my doubts, To sweet mer - cy's gate?
bless me if I firm To his prom - ise hold?

Come to Je - sus, come to - day; He will kind - ly wel-come you, Take your sins a - way.

215 I Come to Thee

Emma A. Tiffany   Geo. C. Hugg

With feeling.

1. Je - sus dear, I come to thee, Thou a - lone canst make me free;
2. Je - sus dear, to thee I bring All of earth to which I cling;
3. Je - sus dear, I come to thee, Wilt thou all my ref - uge be,

I Come to Thee

Thou a - lone canst cleanse from sin, Make me pure with - out, with - in;
All the friends my heart holds dear To thy al - tar now bring near;
Thro' the thorn - y maze of life, Thro' the bat - tles, thro' its strife?

Wound-ed at . . thy feet I lie, Do not, do not pass me by.
Keep them safe with - in thy fold, Grant them rest and joy un - told.
When the fi - nal hour doth come, Wilt thou guide me safe - ly home?

216 ## Depth of Mercy

" God is Love." 1 John, 4: 8.

CHARLES WESLEY   Arr. from BEETHOVEN

1. Depth of mer - cy! can there be Mer - cy still re - served for me?
2. I have long with - stood his grace, Long pro - voked him to his face;
3. Now in - cline me to re - pent; Let me now my sins la - ment;

Can my God his wrath for - bear? Me the chief of sin - ners spare?
Would not heark - en to his calls; Grieved him by a thou-sand falls.
Now my foul re - volt de - plore, Weep, be - lieve, and sin no more.

217 Oh, Why not To-night

"Now is the accepted time. Behold, now is the day of salvation." 2 Cor. 6: 2

Rev. H. Bonar, D.D.   J. Calvin Bushey

1. Oh, do not let the word de-part, And close thine eyes a-gainst the
2. To-mor-row's sun may nev-er rise To bless thy long de-lud-ed
3. Our Lord in pit-y lin-gers still, And wilt thou thus his love re-
4. Our bless-ed Lord re-fus-es none Who would to him their souls u-

light; Poor sin-ner, hard-en not your heart, Be saved, oh, to-night.
sight; This is the time, oh, then be wise, Be saved, oh, to-night.
quite; Re-nounce at once thy stub-born will, Be saved, oh, to-night.
nite. Be-lieve, o-bey, the work is done, Be saved, oh, to-night.

Refrain.

Oh, why not to-night? Oh, why not to-
Oh, why not to-night? Why not to-night? Why not to-night?

night? Wilt thou be saved? Then why not to-night?
Why not to-night? Wilt thou be sav'd, wilt thou be sav'd, Then why not, oh, why not to-night?

Re-entered and copyright, 1895, by J. H. Hall.

218 · **He Died for Thee**

"The Son of man is come to save." Matt. 18: 11

F. J. CROSBY

S. J. VAIL

1. Trou - bled heart, thy God is call - ing, He is draw - ing
2. Come, the Spir - it still is plead - ing, Come to him, the
3. Art thou wait - ing till the mor - row? Thou may'st nev - er
4. Let the an - gels bear the ti - dings Up - ward to the

ver - y near; Do not hide thy deep e - mo - tion,
meek and mild; He is wait - ing now to save you,
see its light; Come at once! ac - cept his mer - cy;
courts of heav'n! Let them sing, with ho - ly rapt - ure,

REFRAIN.

Do not check that fall - ing tear.   Oh, be saved, his grace is free!
Wilt thou not be rec - on - ciled?
He is wait - ing—come to - night.
O'er an - oth - er soul for - giv'n!

rit.

Oh, be saved, he died for thee! Oh, be saved, he died for thee!

219 He Seeks His Wandering Sheep Today

Mrs. Martha Mills Newton

J. Henry Showalter

1. The Shepherd's heart is sad-dened, His sheep have gone a-stray; Thro' summer's heat, and
2. Thro' bri - ers, thorns, and brambles, He seeks with anxious heart, O'er mountain, vale, or
3. He's call - ing for thee, lost one, Can you not hear his voice? Then an-swer to his

win-ter's cold, He seeks his sheep al - way. Some wand'ring sheep he's seeking now, Say
for - est wild, Or in the crowded mart. O'er o-cean's main, o'er des - ert sands, He
lov - ing call, Go meet him and re - joice. Are you not wea - ry wan - der-ing Out

broth - er, is it you? Are you safe sheltered in the fold, Or are you wand'ring too?
seeks the wide world o'er; In gild - ed pal - ace of the rich; In cot-tage of the poor.
in the storm and cold? A- rise, and seek your Shepherd's face, Return un-to the fold.

REFRAIN.

He seeks his wand'ring sheep, Out in the storm and cold;
He seeks his wan - d'ring, wan-d'ring sheep to - day, Out in the storm and cold;

He Seeks His Wandering Sheep Today

Oh, shall he seek in vain, To bring them to the fold?
Oh, shall he seek, oh, shall he seek in vain, To bring them to the fold?

220 Will You Go to Jesus

E. R. Latta   Jacob M. Showalter

1. Wan - der - er in sin - ful ways, Will you go to Je - sus?
2. Wan - der - er on bar - ren ground, Will you go to Je - sus?
3. Wan - der - er, be - fore too late, Will you go to Je - sus?
4. Wan - der - er, do not de - lay! Will you go to Je - sus?

FINE.

He will save you by his grace, Will you go to Je - sus?
On - ly so can peace be found, Will you go to Je - sus?
Death may seal your aw - ful fate, Will you go to Je - sus?
Start for heav - en—Start to - day! Will you go to Je - sus?

D.S. And to him your heart will give, Will you go to Je - sus?

REFRAIN.   D.S.

He is wait - ing to re - ceive, If you on - ly will be - lieve,

By permission of J. Henry Showalter

No Hope in Jesus

"Having no hope, and without God in the world." Eph. 2: 12

Rev. W. O. Cushing

Rev. Robert Lowry

1. Oh, to have no Christ, no Sav - iour! No Rock, no Ref - uge nigh!
2. Oh, to have no Christ, no Sav - iour! How lone - ly life must be!
3. Oh, to have no Christ, no Sav - iour! No hand to clasp thine own!
4. Now, we pray thee, come to Je - sus; His par-d'ning love re - ceive;

When the dark days 'round thee gath - er, When the storms sweep o'er the sky!
Like a sail - or, lost and driv - en On a wide and shore - less sea.
Thro' the dark, dark vale of shad - ows Thou must press thy way a - lone.
For the Sav - iour now is call - ing, And he bids thee turn and live.

Refrain.

1,2,3. Oh, to have no hope in Je - sus! No friend, no light in Je - sus!
4. Come to Je - sus, he will save you; He is the friend of sin - ners;

Oh! to have no hope in Je - sus! How dark this world must be!
Then, when thou hast found the Sav - iour, How bright this world will be!

Remember Me C. M.

"I will arise and go to my Father." Luke 15: 18

J. S. COFFMAN

ASA HULL

1. O wea - ry wan - der - er, come home, Thy Sav - iour bids thee come;
2. Think of thy Fa - ther's house to - day, So blest with plenteous store.
3. Poor prod - i - gal, come home and rest, Come and be rec - on - ciled;
REF. Help me, dear Sav - iour, thee to own, And ev - er faith - ful be;

Thou long in sin didst love to roam, Yet still he calls thee, come.
Think of thy sin - ful, wandering way, Then come, and roam no more.
Here lean up - on thy Fa - ther's breast, He loves his wandering child.
And when thou sit - test on thy throne, O Lord, re - mem - ber me.

223 **Consecration** 7s.

FRANCES E. HAVERGAL

Arr.

1. Take my life, and let it be Con - se - cra - ted, Lord, to thee;
2. Take my feet, and let them be Swift and beau - ti - ful for thee;
3. Take my sil - ver and my gold, Not a mite would I with - hold;
4. Take my will and make it thine, It shall be no lon - ger mine;
5. Take my love; my Lord, I pour At thy feet its treas - ure - store;

CHO. Lord, I give my life to thee, Thine for - ev - er - more to be;

D.C.

Take my hands, and let them move At the im - pulse of thy love.
Take my voice, and let me sing Al - ways, on - ly for my King.
Take my mo - ments and my days, Let them flow in cease - less praise.
Take my heart, it is thine own, It shall be thy roy - al throne.
Take my - self, and I will be Ev - er, on - ly, all for thee.

Lord, I give my life to thee, Thine for - ev - er - more to be.

Bid Them Look to Christ

Mrs. L. M. EVILSIZER

J. C. PERRY, by per.

1. Out in the des-ert the lost are stray-ing, Bid them look to Christ and live;
2. By-ways and high-ways are thronged with dy-ing, Bid them look to Christ and live;
3. Shout ye a warn-ing to ev-'ry na-tion, Bid them look to Christ and live;

Tell them their dear ones for them are pray-ing, Bid them look to Christ and live.
Life is un-cer-tain and time is fly-ing, Bid them look to Christ and live.
This is the day to ac-cept sal-va-tion, Bid them look to Christ and live.

REFRAIN.

Go to the lost and the dy-ing, broth-er, Bid them look to Christ and live;

Sin doth be-set them, for help they're cry-ing, Oh, bid them look to Christ and live.

Come, Ye Wanderers

'Come unto me, all ye that labor and are heavy laden, and I will give you rest." Matt. 11: 28

Words arranged by C. E. P.   CHAS. EDW. POLLOCK

1. Come, ye wan-d'rers, all for-sak-en, Come to Christ for sweet-est
2. Saints are wait-ing, an-gels long-ing, God's in-vit-ing, sin-ner,
3. Christ is wait-ing to for-give you, Seek, and his for-give-ness
4. Come, ye wea-ry, hea-vy la-den, Lay your bur-dens all a-

rest; Come and join the heav'n-ly cho-rus; Come, and be su-preme-ly blessed.
come; Why still lin-ger? Why re-fuse him? And in sin-ful paths still roam?
find; One and all can have sweet par-don; He has died for all man-kind.
side; Come and claim the bless-ed Je-sus; 'Twas for you the dear Lord died.

REFRAIN.

Come, ye wea-ry, hea-vy la-den, Long by sin and care op-

pressed; Hear the pre-cious in-vi-ta-tion; "Come, and I will give you rest."

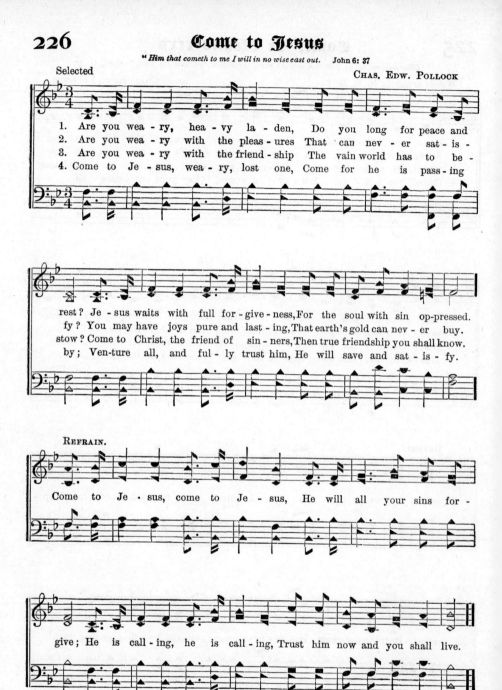

226 Come to Jesus

"Him that cometh to me I will in no wise cast out." John 6: 37

Selected

CHAS. EDW. POLLOCK

1. Are you wea - ry, hea - vy la - den, Do you long for peace and
2. Are you wea - ry with the pleas - ures That can nev - er sat - is -
3. Are you wea - ry with the friend - ship The vain world has to be -
4. Come to Je - sus, wea - ry, lost one, Come for he is pass - ing

rest? Je - sus waits with full for - give - ness, For the soul with sin op - pressed.
fy? You may have joys pure and last - ing, That earth's gold can nev - er buy.
stow? Come to Christ, the friend of sin - ners, Then true friendship you shall know.
by; Ven - ture all, and ful - ly trust him, He will save and sat - is - fy.

REFRAIN.

Come to Je - sus, come to Je - sus, He will all your sins for -

give; He is call - ing, he is call - ing, Trust him now and you shall live.

Dear Lord, I Come

S. B. McManus

A. C. Kolb

With expression.

1. Dear Lord, I come at last, Come with my sin and shame; I
2. Long has my sin-sick soul Sought pleas-ures but in vain; The
3. My friends have sought to cheer My heart with pleas-ures bright, But
4. In ev-'ry wak-ing hour I hear thy lov-ing voice, In

would my sin-ful past Might thro' thy pre-cious name Be washed a-way, and in its
part or e'en the whole Has naught but emp-ty gain; From heart re-pent-ant hear my
thou wast ev-er near, And ev-er in my sight. There stood the cross thou suffer'dst
sweet-ness and in power Bid-ding my soul re-joice. Thy peace shall ev-er with me

place Be found thy sweet a-bid-ing grace. Dear Sav-iour, here am I, Reach
cry, To live with-out thee is to die. Dear Sav-iour, here am I, Stretch
from And felt the pains of mar-tyr-dom. Dear Sav-iour, here am I, Wilt
be; Dear Lamb of God, I come to thee. Dear Sav-iour, here am I, Near

out thine hand to me, And save me else I die; Oh, let me hide in thee.
out thine hand to me, And bid me cease to cry, Blest Lamb of Cal-va-ry.
thou my sins for-give? With-out thee I shall die, But with thee I shall live.
to thy side I'd be, Blest be the ho-ly tie That binds my heart to thee.

228 I Bring My Sins to Jesus

"I will be sorry for my sin." Psalm 38: 18

Dr. Bonar

Chas. Edw. Pollock

1. I bring my sins to Je - sus, To wash my crim - son stains White, in his blood most pre - cious, Till not a spot re - mains.
2. I want to be like Je - sus, Meek, lov - ing, low - ly, mild; I want to love like Je - sus, The Fa - ther's on - ly child.
3. I long to be with Je - sus, A - mid the heav'n - ly throng; To sing with saints and an - gels The ev - er - last - ing song.

REFRAIN.

To Je - sus, to Je - sus, I bring my sins to Je - sus, To wash my crim - son stains White, in his blood most pre - cious, Till not a spot re - mains.

With Je - sus, with Je - sus, I want to be like Je - sus, Meek, lov - ing, low - ly, mild; I want to love like Je - sus, The Fa - ther's on - ly child.

With Je - sus, with Je - sus, I long to be with Je - sus, A - mid the heav'n - ly throng; To sing with saints and an - gels The ev - er - last - ing song.

Come, Ye Sinners

8s. 7s.

"Christ came into the world to save sinners." 1 Tim. 1: 15

JOSEPH HART

JEREMIAH INGALS

1. Come, ye sin-ners, poor and need-y, Weak and wounded, sick and sore,
2. Let not conscience make you lin-ger, Nor of fit-ness fond-ly dream;
3. Ag-o-ni-zing in the gar-den, Lo, your Sav-iour pros-trate lies!
4. Lo! the ris-ing Lord as-cend-ing, Pleads the vir-tue of his blood;
5. Saints and an-gels, joined in con-cert, Sing the prais-es of the Lamb,

Je-sus rea-dy stands to save you, Full of pit-y, love, and pow'r;
All the fit-ness he re-quir-eth Is to feel your need of him;
On the blood-y tree be-hold him! Hear him cry be-fore he dies:
Ven-ture on him, ven-ture free-ly, Let no oth-er trust in-trude;
While the bliss-ful seats of heav-en Sweet-ly ech-o with his name;

He is a-ble, he is a-ble, He is will-ing—doubt no more;
This he gives you, this he gives you, 'Tis the Sav-iour's ris-ing beam;
"It is fin-ished, it is fin-ished!" Sin-ners, will not this suf-fice?
None but Je-sus, none but Je-sus Can do help-less sin-ners good;
Hal-le-lu-jah! Hal-le-lu-jah! Sin-ners here may do the same;

He is a-ble, he is a-ble, He is will-ing—doubt no more.
This he gives you, this he gives you, 'Tis the Sav-iour's ris-ing beam.
"It is fin-ished, it is fin-ished!" Sin-ners, will not this suf-fice?
None but Je-sus, none but Je-sus Can do help-less sin-ners good.
Hal-le-lu-jah! hal-le-lu-jah! Sin-ners here may do the same.

Come, Lost One

"Come, for all things are now ready." Luke 14: 17

Words and melody by J. S. SHOEMAKER.

1. Come, lost one, your Sav-iour is call - ing, He's plead-ing with ten - der-est voice;
2. Come with all thy guilt and pol - lu - tion, And call on the name of the Lord;
3. Thy sins tho' they be red like crim-son, Yea, tho' they be ma - ny and great,
4. The Lord has pro-vid - ed a - bun-dance, Yea, all that ye need is in store;

Come out from your ways of transgres-sion, And has - ten to make him your choice.
He's rea - dy to cleanse and to bless you, And save by his life - giv-ing word.
Shall be blot-ted out by your Sav - iour, If ye come to him ere too late.
Then come and par-take of his boun - ty, And trust him for grace ev - er-more.

REFRAIN.

Oh, why should you wan-der in dark-ness? Oh, why should you lon - ger de - lay, When

Je - sus is rea - dy to save you, And keep you from sin ev - 'ry day?

Jesus Saves

Priscilla J. Owens

Wm. J. Kirkpatrick

1. We have heard a joy-ful sound, Je - sus saves, Je - sus saves;
2. Waft it on the roll - ing tide, Je - sus saves, Je - sus saves;
3. Sing a - bove the bat - tle's strife, Je - sus saves, Je - sus saves;
4. Give the winds a might - y voice, Je - sus saves, Je - sus saves;

Spread the glad - ness all a - round, Je - sus saves, Je - sus saves.
Tell to sin - ners, far and wide, Je - sus saves, Je - sus saves.
By his death and end - less life, Je - sus saves, Je - sus saves.
Let the na - tions now re - joice, Je - sus saves, Je - sus saves.

Bear the news to ev - 'ry land, Climb the steeps and cross the waves,
Sing, ye is - lands of the sea, Ech - o back, ye o - cean caves,
Sing it soft - ly thro' the gloom, When the heart for mer - cy craves,
Shout sal - va - tion full and free, High - est hills and deep - est caves,

On - ward, 'tis our Lord's com - mand, Je - sus saves, Je - sus saves.
Earth shall keep her ju - bi - lee, Je - sus saves, Je - sus saves.
Sing in tri - umph o'er the tomb, Je - sus saves, Je - sus saves.
This our song of vic - to - ry, Je - sus saves, Je - sus saves.

Full Salvation 8s. 7s. D.

" Saved in the Lord with an everlasting salvation." Isa. 45: 17

Rev. W. P. Jackson   Chas. Edw. Pollock

1. To the cross of Christ I'm cling-ing For that cleans-ing pure and
2. Dyed with sins as deep as scar-let, Red, like crim-son is their
3. Lov-er of my death-less spir-it, Un-to thee I flee for
4. Yes, I know the work's ac-com-plished, Je-sus saves me by his

white, Which my stains of sin e-ras-es, Fill me now with joy and
hue; Thou canst make me pure and spot-less, Thou canst form my soul a-
aid; I de-pend a-lone up-on thee; Thou hast full a-tone-ment
might; Faith in his a-ton-ing mer-its Brought me to the pre-cious

light. Thou canst make me pure and ho-ly, Whit-er than the driv-en
new. From my dark im-ag-i-na-tions—Thou wilt help me to re-
made In thy mer-its I am trust-ing, Leav-ing all a-lone to
light. From all sin-ful in-cli-na-tions, Thou hast ful-ly set me

snow;—In thy ho-ly word 'tis prom-ised, And to doubt is sin I know.
call Ev-ry thought and ev-'ry ac-tion, Giv-ing Je-sus Christ my all.
thee, That this cleans-ing ful-ly, free-ly, Now is grant-ed un-to me.
free; Nev-er more to be en-tan-gled, If I al-ways trust in thee.

233 Whiter than Snow

James Nicholson

Wm. G. Fischer

1. Lord Je - sus, I long to be per - fect - ly whole; I
2. Lord Je - sus, look down from thy throne in the skies, And
3. Lord Je - sus, for this I most hum - bly en - treat; I

want thee for - ev - er to live in my soul; Break down ev - 'ry
help me to make a com - plete sac - ri - fice; I give up my -
wait, bless - ed Lord, at thy cru - ci - fied feet; By faith, for my

i - dol, cast out ev - 'ry foe; Now wash me, and I shall be
self, and what - ev - er I know—Now wash me, and I shall be
cleansing, I see thy blood flow— Now wash me, and I shall be

Refrain

whit - er than snow. Whit - er than snow, yes, whit - er than

snow; Now wash me, and I shall be whit - er than snow.

Wonderful Grace

" By grace are ye saved." Eph. 2: 8

Anon.

CHAS. EDW. POLLOCK

With expression.

1. Saved by grace, I live to tell What the love of Christ hath done; He re-
2. In a kind, pro - pi - tious hour, To my heart the Sav - iour spoke; Touch'd me
3. Come, my fel - low sin - ners, try; Je - sus' heart is full of love; Oh, that

deemed my soul from hell, Of a reb - el made a son. Oh, I trem - ble still to
by his spir - it's pow'r, And my dang'rous slumber broke. Then I saw and owned my
you as well as I May his wondrous mer - cy prove. He has sent me to de-

think How se - cure I lived in sin, Sport - ing on de - struction's brink, Yet pre-
guilt; Soon my gra - cious Lord replied, "Fear not; I my blood have spilt;'Twas for
clare, All is read - y, all is free; Why should a - ny soul de - spair, When he

REFRAIN.

served from fall-ing in. Oh, 'tis grace,'tis won-der- ful grace,That full sal - va - tion
such as thou I died."
saved a wretch like me?

Wonderful Grace

brings; Oh, 'tis grace, 'tis won-der-ful grace, My ran-somed spir-it sings.

235

All to Christ I Owe

"Who his own self bare our sins." 1 Peter 2: 24

Mrs. Elvina M. Hall

John T. Grape, by per.

1. I hear the Saviour say, "Thy strength indeed is small; Child of weakness, watch and
2. Lord, now in-deed I find Thy pow'r and thine a-lone Can change the lep-er's
3. For noth-ing good have I Where-by thy grace to claim; I'll wash my gar-ment
4. When from my dy-ing bed My ransomed soul shall rise, Then "Je-sus paid it
5. And when be-fore the throne I stand in him complete, I'll lay my trophies

Refrain.

pray, Find in me thine all in all." Je-sus paid it all,
spots, And melt the heart of stone.
white In the blood of Calvary's Lamb.
all" Shall rend the vault-ed skies.
down, All down at Je-sus' feet.

All to him I owe; Sin had left a crim-son stain: He washed it white as snow.

236 Cleansing Fountain C. M. D.

" The fountain for sin." Zach. 13: 1

WM. COWPER, 1779　　　　　　　　　　　　　　　　　　Unknown

1. There is a foun-tain filled with blood, Drawn from Im-man-uel's veins;
2. The dy-ing thief re-joiced to see That foun-tain in his day;
3. Thou dy-ing Lamb, thy pre-cious blood Shall nev-er lose its pow'r,
4. E'er since, by faith, I saw the stream Thy flow-ing wounds sup-ply,
5. And when this fee-ble, fal-t'ring tongue Lies si-lent in the grave,

And sin-ners wash-ing in that flood, Lose all their guilt-y stains;
And may I there, tho' vile as he, Wash all my sins a-way;
Till all the ran-somed church of God Are saved to sin no more,
Re-deem-ing love has been my theme, And shall be, till I die,
Then in a no-bler, sweet-er song I'll sing thy pow'r to save;

Lose all their guilt-y stains, .. Lose all their guilt-y stains,
Wash all my sins a-way, .. Wash all my sins a-way,
Are saved to sin no more, .. Are saved to sin no more,
And shall be, till I die, ... And shall be, till I die,
I'll sing thy pow'r to save, ... I'll sing thy pow'r to save,

And sin-ners, wash-ing in that flood, Lose all their guilt-y stains.
And may I there, tho' vile as he, Wash all my sins a-way.
Till all the ran-somed church of God Are saved to sin no more.
Re-deem-ing love has been my theme, And shall be till I die.
Then in a no-bler, sweet-er song I'll sing thy pow'r to save.

237 **Coming Now, O Lord, to Thee!**

Rev. Geo. P. Hott   Aldine S. Kieffer

1. Sav - iour, to thee I come, Bur - dened with sin; O - pen the
2. Plead - ing thy grace a - lone, Hum - bly I bow; No oth - er
3. Trust - ing thy mer - cy, Lord, Night turns to day; Rest - ing up -

door, I pray, Oh, let me in! How can I lon - ger stay,
help I know, Save me just now. Heal thou my bro - ken heart,
on thy word, Doubts flee a - way. Ev - er my path shall be

My God, from thee? Thou art the Life, the Way, All in all to me.
Sav - iour di - vine; On me thy love be - stow, Make me whol - ly thine.
Where thou hast trod; I come, O Christ, to thee, Bless - ed Lamb of God.

Copyright, 1898, by A. S. Kieffer and G. P. Hott.

238 **The Lord's Prayer**

1. Our Father who art in heaven, hallowed be thy name,
2. Give us this day our dai - ly bread,
3. And lead us not into temptation, but deliver us from evil,

Thy kingdom come, thy will be done on earth as it is in heaven.
And forgive us our trespasses, as we forgive them that trespass a - gainst us.
For thine is the kingdom, and the power, and the glory, for - ever, A - men.

239 Jesus Has Died for Me

A. H. A.   A. H. A.

1. Oh, to be there, where the songs of glo-ry Float o'er the waves of the bright crystal sea;
2. Oh, for a voice to pro-claim the mes-sage In ev-'ry land and the isles of the sea,
3. Now that I've tast-ed thy love, O Je-sus, Tak-en my cross and am fol-low-ing thee,
4. Oh, for a heart that will al-ways love him, Trusting his promise wherev-er I be;

This the re-frain of the won-drous sto-ry, "Je-sus has died for me."
"God's on-ly Son is the friend of sin-ners, "Je-sus has died for me."
Help me to tell this great truth to oth-ers, "Je-sus has died for me."
Bear-ing in mind this sweet truth so pre-cious, "Je-sus has died for me."

While still I lin-ger in this world be-low, Wait-ing till homeward I am called to go,
'Tis but a lit-tle that my hands can do For this dear lov-ing One so kind and true,
Oh, that the world would seek the Father's face, Trust in his mer-cy and for-giv-ing grace;
Washed in the blood of Je-sus Christ my King, Thro' endless a-ges I this song shall sing,

I will re-peat o'er and o'er the sto-ry, "Je-sus has died for me."
But I can tell to the world the sto-ry, "Je-sus has died for me."
Then how all hearts would re-joice in sing-ing, "Je-sus has died for me."
"Glo-ry to God, ev-er-last-ing glo-ry, "Je-sus has died for me."

Copyright, 1898, by GEO. C. HUGG. By per.

The Blood of the Lamb

Foote Bros.

J. Henry Showalter, by per.

1. Christ, our Re-deem-er, died on the cross, Died for the sin-ner, paid all his due;
2. Chief-est of sin-ners Je-sus can save, As he has prom-ised, so will he do;
3. Judg-ment is com-ing, all will be there Who have re-ject-ed, who have re-fused:
4. Oh, what compas-sion! oh, boundless love! Je-sus hath pow-er, Je-sus is true:

All who re-ceive him need nev-er fear, For he will pass, will pass o-ver you.
O, sin-ner, hear him, trust in his word, Then he will pass, will pass o-ver you.
O, sin-ner, hast-en, let Je-sus in, Then God will pass, will pass o-ver you.
All who be-lieve are safe from the storm, Oh, he will pass, will pass o-ver you.

REFRAIN.

When I see the blood, I will pass o-ver you;
Yes, when I see the blood, I will pass o-ver you;

When I see the blood, I will pass, I will pass o-ver you.
Yes, when I see the blood of the Lamb, I will pass, I will pass o-ver you.

241 Zion 8s. 7s. 4s.

"How beautiful upon the mountains."—Isa. 52: 7

THOS. KELLY   THOS. HASTINGS

1. On the mountain's top ap - pear - ing, Lo ! the sa - cred her - ald stands, Wel-come
2. Has thy night been long and mournful ? Have thy friends unfaithful prov'd? Have thy
3. God, thy God, will now re-store thee : He him-self ap-pears thy friend ; All thy
4. Peace and joy shall now at-tend thee ; All thy war-fare now be past ; God, thy

news to Zi - on bear - ing—Zi - on, long in hos - tile lands ;Mourning cap - tive,
foes been proud and scorn-ful, By thy sighs and tears unmoved?Cease thy mourn-ing,
foes shall flee be - fore thee; Here their boasts and triumphs end. Great de - liv-'rance
Sav - iour,will de - fend thee; Vic - to - ry is thine at last; All thy con - flicts

God him-self will loose thy bands; Mourning cap-tive,God him-self will loose thy bands.
Zi - on still is well be - loved;Cease thy mourning,Zi-on still is well be - loved.
Zi - on's King will sure - ly send;Great de - liv-'rance Zi-on's King will sure - ly send.
End in ev - er - last - ing rest ; All thy con-flicts End in ev - er - last - ing rest.

242

"Glory to God in the highest, and on earth, peace, good-will toward men." Luke 2: 14.

1 Angels! from the realms of glory,
Wing your flight o'er all the earth;
Ye who sang creation's story,
Now proclaim Messiah's birth :
‖:Come and worship—
Worship Christ, the new-born King. :‖

2 Shepherds! in the field abiding,
Watching o'er your flocks by night,
God with man is now residing ;
Yonder shines the heavenly light :
‖:Come and worship—
Worship Christ, the new-born King. :‖

3 Saints ! before the altar bending,
Watching long in hope and fear,
Suddenly the Lord, descending,
In his temple shall appear :
‖:Come and worship—
Worship Christ, the new-born King. :‖

4 Sinners ! wrung with true repentance,
Doomed for guilt to endless pains :
Justice now revokes the sentence,
Mercy calls you, break your chains :
‖:Come and worship—
Worship Christ, the new-born King. :‖

243

"Behold, I bring you good tidings of great joy." Luke 2: 10

JOHN CAWOOD, 1819

1. { Hark ! what mean those ho - ly voi - ces, Sweet-ly sounding thro' the skies ?
   Lo ! th'angel - ic host re - joi - ces ; Heavenly hal - le - lu - jahs rise.
2. { Peace on earth, good- will from hea - ven, Reaching far as man is found ;
   Souls redeemed, and sins for - giv - en, Loud our gold - en harps shall sound.
3. { Haste, ye mor- tals, to a - dore him ; Learn his name and taste his joy !
   Till in heav'n ye sing be - fore him, "Glo - ry be to God most high !"

Hear them tell the won - drous sto - ry, Hear them chant in hymns of joy :
Christ is born, the great A - noint - ed ; Heaven and earth his prais - es sing !
Let us learn the won - drous sto - ry, Of our great Re - deem - er's birth,

"Glo - ry in the high - est, glo - ry ! Glo - ry be to God most high !"
Oh, re-ceive whom God ap - point - ed For your Pro - phet, Priest, and King !
Spread the brightness of his glo - ry, Till it cov - er all the earth.

244

"Bless me, even me also." Gen. 27: 34

1 Lord, I hear of showers of blessing
    Thou art scattering, full and free ;
Showers the thirsty land refreshing ;
    Let some droppings fall on me.
Pass me not, O gracious Father !
    Sinful though my heart may be ;
Thou might'st leave me, but the rather
    Let thy mercy light on me.

2 Pass me not, O tender Saviour !
    Let me love and cling to thee ;
I am longing for thy favor ;
    When thou comest, call for me.

Pass me not, O mighty Spirit !
    Thou canst make the blind to see;
Witnesser of Jesus' merit,
    Speak the word of power to me.

3 Love of God, so pure and changeless,
    Blood of Christ, so rich and free,
Grace of God, so strong and boundless,
    Magnify them all in me.
Pass me not ! thy lost one bringing,
    Bind my heart, O Lord, to thee ;
While the streams of life are springing,
    Blessing others, oh, bless me.

ELIZABETH CODNER, 1860

245　Christ is Born in Bethlehem

CHARLES WESLEY　　　　　　　　　　　　　　　　GEO. C. HUGG

1. Hark! the her - ald an - gels sing: Glo - ry to the new - born
2. Christ by high - est heav'n a - dored; Christ the ev - er - last - ing
3. Hail, the heav'n - born Prince of Peace, Hail, the Sun of Right - eous -

King; .. Peace on earth and mer - cy mild,
Lord; .. Late in time be - hold him come,
ness! .. Light and life to all he brings,

God and sin - ners rec - on - ciled! Joy - ful all ye
Off - spring of the Vir - gin's womb. Veiled in flesh the
Ris'n with heal - ing in his wings. Mild he lays his

na - tions rise, Join the tri - umph of the skies;
God - head see; Hail th'in - car - nate De - i - ty: ..
glo - ry by, Born that man no more may die: ..

Christ is Born in Bethlehem

With th'an-gel - ic host pro-claim, Christ is born in Beth - le - hem.
Pleased as Man with men to dwell; Je - sus our Em - man - u - el!
Born to raise the sons of earth, Born to give them sec - ond birth.

REFRAIN.

O Beth - le - hem, dear Beth - le - hem, Hark how the glad notes ring!

Ho - san - na in the high - est, Ex - alt the new - born King!

The an - gel throng his praise pro-long, Glo - ry to God they sing,

While heav'n and earth pro-claim the birth of Christ, the new - born King!

246 **Markell** C. M.

A. S. KIEFFER, by per.

1. And now, my soul, an - oth - er year Of thy short life is past;
2. Much of my has - ty life is gone, Nor will re - turn a - gain;
3. A - wake, my soul, with ut - most care Thy true con - di - tion learn:
4. Be - hold an - oth - er year be - gins; Set out a - fresh for heav'n;
5. De - vout - ly yield thy - self to God, And on his grace de - pend;

I can - not long con - tin - ue here, And this may be my last.
And swift my pass - ing mo - ments run, The few that yet re - main.
What are thy hopes? how sure? how fair? What is thy great con - cern?
Seek par - don for thy for - mer sins, In Christ so free - ly given.
With zeal pur - sue the heav'n - ly road, Nor doubt a hap - py end.

247 **Evening Twilight** C. M.

"Remember, O Lord, thy tender mercies." Psalm 25: 6

1. Now, gra - cious Lord, thine arm re - veal, And make thy glo - ry known;
2. From all the guilt and for - mer sin, May mer - cy set us free;
3. Send down thy spir - it from a - bove, That saints may love thee more;
4. And when be - fore thee we ap - pear In our e - ter - nal home,

Now let us all thy pres - ence feel, And soft - en hearts of stone.
And let the year we now be - gin, Be - gin and end with thee.
And sin - ners now may learn to love, Who nev - er loved be - fore.
May grow - ing num - bers wor - ship here, And praise thee in our room.

248 Dear Saviour, When I Think of Thee

" Who his own self bare our sins in his own body on the tree." 1 Pet. 2: 24

A. B. K.　　　　　　　　　　　　　　　　　　　　　　　A. B. Kolb

1. Dear Sav - iour, when I think of thee . . . . In an-guish hanging on the
2. O bless - ed Mas - ter, help me still . . . . To know and do thy ho - ly
3. What-ev - er ill may then be - tide, ... With thee, dear Sav-iour, at my
4. Then as I cross those por-tals wide, ... And min - gle with the glo - ri

1. Dear Sav - iour, . . . when I think of thee, In an - guish . . .

tree, ... My heart grows sad; But when I see thee sent by
will; . . . . 'Tis my de - sire To be from sin for - ev - er
side, ... I feel no fear; And when this earth - ly house shall
fied, ... My voice I'll raise In songs of heav'n - ly mel - o -
hang-ing on the tree. My heart grows sad; But when I

God . . . . . To bear for me sin's crush-ing load, . . . And
free, ... To live and la - bor but for thee, . . . And
fail . . . . And I must cross the gloom - y vale, ... The
dy, ... To him who gave his life for me ; . . . . And
see thee sent by God To bear for me sin's crushing load, And

lead me to thy blest a - bode, ... My soul is glad.
feel with - in, con - tin - ual - ly, ... A liv - ing fire.
pow'rs of death shall not pre - vail, ... For thou art near.
spend a blest e - ter - ni - ty . . . . . . In cease - less praise
lead me . . . to thy blest a - bode, My soul is glad.

249   He Loves Me

Slow.

1. A - las! and did my Sav - iour bleed? And did my Sov - 'reign die?
2. Was it for crimes that I have done, He groaned up - on the tree?
3. Well might the sun in dark - ness hide, And shut his glo - ries in;
4. Thus might I hide my blush - ing face While his dear cross ap - pears;
5. But drops of grief can ne'er re - pay The debt of love I owe;

Would he de - vote that sa - cred head For such a worm as I?
A - maz - ing pit - y! grace un - known! And love be - yond de - gree!
When God's own Son was cru - ci - fied For man, the crea - ture's sin.
Dis - solve my heart in thank - ful - ness, And melt mine eyes to tears.
Here, Lord, I give my - self a - way; 'Tis all that I can do.

REFRAIN. *Faster.*

He loves me, he loves me, He loves me this I know; (I know;)

He gave him - self to die for me, Be - cause he loves me so.

250 Divine Compassion 8s. 7s.

JAMES ALLEN

FINE.

1. { Sweet the mo-ments, rich in bless-ing, Which be - fore the cross I spend;
   Life and health and peace pos-sess-ing From the sin-ner's dy - ing Friend.
2. { Tru - ly bless-ed is this sta - tion, Low be - fore his cross to lie;
   While I see di - vine com-pas-sion Float - ing in his lan - guid eye.
3. { Love and grief my heart di - vid-ing, With my tears his feet I bathe;
   Con-stant still in faith a - bid-ing, Life de - riv-ing from his death.

D.C. Pre-cious drops my soul be - dew-ing, Plead and claim my peace with God.
Love I much—I've much for - giv - en; I'm a mir - a - cle of grace.
Prove his wounds each day more heal-ing, And him-self more deep-ly known.

D.C.

Here I'll sit for - ev - er view-ing Mer-cy's streams in streams of blood,
Here it is I find my heav - en, While up - on the Lamb I gaze,
May I still en - joy this feel-ing, In all need to Je - sus go,

251 Harmony Grove C. M.

Father, into thy hands I commend my spirit. Luke 23: 46

Southern Melody

1. Be - hold the Sav - iour of man-kind Nailed to the shame-ful tree;
2. Hark! how he groans while na - ture shakes, And earth's strong pil - lars bend;
3. 'Tis done! the pre - cious ran-som's paid! "Re-ceive my soul!" he cries;
4. But soon he'll break death's en-vious chain, And in full glo - ry shine;

How great the love that him in-clined To bleed and die for thee!
The tem - ple's vale in sun - der breaks, The sol - id mar - bles rend.
See where he bows his sa - cred head! He bows his head, and dies.
O Lamb of God, was ev - er pain, Was ev - er love, like thine!

252

The Pilgrim S. M.

"A little while." John 16: 16

BONAR

Arr.

1. A few more years shall roll, .. A few more sea-sons come; And
2. A few more storms shall beat .. On this wild, rock-y shore; And
3. A few more strug-gles here, .. A few more part-ings o'er, A
4. A few more meet-ings here .. Shall cheer us on our way; And

we shall lie with them that rest, A-sleep with-in the tomb.
we shall be where tem-pests cease, And sur-ges swell no more.
few more toils, a few more tears, And we shall weep no more.
we shall reach the end-less rest, Th'e-ter-nal Sab-bath day.

REFRAIN.

Then oh, my Lord, pre-pare .. My soul for that great day; .. Oh,
Then oh, ... my Lord, prepare My soul ... for that great day; Oh,

wash me in thy pre-cious blood, And take my sins a-way.

253

Atonement P. M.

"And they crucified him." Matt. 27: 35

1. Saw ye my Sav-iour, saw ye my Sav-iour, Saw ye my
2. He was ex-tend-ed, he was ex-tend-ed, Pain-ful-ly
3. Je-sus hung bleed-ing, Je-sus hung bleed-ing Three dread-ful
4. Dark-ness pre-vail-ed, dark-ness pre-vail-ed, dark-ness pre-

Atonement

Sav - iour and God? Oh! he died on Cal - va - ry, To a -
nailed to the cross; Here he bowed his head and died, Thus my
hours . . in pain; And the sol - id rocks were rent, Through cre -
vailed o'er the land; And the sun re - fused to shine When his

tone for you and me, And to pur - chase our par - don with blood.
Lord was cru - ci - fied, To a - tone for a world that was lost.
a - tion's vast ex - tent, When the Jews cru - ci - fi - ed the Lamb.
Ma - jes - ty di - vine Was de - rid - ed, in - sult - ed, and slain.

254   **Gethsemane**   7s. 5l.

"My soul is exceeding sorrowful even unto death." Matt. 26: 38

THOS. MACKELLER   C. H. BRUNK

1. O the ag - o - niz - ing prayer Ris - ing on the mid-night air! "Let this cup pass
2. O the tears and blood - y sweat Fall - ing fast on Ol - i - vet! In thy lone - ly
3. O what wrath of earth and hell On thy head un - pity - ing fell, When thy passion
4. Sor - row none had ev - er known Came up - on thy soul a - lone; While its bil - lows
5. Wa - ken me from sin - ful sleep; Faithful, lov - ing, make me keep, Watching ev - 'ry

from thy Son: Not my will, but thine be done!"Je - sus in Geth-sem - a - ne!
ag - o - ny, Shed-ding crim - son tears for me, Je - sus in Geth-sem - a - ne!
time be - gan, Bear - er of the sin of man, Je - sus in Geth-sem - a - ne!
o'er thee swept, Near at hand thy followers slept, Je - sus in Geth-sem - a - ne!
hour with thee Who didst ag - o - nize for me, Je - sus in Geth-sem - a - ne!

255 **Balerma** C. M.

"In remembrance of me." Luke 22: 19

THOMAS COTTERILL, 1812

ARR. from HUGH WILSON

1. In mem - 'ry of the Sav - iour's love, We keep the sa - cred feast,
2. Here let our ran - som'd pow'rs u - nite, His hon - or'd name to raise;
3. One fold, one faith, one hope, one Lord, One God a - lone we know;
4. By faith we take the bread of life, With which our souls are fed;
5. Un - der his ban - ner thus we sing The won - ders of his love.

Where ev - 'ry hum - ble, con - trite heart Is made a wel - come guest.
Let grate - ful joy fill ev - 'ry mind, And ev - 'ry voice be praise.
Breth - ren we are; let ev - 'ry heart With kind af - fec - tions glow.
And cup, in to - ken of his blood That was for sin - ners shed.
And thus an - ti - ci - pate by faith The heav'n - ly feast a - bove.

256 **Gouldie** 8s. 7s.

T. HASTINGS

CHAS. EDW. POLLOCK

1. He that go - eth forth with weep - ing, Bear - ing pre - cious seed in
2. Soft de - scend the dews from hea - ven, Bright the rays ce - les - tial
3. Sow thy seed, be nev - er wea - ry, Let no fears thy soul an -
4. "Lo, the scene of ver - dure bright'ning! See the ris - ing grain ap -

love, Nev - er tir - ing, nev - er sleep - ing, Find - eth mer - cy from a - bove.
shine; Precious fruits will thus be giv - en, Thro' an in - fluence all di - vine.
noy; Be the pros - pect ne'er so drear - y, Thou shalt reap the fruits of joy.
pear, Look a - gain, the fields are whit'ning, For the har - vest time is near.

257

Solon C.M.

" Ye show forth the Lord's death till he come." 1 Cor. 11: 26

JAS. HART

JEREMIAH INGALS, 1805

1. That dole - ful night be - fore his death, The Lamb, for sin - ners slain,
2. To keep the feast, Lord, we are met, And to re - mem - ber thee;
3. Thy suf -f'rings, Lord, each sa - cred sign To our re - membrance brings;
4. Oh, tune our tongues, and set in frame Each heart that pants for thee,

Did, al - most with his lat - est breath This sol - emn feast or - dain.
Help each poor trem - bler to re - peat, "The Sav - iour died for me."
We eat the bread and drink the wine, But think on no - bler things.
To sing "Ho - san - na to the Lamb, The Lamb that died for me."

258

Sadie C.M.

CHAS. EDW. POLLOCK

Rather slow.

1. For - ev - er here my rest shall be, Close to thy bleed - ing
2. My dy - ing Sav - iour and my God, Foun - tain for guilt and
3. Wash me and make me thus thine own; Wash me, and mine thou
4. Th' a - tone - ment of thy blood ap - ply, Till faith my sight im -

side; This all my hope, and all my plea; For me the Sav - iour died.
sin, Sprin - kle me ev - er with thy blood, And cleanse and keep me clean.
art; Wash me, but not my feet a - lone, My hands, my head, my heart.
prove; Till hope in full fru - i - tion die, And all my soul be love.

259   **Hamburg**   L. M.

" The effects of a view of the Cross." Gal. 6: 14.

I. WATTS   ARR. BY LOWELL MASON

1. When I sur-vey the won-drous cross On which the Prince of glo-ry died,
2. For-bid it, Lord, that I should boast, Save in the death of Christ my Lord:
3. See, from his head, his hands, his feet, Sor-row and love flow min-gled down;
4. Were the whole realm of na-ture mine, That were a pres-ent far too small;

My rich-est gain I count but loss, And pour con-tempt on all my pride.
All the vain things that charm me most, I sac-ri-fice to Je-sus' blood.
Did e'er such love and sor-row meet, Or thorns compose so rich a crown?
Love so a-maz-ing, so di-vine, Demands my soul, my life, my all.

260   **Endor**   P. M.

" For a parting blessing." Luke 23: 33

C. WESLEY   S. B. MARSH
                                      FINE.

1. { Lamb of God, whose bleed-ing love We now re-call to mind, }
   { Send the an-swer from a-bove, And let us mer-cy find; }
2. { Let thy blood, by faith ap-plied, The sin-ner's par-don seal; }
   { Speak us free-ly jus-ti-fied, And all our sick-ness heal; }
3. { Let thy blood, by faith ap-plied, The sin-ner's par-don seal; }
   { Speak us free-ly jus-ti-fied, Our wound-ed spir-its heal; }

D.C. *Oh, re-mem-ber Cal-va-ry, And bid us go in peace!*
                                                  D.C.

Think on us who think on thee, And ev'ry strug-gling soul re-lease;
By thy pas-sion on the tree, Let all our griefs and trou-bles cease;
By thy pas-sion on the tree, Let all our griefs and trou-bles cease;

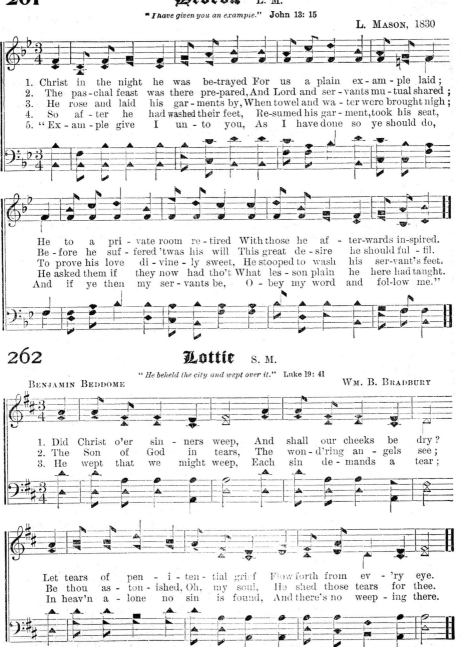

261 **Hebron** L. M.

"I have given you an example." John 13: 15

L. Mason, 1830

1. Christ in the night he was be-trayed For us a plain ex - am - ple laid;
2. The pas-chal feast was there pre-pared, And Lord and ser - vants mu - tual shared;
3. He rose and laid his gar - ments by, When towel and wa - ter were brought nigh;
4. So af - ter he had washed their feet, Re-sumed his gar - ment, took his seat,
5. "Ex - am - ple give I un - to you, As I have done so ye should do,

He to a pri - vate room re - tired With those he af - ter-wards in-spired.
Be - fore he suf - fered 'twas his will This great de - sire he should ful - fil.
To prove his love di - vine - ly sweet, He stooped to wash his ser-vant's feet.
He asked them if they now had tho't What les - son plain he here had taught.
And if ye then my ser - vants be, O - bey my word and fol-low me."

262 **Lottie** S. M.

"He beheld the city and wept over it." Luke 19: 41

Benjamin Beddome

Wm. B. Bradbury

1. Did Christ o'er sin - ners weep, And shall our cheeks be dry?
2. The Son of God in tears, The won - d'ring an - gels see;
3. He wept that we might weep, Each sin de - mands a tear;

Let tears of pen - i - ten - tial grief Flow forth from ev - 'ry eye.
Be thou as - ton - ished, Oh, my soul, He shed those tears for thee.
In heav'n a - lone no sin is found, And there's no weep - ing there.

263 Lenox H. M.

C. Wesley

J. Edson, 1782

1. A - rise, my soul, a - rise, Shake off thy guilt - y fears; A bleed-ing
2. Five bleed-ing wounds he bears, Re - ceived on Cal - va - ry; They pour ef -
3. My God is rec - on - ciled, His pard'ning voice I hear, He owns me

sac - ri - fice In my be - half ap - pears ; Be - fore the throne my sure-ty stands,
fect - ual pray'rs, They strongly speak for me ; For - give him, Oh ! for-give, they cry,
for a child, I can no lon - ger fear ; With con - fi - dence I now draw nigh,

Be - fore the throne my sure - ty stands, My name is writ - ten on his hands.
For - give him, Oh ! for - give, they cry, Nor let the ran - somed sin - ner die.
With con - fi - dence I now draw nigh, And Fa - ther, Ab - ba, Fa - ther, cry.

264 Come, My Redeemer, Come

1 Come, my Redeemer, come,
    And deign to dwell with me ;
  Come and thy right assume,
    And bid thy rivals flee ;
  Come, my Redeemer, quickly come,
  Come, my Redeemer, quickly come,
  And make my heart thy lasting home.

2 Exert thy mighty power,
    And banish all my sin ;
  In this auspicious hour,
    Bring all thy graces in ;
  Come, my Redeemer, quickly come,
  Come, my Redeemer, quickly come,
  And make my heart thy lasting home.

3 Rule thou in every thought
    And passion of my soul,
  Till all my powers are brought
    Beneath thy full control ;
  Come, my Redeemer, quickly come,
  Come, my Redeemer, quickly come,
  And make my heart thy lasting home.

4 Then shall my days be thine,
    And all my heart be love,
  And joy and peace be mine,
    Such as are known above ;
  Come, my Redeemer, quickly come,
  Come, my Redeemer, quickly come,
  And make my heart thy lasting home.

265 He Arose

GEO. C. HUGG

GEO. C. HUGG

Slowly.

1. Low - ly en-tombed he lay, My bless - ed Sav - iour; Wait-ing the
2. Vain - ly they watch him now, My bless - ed Sav - iour; Sure - ly he'll
3. Burst - ing the seal, he rose, My bless - ed Sav - iour; Scat-t'ring his

prom - ised day, My pre - cious Lord.
keep his vow, My pre - cious Lord.
arm - ed foes, My pre - cious Lord.

REFRAIN. *Faster.*

Up from the tomb he a - rose! And in tri - umph, vanquish'd all his foes, He a - rose a vic - tor o'er the realms of night; And he reigns for - ev - er with his saints in light, He a - rose, he a - rose, Vic - tor o - ver all his foes.

He a - rose!

All his foes,

He a - rose, He a - rose,

Christ is Risen

"He is risen, as he said." Matt. 28: 6

A. B. K.

A. B. KOLB

Joyfully.

1. Christ who left his home in glo-ry, And up-on the cross was slain,
2. While the world in peace was sleep-ing, Ear-ly on that Eas-ter day,
3. Christ, our lov-ing Me-di-a-tor, Now with God for you and me

Now is ris'n! Oh, tell the sto-ry That the Sav-iour lives a-gain.
Came the faith-ful wo-men weep-ing, But the stone was rolled a-way.
In-ter-cedes, and our Cre-a-tor, Hears and an-swers ev-'ry plea.

REFRAIN.

Hail him! Hail him! Tell the sto-ry
Hail to the King, the might-y Re-deem-er! Hail him who robbed the grave of its pow'r!

Hail! all hail!... Je-sus lives for-ev-er-more.
Tell ev-'ry na-tion, all is well,

Crown Him

" Thou hast crowned him with glory and honor." **Ps. 8: 5**

Rev. Thos. Kelly

Arr. by Geo. C. Stebbins

1. Look, ye saints, the sight is glo-rious, See the "Man of sor-rows" now,
2. Crown the Sav-iour! An-gels crown him, Rich the tro-phies Je-sus brings;
3. Sin-ners in de-ri-sion crown'd him, Mock-ing thus the Sav-iour's claim;
4. Hark! the bursts of ac-cla-ma-tion! Hark! these loud tri-um-phant chords;

From the fight re-turn vic-to-rious, Ev-'ry knee to him shall bow.
In the seat of pow'r en-throne him, While the vault of heav-en rings.
Saints and an-gels crowd a-round him, Own his ti-tle, praise his name.
Je-sus takes the high-est sta-tion, Oh, what joy the sight af-fords.

Refrain.

Crown him! crown him, an-gels crown him! Crown the Sav-iour "King of kings."

Crown him! crown him, an-gels crown him! Crown the Sav-iour "King of kings."

268 Love's Consecration C. M.

S. B. McManus

A. B. Kolb

1. Love con - se - crates the hum - blest act, And sanc - ti - fies each deed,
2. When, in the sha - dow of the cross, Christ bowed and wash'd the feet
3. "Ye call me Lord and Mas - ter, all Yet I would hum - bly bow
4. "As I have done this un - to you, My breth - ren, here this night
5. Love serves, yet will - ing stoops to serve, What Christ in love so true,

It sheds a ben - e - dic - tion sweet, And hal - lows ev - 'ry need.
Of his dis - ci - ples, 'twas a sign Of his great love com - plete.
And con - se - crate this low - ly deed, As ye be - hold me now.
Thus would I have you do to each When I have passed from sight."
Hath free - ly done for one and all,—Shall we not glad - ly do?

269 Marlow C. M

Mary P. Bowly

John Chetham

1. O Lord, while we con - fess the worth Of this the out - ward seal,
2. Death to the world we here a - vow, Death to each flesh - ly lust;
3. And we, O Lord, who now par - take Of res - ur - rec - tion life,
4. Bap - tized in - to the Fa - ther's name, We'd walk as sons of God,
5. Bap - tized in - to the Ho - ly Ghost, We'd keep his tem - ple pure,

Marlow C. M.

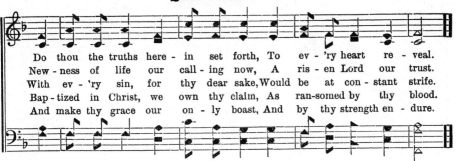

Do thou the truths here - in set forth, To ev - 'ry heart re - veal.
New - ness of life our call - ing now, A ris - en Lord our trust.
With ev - 'ry sin, for thy dear sake, Would be at con - stant strife.
Bap - tized in Christ, we own thy claim, As ran-somed by thy blood.
And make thy grace our on - ly boast, And by thy strength en - dure.

270 Booker C. M.

"My soul shall make her boast in the Lord." Ps. 34: 2

J. H. RUEBUSH, by per.

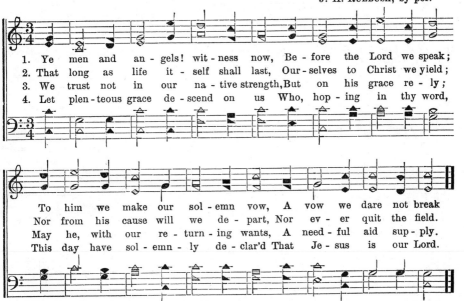

1. Ye men and an - gels! wit - ness now, Be - fore the Lord we speak;
2. That long as life it - self shall last, Our - selves to Christ we yield;
3. We trust not in our na - tive strength, But on his grace re - ly;
4. Let plen - teous grace de - scend on us Who, hop - ing in thy word,

To him we make our sol - emn vow, A vow we dare not break
Nor from his cause will we de - part, Nor ev - er quit the field.
May he, with our re - turn - ing wants, A need - ful aid sup - ply.
This day have sol - emn - ly de - clar'd That Je - sus is our Lord.

5 With cheerful feet may we advance,
　And run the Christian race,
　And, through the troubles of the way,
　　Find all-sufficient grace.

6 Oh, guide our doubtful feet aright,
　And keep us in thy ways;
　And while we turn our vows to pray'rs,
　　Turn thou our prayers to praise.

Happy Day

"Happy is that people whose God is the Lord." Psalm 144: 15

F. DODDRIDGE

From E. T. RIMBAULT

1. O hap-py day that fixed my choice On thee, my Sav-iour and my God!
2. O hap-py bond that seals my vows To him who mer-its all my love;
3. 'Tis done, the great tran-saction's done; I am my Lord's and he is mine;
4. Now rest, my long di-vid-ed heart, Fix'd on this bliss-ful cen-tre, rest;
5. High heaven that heard the sol-emn vow, That vow re-newed shall dai-ly hear,

Well may this glow-ing heart re-joice, And tell its rap-tures all a-broad.
Let cheer-ful an-thems fill his house, While to that sa-cred shrine I move.
He drew me and I followed on, Charm'd to con-fess the voice di-vine.
Nor ev-er from thy Lord de-part, With him of ev-'ry good pos-sess'd.
Till in life's la-test hour I bow, And bless in death a bond so dear.

:S: REFRAIN.

FINE.

Hap-py day, hap-py day, When Je-sus washed my sins a-way;

D.S. *Hap-py day, hap-py day, When Je-sus washed my sins a-way;*

D.S.

He taught me how to watch and pray, And live re-joic-ing ev-'ry day.

272

Welcome 7s. D.

"Return unto thy rest, O my soul." Psalm 116: 7

G. W. Linton

1. Wel-come, wel-come, day of rest, To the world in kind-ness giv'n;
   Wel-come to this care-worn breast, As the beam-ing light from heav'n;
D.C. *As the peace-ful stream-let flows, Ra-diant with a sum-mer's sun.*

2. Day of tid-ings from the skies, Day of sol-emn praise and pray'r,
   Day to make the sim-ple wise, Oh, how great thy bless-ings are!
D.C. *May thy hal-lowed hours be blest, To this fee-ble heart of mine.*

Day of soft and sweet re-pose, Gen-tly now thy mo-ments run;
Wel-come, wel-come, day of rest, With thy in-flu-ence di-vine;

273

Winston L. M.

"And the blood of Christ cleanseth us from all sin." 1 John 1: 7

I. Watts

E. T. Hildebrand, by per.

Slow.

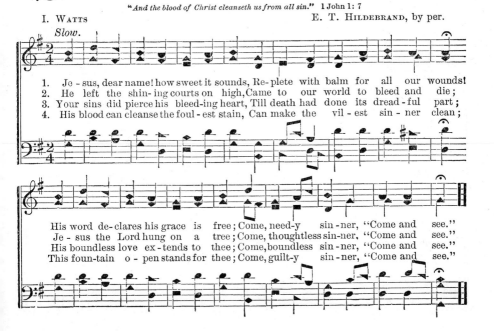

1. Je-sus, dear name! how sweet it sounds, Re-plete with balm for all our wounds!
2. He left the shin-ing courts on high, Came to our world to bleed and die;
3. Your sins did pierce his bleed-ing heart, Till death had done its dread-ful part;
4. His blood can cleanse the foul-est stain, Can make the vil-est sin-ner clean;

His word de-clares his grace is free; Come, need-y sin-ner, "Come and see."
Je-sus the Lord hung on a tree; Come, thoughtless sin-ner, "Come and see."
His boundless love ex-tends to thee; Come, boundless sin-ner, "Come and see."
This foun-tain o-pen stands for thee; Come, guilt-y sin-ner, "Come and see."

274 O Holy Day

" The Son of man is Lord of the sabbath." Luke 6: 5

Rev. Elisha A. Hoffman

Chas. Edw. Pollock

Rather slow.

1. How calm and how bright is this ho- ly day! We haste to the courts of the Lord a- way; We wor-ship and pray and ex- ult in his praise, And we hal- low and hon- or this best of all days.

2. The courts of the tem- ple of God we love; We en- ter and here our de- vo- tion prove; We lay our ob- la- tions down low at his feet, And in songs of re- joic- ing our thanks we re- peat.

3. No day brings so ho- ly a calm and rest; No day is so rich- ly with com- fort blest; Our faith is in-creased and our love is re- newed, And our hearts are with pow- er from heav- en en- dued.

Refrain.

O ho- ly day! O hap- py day! O day of days the best! We wor- ship at God's glo- rious throne, And there find peace and rest.

275

Sabbath 7s. D.

" Safely through another week." Isaiah 58: 13

JOHN NEWTON   LOWELL MASON

1. Safe - ly thro' an - oth - er week God has brought us on our way:
2. While we seek sup - plies of grace, Through the blest Re - deem - er's name,
3. Here we come, thy name to praise: Let us feel thy pres - ence near;
4. May the Gos - pel's joy - ful sound Con - quer sin - ners, com - fort saints,

Let us each a bless - ing seek, Wait - ing in his courts to - day—
Show thy rec - on - cil - ing face, Take a - way our sin and shame;
May thy glo - ry meet our gaze, While we in thy house ap - pear;
Make the fruits of grace a - bound, Bring re - lief to all com - plaints;

Day of all the week the best, Em - blem of e - ter - nal rest,
From our world - ly care set free, May we rest this day in thee,
Here af - ford us, Lord, a taste Of our ev - er - last - ing rest,
Thus let all our wor - ship prove, Till we join thy courts a - bove,

Day of all the week the best, Em - blem of e - ter - nal rest.
From our world - ly care set free, May we rest this day in thee.
Here af - ford us, Lord, a taste Of our ev - er - last - ing rest.
Thus let all our wor - ship prove, Till we join thy courts a - bove.

276

Victory S. M.

GEO. HARTMAN

Arr. from C. U. LINK

1. O Christ, to thee we come, With tri - umph songs of praise,
2. Re - deemed from Sa - tan's pow'rs, Un - fet - tered now we stand,
3. We pledge to thee our might, And waft thy ban - ners high,
4. We'll not from du - ty shrink, But for the right we'll stand,

Our ran-somed souls in ec - sta - sy Burst forth in won - drous lays.
And hail thee, Great De - liv - er - er, To fol - low thy com - mand.
While all the val - iant hosts of right Will join the bat - tle cry.
And march - ing on to vic - to - ry, We'll tri - umph in the end.

277

Vesper S. M.

JEREMIAH INGALLS, 1804

1. Be - gin the day with God, Kneel down to him in pray'r,
2. O - pen the book of God, And read a por - tion there,
3. Go thro' the day with God, What - e'er thy work may be,
4. Con - verse in mind with God, Thy spir - it heav'n-ward raise,
5. Con - clude the day with God, Thy sins to him con - fess,

Lift up thine heart to his a - bode, And seek his love to share.
That it may hal - low all thy tho'ts, And sweet - en all thy care.
Wher - e'er thou art, at home, a - broad, He still is near to thee.
Ac - knowledge ev - 'ry good be - stowed, And of - fer grate - ful praise.
Trust in the Lord's a - ton - ing blood, And plead his right - eous-ness.

Gratitude C. M.

"I will sing aloud of thy mercy in the morning." Psalm 59: 16

Amos Herr   From "Hymns and Tunes"

1. I owe the Lord a morn-ing song Of grat - i-tude and praise,
2. He kept me safe an-oth-er night; I see . . an-oth-er day,
3. Keep me from dan - ger and from sin; Help me . . thy will to do,
4. Keep me till thou wilt call me hence, Where nev - er night can be,

For the kind mer - cy he has shown In length-ning out my days.
Now may his Spir - it as the light Di-rect me in his way.
So that my heart be pure with - in; And I thy good-ness know.
And save me Lord, for Je - sus' sake,—He shed his blood for me.

---

279 *"Day unto day uttereth speech."* Ps. 19: 2

1 Once more, my soul, the rising day
   Salutes thy waking eyes;
Once more, my voice, thy tribute pay
   To him that rules the skies.

2 Night unto night his name repeats,
   The day renews the sound,
Wide as the heaven on which he sits,
   To turn the seasons round.

3 'Tis he supports my mortal frame;
   My tongue shall speak his praise;
My sins would rouse his wrath to flame,
   And yet his wrath delays.

4 O God, let all my hours be thine,
   Whilst I enjoy the light;
Then shall my sun in smiles decline,
   And bring a peaceful night.

---

280 *"The Lord sustained me."* Ps. 3: 5

1 Lord, for the mercies of the night
   My humble thanks I pay;
And unto thee I dedicate
   The first-fruits of the day.

2 Let this day praise thee, O my God,
   And so let all my days;
And oh, let mine eternal day
   Be thine eternal praise.
                                   John Mason, 1683

---

281 *"My voice shalt thou hear in the morning."* Ps. 5: 3

1 Lord, in the morning thou shalt hear
   My voice ascending high;
To thee will I direct my prayer,
   To thee lift up mine eye.

2 Oh, may thy Spirit guide my feet
   In ways of righteousness,
Make every path of duty straight
   And plain before my face.

282 **Trusting** 7s.

" I will guide thee." Ps. 32: 8. M. 5

W. G. FISCHER

1. Now the shades of night are gone; Now the morn - ing light is come;
2. Fill my soul with heav'n - ly light, Ban - ish doubt, and cleanse my sight:
3. Keep my haugh - ty pas - sions bound, Save me from my foes a - round;
4. When my work of life is past, Oh! re - ceive me then at last!

Lord, may I be thine to - day,— Drive the shades of sin a - way.
In thy ser - vice, Lord, to - day, Help me la - bor, help me pray.
Go - ing out and com - ing in, Keep me safe from ev - 'ry sin.
Night of sin will be no more When I reach the heav'n - ly shore.

---

283 *" The fountain of Life.* Ps. 36: 9

1 Blessed fountain full of grace!
    Grace for sinners, grace for me!
To this source alone I trace,
    What I am, and hope to be.

2 What I am, as one redeemed,
    Saved and rescued by the Lord;
Hating what I once esteemed,
    Loving what I once abhorred.

3 What I hope to be ere long,
    When I take my place above,
When I join the heavenly throng,
    When I see the God of Love.

4 Then I hope like him to be
    Who redeemed his saints from sin,
Whom I now obscurely see,
    Through a vail that stands between.

KELLY

284 *" Even the sure mercies of David."* Is. 55: 3

1 As the sun doth daily rise,
    Bright'ning all the morning skies,
So to thee with one accord,
    Lift we up our hearts, O Lord.

2 Day by day provide us food,
    For from thee come all things **good.**
Strength unto our souls afford
    From thy living bread, O Lord.

3 Be our guide 'mid sin and strife,
    Be the leader of our life,
Lest like sheep we go abroad;
    Stay our wayward feet, O Lord.

4 Quickened by thy Spirit's grace,
    All thy holy will to trace,
While we daily search thy word
    Wisdom true impart, O Lord.

King ALFRED, 848-901. Tr. EARL NELSON, 1864

J. H. HALL

Not too fast.

1. Sav - iour, breathe an eve-ning bless - ing,   Ere re-pose our spir - its seal;
2. Tho' the night be dark and drear - y,   Dark - ness can - not hide from thee;

Sin and want we come con - fess - ing;   Thou canst save and thou canst heal.
Thou art he who dost not wea - ry,   Watch - est where thy peo - ple be.

Tho' de - struc-tion walk a - round us,   Tho' the ar - rows past us fly,
Should swift death this night o'er-take us,   And com-mand us to the tomb,

An - gel guards from thee surround us;   We are safe, if thou art nigh.
May the morn in heav'n a - wake us,   Clad in bright e - ter - nal bloom.

286

Matt. 5: 4

1 Can my soul find rest from sorrow?
   Can my sins forgiven be?
Must I wait until to-morrow
   Ere my Saviour speak to me?
Will he speak in words of kindness,
   Will he wash away my sin?
Will he lift this vale of blindness,
   And remove this deadly pain?

2 Oh, the darkness, how it thickens,
   Like the brooding of despair!
And my soul within me sickens—
   God, in mercy, hear my prayer!
Give me but a hope to cherish,
   Give me just one ray of light—
Help me, save me, or I perish,
   Take away this awful night!

287   Vespers   S. M.

John Leland

J. D. Brunk

Gently.

1. The day is past and gone: The eve-ning shades ap - pear;
2. Lord, keep me safe this night, Se - cure from all our fears;
3. And when our days are past, And we from time re - move,

Oh, may we all re - mem - ber well, The night of death draws near.
May an - gels guard us while we sleep, Till morn - ing light ap - pears.
Oh, may we in thy bo - som rest, The bo - som of thy love.

288   Evening Prayer

A. B. K.

A. B. Kolb

1. Ma - ker, keep - er, thou, Be my Guar-dian now, Thro' the shades of night,
2. Ere the light de - cay, God, to thee I pray, Par - don ev - 'ry sin,
3. And when morn shall call, Then, what - e'er be - fall, May I still o - bey

Guard me while I sleep; An - gels vig - ils keep, Till the morn-ing light.
That my soul may be From all care set free, And at peace with - in.
Ev - 'ry wish of thine, Ev - 'ry truth di - vine, All the live - long day.

289 **Ninety=Third** S. M.

"Peace be unto you." Luke 24: 30

ELEAZAR T. FITCH, 1845

WATTS

1. Lord, at this clos - ing hour, Es - tab - lish ev - 'ry heart Up -
2. Peace to our breth - ren give; Fill all our hearts with grace; In
3. Thro' chan - ges bright or drear, We would thy will pur - sue; And
4. To God, the on - ly Wise, In ev - 'ry age a - dored, Let

on thy word of truth and pow'r, To keep us when we part.
faith and pa - tience may we live, Till we shall see thy face.
toil to spread thy gos - pel here, Till we thy glo - ry view.
glo - ry from the church a - rise Thro' Je - sus Christ our Lord!

290 **Evening** 8s 7s

"I will fear no evil." Ps. 23: 4

P. S. GOOD

FINE.

1. Tar - ry with me, O my Sav - iour! For the day is pass - ing by;
   See! the shades of eve - ning gath - er, And the night is draw - ing nigh.
   D.C. *Swift the night of death ad - vanc - es, Shall it be the night of rest?*

2. Fee - ble, trem - bling, faint - ing, dy - ing, Lord, I cast my - self on Thee;
   Tar - ry with me thro' the dark - ness; While I sleep, still watch o'er me.
   D.C. *Till the morn - ing; then a - wake me—Morn - ing of e - ter - nal rest.*

D.C.

Deep - er, deep - er grow the shad - ows, Pal - er now the glow - ing west,
Tar - ry with me, O my Sav - iour! Lay my head up - on thy breast

291   **Lella** C. M.

P. H. BROWN

CHAS. EDW. POLLOCK, by per.

Softly with expression.

1. I love to steal a-while a-way From ev-'ry cum-b'ring care,
2. I love in sol - i-tude to shed The pen-i-ten-tial tear,
3. I love to think on mer-cies past, And fu-ture good im-plore,
4. I love by faith to take a view Of bright-er scenes in heaven,
5. Thus, when life's toil-some day is o'er, May its de-part-ing ray

And spend the hours of set-ting day In hum-ble grate-ful prayer.
And all his prom-is-es to plead, Where none but God can hear.
And all my cares and sor-rows cast On him whom I a-dore.
The pros-pect doth my strength re-new, While here by tem-pests driven.
Be calm as this im-pres-sive hour, And lead to end-less day.

292   **Brown** C. M.

Scripture instruction. Psa. 119: 9

I. WATTS

WM. B. BRADBURY, 1840

1. In mer-cy, Lord, re-mem-ber me Thro' all the hours of night,
2. With cheer-ful heart I close my eyes, Since thou wilt not re-move:
3. Or if this night should prove the last, And end my tran-sient days,

And grant to me most gra-cious-ly The safe-guard of thy might.
Oh, in the morn-ing let me rise Re-joic-ing in thy love.
Then take me to thy prom-ised rest, Where I may sing thy praise.

293

Enon 10s

Abide with us. Luke 84: 29

LYTE   Rev. E. S. WIDDEMAN

1. A - bide with me ! Fast falls the e - ven-tide, The darkness deepens— Lord, with me abide ;
2. Swift to its close ebbs out life's lit - tle day : Earth's joys grow dim, its glories pass a-way ;
3. I need thy pres-ence ev - 'ry passing hour, What but thy grace can foil the tempter's pow'r?
4. Hold thou thy cross be-fore my clos-ing eyes; Shine thro' the gloom, and point me to the skies;

When oth - er help-ers fail, and comforts flee, Help of the help-less, oh, a-bide with me !
Change and de-cay in all a-round I see ; O thou who changest not, a-bide with me !
Who, like thy-self, my guide and stay can be? Thro' cloud and sunshine, oh, a-bide with me !
Heav'n's morn-ing breaks and earth's vain shadows flee ! In life, in death, O Lord, a-bide with me !

294

Violet S. M.

J. NEWTON   CHAS. EDW. POLLOCK

1. Je - sus, who knows full well The heart of ev - 'ry saint,
2. He bows his gra - cious ear, — We nev - er plead in vain ;
3. Je - sus, the Lord will hear His cho - sen when they cry ;
4. Then let us ear - nest cry, And nev - er faint in pray'r ;

In - vites us all, our grief to tell ; To pray and nev - er faint.
Then let us wait till he ap - pear, And pray and pray a - gain.
Yes, tho' he may a while for - bear, He'll help them from on high.
He sees, he hears, and, from on high, Will make our cause his care.

295

Jesus a Wedding Guest

"And Jesus was called to the marriage." John 2: 2

FLORA H. GOOD

1. Since Jesus free-ly did ap-pear To grace a mar-riage feast,
2. Up - on the bri-dal pair look down, Who now have plight-ed hands;
3. In pur - est love these souls u - nite, That they with Chris-tian care,
4. And when that sol-emn hour shall come, And life's short space be o'er,

O Lord, we ask thy pres-ence here, To be a wed-ding guest.
Their un - ion with thy fa - vor crown, And bless the nup-tial bands.
May make do - mes-tic bur-dens light By tak - ing mu-tual share.
May they in tri-umph reach that home, Where they shall part no more.

296

Hand in Hand

"Marriage is honorable." Heb. 13: 4

EDWARD D. NAFF

1. We join to pray, with wish - es kind, A bless-ing, Lord, from thee,
2. We know that scenes not al - ways bright Must un - to them be given;
3. Still hand in hand, their jour - ney thro' Joint pil - grims may they go;
4. May each in each still feed the flame Of pure and ho - ly love;

On those who now the bands have twined Which ne'er may bro-ken be.
But o - ver all give thou the light Of love, and truth, and heaven.
Min - gling their joys as help - ers true, And shar-ing ev - 'ry woe.
In faith, and trust, and heart the same, The same their home a - bove.

Non=Resistance L. M. D.

Melody by L. J. HEATWOLE
Harmony by J. H. HALL

L. J. H.

1. The ten-or of the gos-pel word For-bids that men rule by the sword, Is
2. To reg-u-late the car-nal mind, And ful-ly lev-el all man-kind, Is to
3. The great im-pulse to Chris-tian pow'r Is best main-tained in tri-al's hour; The

so com-plete with-in it-self, Think all men bet-ter than your-self. The
pay with good all e-vil deeds, And walk the way the Christ-life leads; No
test that yields the pur-est gold Is live for right and truth up-hold. The

"eye for eye" or "tooth for tooth" Forms not a text for gos-pel truth; For
civ-il code of hu-man laws Has yet sus-tained so true a cause, Which
saint who thus has no-bly stood, With hands unstained from hu-man blood, Shall

now the law that sways the throng, Leads where the weak e-qual the strong.
needs no pri-son house or jails, For keep-ing this none ev-er fails.
la-ter hear the an-swer true, "En-ter the joys pre-pared for you."

298

Wayland L. M.

Be kind to one another. Eph. 4 : 32

Geo. B. Holsinger, by per.

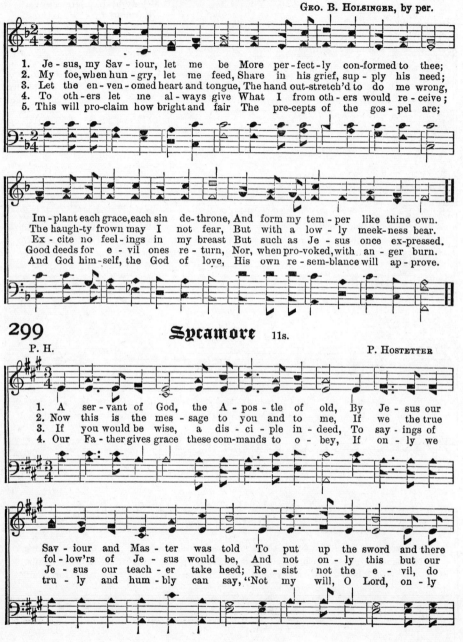

1. Je - sus, my Sav - iour, let me be More per - fect - ly con-formed to thee;
2. My foe, when hun - gry, let me feed, Share in his grief, sup - ply his need;
3. Let the en - ven - omed heart and tongue, The hand out-stretch'd to do me wrong,
4. To oth - ers let me al - ways give What I from oth - ers would re - ceive;
5. This will pro-claim how bright and fair The pre-cepts of the gos - pel are;

Im - plant each grace, each sin de - throne, And form my tem - per like thine own.
The haugh-ty frown may I not fear, But with a low - ly meek-ness bear.
Ex - cite no feel - ings in my breast But such as Je - sus once ex-pressed.
Good deeds for e - vil ones re - turn, Nor, when pro-voked, with an - ger burn.
And God him - self, the God of love, His own re - sem-blance will ap - prove.

299

Sycamore 11s.

P. H.

P. Hostetter

1. A ser - vant of God, the A - pos - tle of old, By Je - sus our
2. Now this is the mes - sage to you and to me, If we the true
3. If you would be wise, a dis - ci - ple in - deed, To say - ings of
4. Our Fa - ther gives grace these com-mands to o - bey, If on - ly we

Sav - iour and Mas - ter was told To put up the sword and there
fol - low'rs of Je - sus would be, And not on - ly this but our
Je - sus our teach - er take heed; Re - sist not the e - vil, do
tru - ly and hum - bly can say, "Not my will, O Lord, on - ly

Sycamore

let it re - main: Who - ev - er will take it by it shall be slain.
Lead - er did say, "Your en - e - mies love, and for them you shall pray."
good un - to those Who do you in ha - tred and mal - ice a - buse.
thy will be done." Praise God for such grace thro' his dear lov - ing Son.

300 Two Little Hands

W. A. O.

W. A. OGDEN

1. I've two lit - tle hands to work for Je - sus, One lit - tle tongue his praise to tell,
2. I've two lit - tle feet to tread the path - way Up to the heav'nly courts a - bove;
3. I've one lit - tle heart to give to Je - sus, One lit - tle soul for him to save,

Two lit - tle ears to hear his coun - sel, One lit - tle voice a song to swell.
Two lit - tle eyes to read the Bi - ble, Tell - ing of Je - sus' won - drous love.
One lit - tle life for his dear ser - vice, One lit - tle self that he must have.

CHORUS.

1 2

Lord, we come, Lord, we come, In our childhood's early morning Come to learn of thee.

By permission of DAVID C. COOK

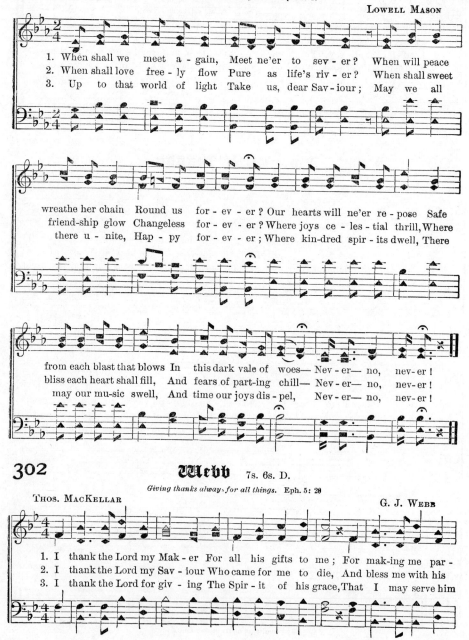

301

Unity 6s. 5s. P.

"When shall we meet again?" Eph. 1: 10

LOWELL MASON

1. When shall we meet a - gain, Meet ne'er to sev - er? When will peace
2. When shall love free - ly flow Pure as life's riv - er? When shall sweet
3. Up to that world of light Take us, dear Sav - iour; May we all

wreathe her chain Round us for - ev - er? Our hearts will ne'er re - pose Safe
friend-ship glow Changeless for - ev - er? Where joys ce - les - tial thrill, Where
there u - nite, Hap - py for - ev - er; Where kin-dred spir - its dwell, There

from each blast that blows In this dark vale of woes— Nev - er— no, nev - er!
bliss each heart shall fill, And fears of part-ing chill— Nev - er— no, nev - er!
may our mu - sic swell, And time our joys dis - pel, Nev - er— no, nev - er!

302

Webb 7s. 6s. D.

Giving thanks always, for all things. Eph. 5: 20

THOS. MACKELLAR

G. J. WEBB

1. I thank the Lord my Mak - er For all his gifts to me; For mak-ing me par -
2. I thank the Lord my Sav - iour Who came for me to die, And bless me with his
3. I thank the Lord for giv - ing The Spir - it of his grace, That I may serve him

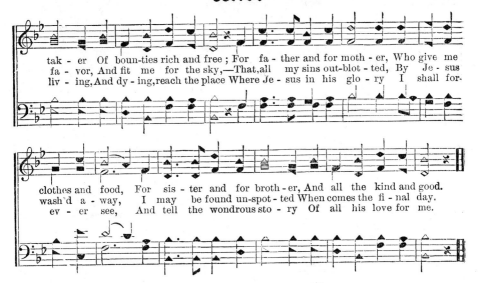

tak - er Of boun-ties rich and free ; For fa - ther and for moth - er, Who give me
fa - vor, And fit me for the sky,—That, all my sins out-blot - ted, By Je - sus
liv - ing, And dy - ing, reach the place Where Je - sus in his glo - ry I shall for-

clothes and food, For sis - ter and for broth - er, And all the kind and good.
wash'd a - way, I may be found un-spot - ted When comes the fi - nal day.
ev - er see, And tell the wondrous sto - ry Of all his love for me.

303

1 Stand up! stand up for Jesus!
　Ye soldiers of the cross;
Lift high his royal banner,
　It must not suffer loss;
From victory unto victory
　His army he shall lead,
Till every foe is vanquished,
　And Christ is Lord indeed.

2 Stand up! stand up for Jesus!
　Stand in his strength alone;
The arm of flesh will fail you—
　Ye dare not trust your own;
Put on the gospel armor,
　And, watching unto prayer,
Where duty calls, or danger,
　Be never wanting there.

3 Stand up! stand up for Jesus!
　The strife will not be long;
This day the noise of battle,
　The next the victor's song;
To him that overcometh,
　A crown of life shall be;
He with the King of Glory
　Shall reign eternally

Rev. Geo. Duffield, Jr., 1858

304　　Psalm 91: 9, 10

1 In heavenly love abiding,
　No change my heart shall fear,
And safe is such confiding,
　For nothing changes here:
The storm may roar without me,
　My heart may low be laid,
But God is round about me,
　And can I be dismayed?

2 Wherever he may guide me,
　No want shall turn me back;
My Shepherd is beside me,
　And nothing can I lack;
His wisdom ever waketh,
　His sight is never dim:
He knows the way he taketh,
　And I will walk with him.

3 Green pastures are before me,
　Which yet I have not seen;
Bright skies will soon be o'er me,
　Where darkest clouds have been:
My hope I cannot measure;
　My path to life is free:
My Saviour has my treasure,
　And he will walk with me.

Anna L. Waring

305 Bound Brook 7s. 6s. D.

"Follow his steps." 1 Pet. 2: 21

From "Hymns and Tunes"

1. Fol-low the path of Je-sus, Walk where his foot-steps lead, Keep in his beam-ing
2. Cling to the hand of Je-sus, All thro' the day and night, Dark tho' the way and

pres - ence, Ev - 'ry coun - sel heed'; Watch, while the hours are fly - ing,
drear - y, He will guide you right; Live for the good of oth - ers,

Rea-dy some good to do; Quick, while his voice is call -ing, Yield o - be-dience true!
Help-less, oppressed and wrong; Lift them from depths of sor - row, In his strength be strong!

306 We'll Work till Jesus Comes

"Thy work shall be rewarded." Jer. 31: 16

Mrs. Elizabeth Mills   Dr. Wm. Miller

1. O land of rest, for thee I sigh, When will the mo - ment come,
2. No tran - quil joys on earth I know, No peace - ful, shel - t'ring dome;
3. To Je - sus Christ I fled for rest; He bade me cease to roam,
4. I sought at once my Sav-iour's side, No more my steps shall roam;

When I shall lay my ar - mor by, And dwell in peace at home?
This world's a wil - der - ness of woe, This world is not my home.
And lean for suc - cor on his breast, Till he con - duct me home.
With him I'll brave death's chill - ing tide, And reach my heav'n - ly home.

We'll Work till Jesus Comes

REFRAIN.

We'll work till Je-sus comes, We'll work till Je-sus comes, We'll
We'll work till Je-sus comes, We'll work till Je-sus comes,

work till Je-sus comes, And we'll be gath-ered home.
We'll work till Je-sus comes,

307 In that Day

J. McPhail   JOHN McPhail

1. All those who love and o-bey my word, In that day, In that day, They shall re-ceive a
2. They shall be mine, saith the Lord of hosts, In that day, In that day, When I shall make my
3. They shall be with me for ev-er-more, In that day, In that day, And all their tri-als

REFRAIN.

great re-ward In that day. They to my pre-cepts are al-ways true, Do-ing my will
jew-els up, In that day.
will be o'er In that day.

in the work they do; I shall be with them and crown them too, In that day.

308 **Jesus, Saviour, Pilot Me**

Rev. Edward Hopper

J. E. Gould

FINE

1. Je - sus, Sav - iour, pi - lot me, O - ver life's tem - pest-uous sea;
D.C. *Chart and com - pass came from thee; Je - sus, Sav - iour, pi - lot me.*
2. As a moth - er stills her child, Thou canst hush the o - cean wild;
D.C. *Won-drous Sov - 'reign of the sea, Je - sus, Sav - iour, pi - lot me.*
3. When at last I near the shore, And the fear - ful break-ers roar,
D.C. *May I hear thee say to me, "Fear not, I will pi - lot thee!"*

D.C.

Unknown waves be - fore me roll, . . Hid - ing rocks and treacherous shoal;
Boisterous waves o - bey thy will . . When thou say'st to them, "Be still!"
'Twixt me and the peace - ful rest, . . Then while lean - ing on thy breast,

309 **Lyte** 11s

Faint, yet pursuing. Judges 8: 4

John N. Darby, 1861

From Temple Star

1. Though faint, yet pur - su - ing, we go on our way; The Lord is our
2. He rais - eth the fall - en, he cheer - eth the faint; The weak and op -
3. In - to his green pas-tures our foot - steps he leads, His flock in the
4. Though clouds may sur-round us, our God is our light; Though storms rage a -
5. And there all his peo - ple e - ter - nal - ly dwell, With him who hath

lead - er, his word is our stay; Though suf - f'ring, and sor - row, and
press'd, he will hear their com - plaint; The way may be wea - ry, and
des - ert how kind - ly he feeds! The lambs in his bos - om he
round us, our God is our might; So faint, yet pur - su - ing, still
led them so safe - ly and well; The toil - some way o - ver, the

310

Nearer, Still Nearer

C. H. M.

Mrs. C. H. MORRIS

1. Near - er, still near - er, close to thy heart, Draw me, my Sav - iour, so
2. Near - er, still near - er, noth - ing I bring, Naught as an off - 'ring to
3. Near - er, still near - er, Lord, to be thine, Sin, with its fol - lies, I
4. Near - er, still near - er, while life shall last, Till safe in glo - ry my

pre - cious thou art; Fold me, O fold me close to thy breast, Shel - ter me
Je - sus my King; On - ly my sin - ful, now con-trite heart, Grant me the
glad - ly re - sign; All of its pleasures, pomp and its pride, Give me but
an - chor is cast; Thro' end-less a - ges, ev - er to be, Near - er, my

safe in that "Ha-ven of Rest," Shel - ter me safe in that "Ha - ven of Rest."
cleansing thy blood doth im-part, Grant me the cleans-ing thy blood doth impart.
Je - sus, my Lord cru - ci - fied, Give me but Je - sus, my Lord cru - ci - fied.
Sav-iour, still near - er to thee, Near - er, my Sav - iour, still near - er to thee.

311 Closer Cling to Jesus

IDA L. REED

GEO. C. HUGG

1. Do life's storms a - bove thee roll? Clos - er cling to Je - sus;
2. Are there griefs that bow thee low? Clos - er cling to Je - sus;
3. Are thy days full oft - en drear? Clos - er cling to Je - sus;

There is ref - uge for thy soul, Clos - er cling to Je - sus.
He thine ev - 'ry care doth know, Clos - er cling to Je - sus.
He will give thee joy and cheer, Clos - er cling to Je - sus.

Near - er press - ing to his side, 'Neath his wing se - cure - ly hide,
Do not stand a - part and grieve, At his feet thy bur - den leave;
Trust him, love him, to him cling, Crown him ev - er - more thy King;

Safe - ly in his love a - bide, Clos - er cling to Je - sus.
Ask, and his strong help re - ceive, Clos - er cling to Je - sus.
Glad - ness, peace and rest 'twill bring, Clos - er cling to Je - sus.

Rock of Ages 7s.

"And that Rock was Christ." 1 Cor. 10: 4

A. M. TOPLADY, 1776   Dr. THOMAS HASTINGS, 1830

1. Rock of A - ges, cleft for me, Let me hide my - self in thee,
2. Not the la - bor of my hands Can ful - fill the law's de-mands;
3. Noth - ing in my hands I bring, Sim - ply to thy cross I cling;
4. While I draw this fleet - ing breath, When my heart-strings break in death,

Let the wa - ter and the blood, From thy riv - en side which flowed,
Could my zeal no res - pite know, Could my tears for - ev - er flow,
Na - ked, come to thee for dress; Help - less, look to thee for grace,
When I soar to worlds un-known, See thee on thy judg-ment throne,

Be of sin the dou - ble cure; Cleanse me from its guilt and pow'r.
All for sin could not a - tone, Thou must save, and thou a - lone.
Foul, I to the foun - tain fly, Wash me, Sav - iour, or I die.
Rock of A - ges, cleft for me, Let me hide my - self in thee.

To-day 6s. 4s.

REV. SAMUEL FRANCIS SMITH   LOWELL MASON, 1831

1. To - day the Saviour calls: Ye wand'rers, come; O ye benighted souls, Why longer roam ?
2. To - day the Saviour calls: Oh, hear him now; With-in these sa-cred walls To Je - sus bow.
3. To - day the Saviour calls: For ref - uge fly; The storm of justice falls, And death is nigh.
4. The Spir - it calls to - day: Yield to his pow'r; Oh, grieve him not away, 'Tis mercy's hour.

314

Martyn 7s. D

The Lord is my refuge. Psalm 91: 1

CHARLES WESLEY

S. B. MARSH

FINE.

1. { Je - sus, lov - er of my soul, Let me to thy bo - som fly,
While the near - er wa - ters roll, While the tem - pest still is high!

D.C. Safe in - to the ha - ven guide, Oh, re - ceive my soul at last.

Hide me, O my Sav - iour, hide, Till the storm of life is past;

2 Other refuge have I none,
    Hangs my helpless soul on thee;
Leave, oh, leave me not alone!
    Still support and comfort me:
All my trust on thee is stayed,
    All my help from thee I bring;
Cover my defenceless head
    With the shadow of thy wing.

3 Thou, O Christ, art all I want;
    All I need in thee I find;
Raise the fallen, cheer the faint,
    Heal the sick, and lead the blind.
Just and holy is thy name,
    I am all unrighteousness;
False and full of sin I am,
    Thou art full of truth and grace.

4 Plenteous grace with thee is found,
    Grace to pardon all my sins:
Let the healing streams abound;
    Make and keep me pure within.
Thou of life the Fountain art,
    Freely let me take of thee;
Spring thou up within my heart,
    Rise to all eternity.

315 *Woman, why weepest thou?* John 20: 13

1 Mary to the Saviour's tomb
    Hasted at the early dawn;
Spice she brought and rich perfume,
    But the Lord she loved was gone.
For a while she lingering stood,
    Filled with sorrow and surprise,
Trembling, while a crystal flood
    Issued from her weeping eyes.

2 But her sorrows quickly fled
    When she heard her Saviour's voice;
Christ has risen from the dead,
    Now he bids her heart rejoice.
What a change his word can make,
    Turning darkness into day!
You who weep for Jesus' sake,
    He will wipe your tears away.

3 He who came to comfort her,
    When she thought her all was lost,
Will for your relief appear,
    Though you now are tempest-tossed.
On his word your burden cast;
    On his love your thoughts employ;
Weeping for a night may last,
    But the morning bringeth joy.

JOHN NEWTON, ab. 1779

316 He Keepeth Me Ever

E. R. LATTA

GEO. F. ROSCHE

1. He keep-eth me ev - er, Wher - e'er be the place! I've on - ly to
2. He keep-eth me ev - er, With ten - der-est care! I've on - ly to
3. He keep-eth me ev - er From yield-ing to dread; Though darkness be

ask it— Most won - der-ful grace! Though sor - est temp - ta - tions
ask him My bur - dens to bear! A word of his prom - ise
round me, And clouds o - ver-head! He still - eth my doubt - ings,

My spir - it may try, . . I know my Re - deem - er
He nev - er will break! Who - ev - er may leave me,
He light - ens my grief! I've on - ly to trust him—

REFRAIN.

Will ev - er be nigh! He keep-eth me ev - er! His love end - eth
He ne'er will for - sake!
He'll give me re - lief!

nev - er! From him naught shall sev - er! He keep - eth my soul!

317 He Knoweth Thy Grief

IDA L REED

J. H. HALL

1. He know-eth thy grief, . He know-eth thy care, .
2. He know-eth thy pain, . Thy tears he doth see, .
3. He know-eth it all, . . The wea-ri-some way, .

He giv-eth re-lief, . . Go find it in prayer.
And nev-er in vain . . Thy suf-f'ring shall be. . .
And when thou dost fall, . . He'll lift thee each day. .

REFRAIN.

He know-eth thy grief, . Each pang thou dost feel, . .
He know-eth thy grief, . . Each pang thou dost feel, . .

And all of thy wounds, Thy Sav-iour will heal. . . .
And all of thy wounds, Thy Sav-iour will heal, will heal.

318 The Hallowed Spot

Rev. Wm. Hunter, D.D.   Arr. by T. C. O'Kane

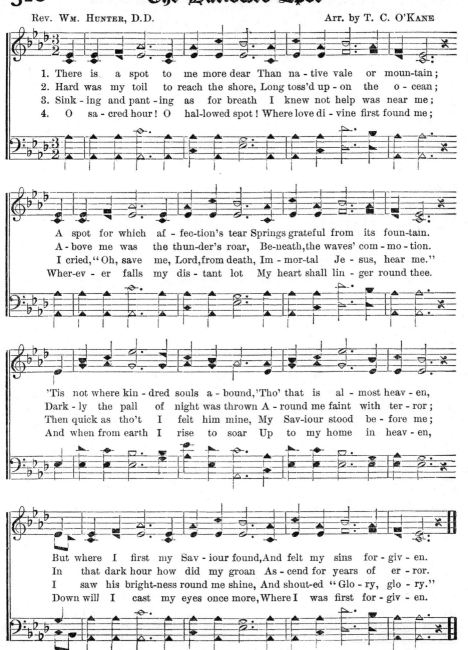

1. There is a spot to me more dear Than na-tive vale or moun-tain;
2. Hard was my toil to reach the shore, Long toss'd up-on the o-cean;
3. Sink-ing and pant-ing as for breath I knew not help was near me;
4. O sa-cred hour! O hal-lowed spot! Where love di-vine first found me;

A spot for which af-fec-tion's tear Springs grateful from its foun-tain.
A-bove me was the thun-der's roar, Be-neath, the waves' com-mo-tion.
I cried, "Oh, save me, Lord, from death, Im-mor-tal Je-sus, hear me."
Wher-ev-er falls my dis-tant lot My heart shall lin-ger round thee.

'Tis not where kin-dred souls a-bound, 'Tho' that is al-most heav-en,
Dark-ly the pall of night was thrown A-round me faint with ter-ror;
Then quick as tho't I felt him mine, My Sav-iour stood be-fore me;
And when from earth I rise to soar Up to my home in heav-en,

But where I first my Sav-iour found, And felt my sins for-giv-en.
In that dark hour how did my groan As-cend for years of er-ror.
I saw his bright-ness round me shine, And shout-ed "Glo-ry, glo-ry."
Down will I cast my eyes once more, Where I was first for-giv-en.

319 A Shelter in the Time of Storm

Mrs. Harriet E. Jones

Geo. F. Rosche

1. We have a Rock, a safe re-treat, A shel-ter in the time of storm;
2. O Rock of A-ges, al-ways sure, A shel-ter in the time of storm;
3. With-in the cleft we safe-ly hide, A shel-ter in the time of storm;
4. O Rock of A-ges, hide thou me, A shel-ter in the time of storm;

A sure foun-da-tion for our feet, A shel-ter in the time of storm.
Where wea-ry pil-grims rest se-cure, A shel-ter in the time of storm.
And there would ev-er-more a-bide, A shel-ter in the time of storm.
And ev-er keep me close to thee, A shel-ter in the time of storm.

REFRAIN.

Our Je-sus is the Rock where we safe-ly rest, We

safe-ly rest, we safe-ly rest; Our Je-sus is the Rock where we

safe-ly rest, A shel-ter in the time of storm.

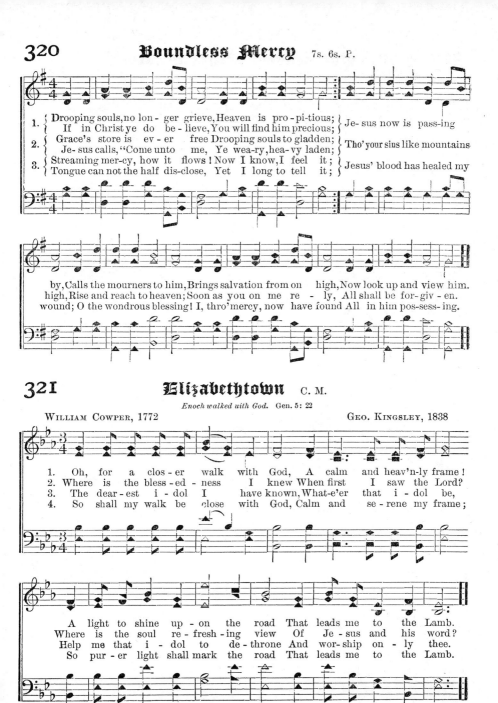

322

God Knows What is Best

Rev. G. P. Hott

J. H. Ruebush

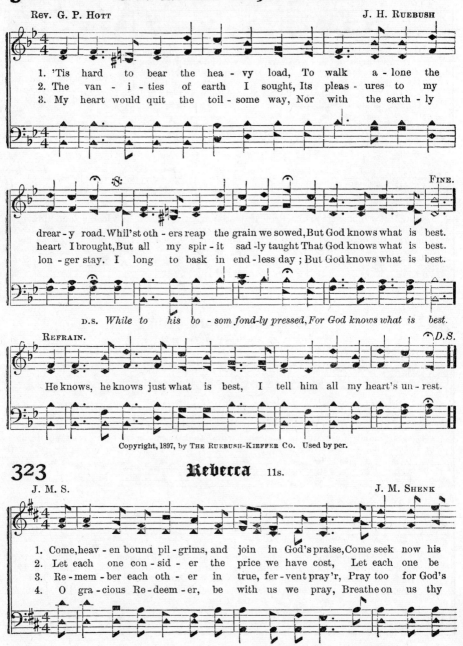

1. 'Tis hard to bear the hea-vy load, To walk a-lone the
2. The van-i-ties of earth I sought, Its pleas-ures to my
3. My heart would quit the toil-some way, Nor with the earth-ly

drear-y road. Whil'st oth-ers reap the grain we sowed, But God knows what is best.
heart I brought, But all my spir-it sad-ly taught That God knows what is best.
lon-ger stay. I long to bask in end-less day; But God knows what is best.

D.S. *While to his bo-som fond-ly pressed, For God knows what is best.*

REFRAIN.

He knows, he knows just what is best, I tell him all my heart's un-rest.

Copyright, 1897, by THE RUEBUSH-KIEFFER CO. Used by per.

323

Rebecca 11s.

J. M. S.

J. M. SHENK

1. Come, heav-en bound pil-grims, and join in God's praise, Come seek now his
2. Let each one con-sid-er the price we have cost, Let each one be
3. Re-mem-ber each oth-er in true, fer-vent pray'r, Pray too for God's
4. O gra-cious Re-deem-er, be with us we pray, Breathe on us thy

Rebecca

bless - ing and learn of his ways, In hum - ble de - vo - tion bow
bur - dened with souls that are lost, And seek that in - fill - ing of
ser - vants that they may de - clare The mes - sage of truth with an
Spir - it to show us the way, And fill us with good - ness, with

low at his feet, In true spir - it wor - ship, his fa - vor en - treat.
pow'r from a - bove, That fits us for ser - vice and fills us with love.
anx - ious de - sire, That all be en - kin - dled with heav - en - ly fire.
peace and de - light, That all to thy glo - ry may shine as a light.

324 Praise the Lord

For Little Children

C. E. P.

CHARLES EDW. POLLOCK

1. Lit - tle chil - dren, praise the Lord, Praise the Lord, Praise the Lord,
2. Praise him for his bless - ed Word, Bless - ed Word, Bless - ed Word,
3. Praise him for the Sab - bath day, Sab - bath day, Sab - bath day,
4. Praise him for the Sun - day - school, Sun - day - school, Sun - day - school,
5. Praise him for your teach - ers dear, teach - ers dear, teach - ers dear,

Lit - tle chil - dren, praise the Lord, Praise ye the Lord.
Praise him for his bless - ed Word, Praise ye the Lord.
Praise him for the Sab - bath day, Praise ye the Lord.
Psaise him for the Sun - day - school, Praise ye the Lord.
Praise him for your teach - ers dear, Praise ye the Lord.

By per. David C. Cook Pub. Co.

325 Scattering Precious Seed

W. A OGDEN

GEO. C. HUGG

1. Scat - ter - ing pre - cious seed by the way - side, Scat - ter - ing
2. Scat - ter - ing pre - cious seed for the grow - ing, Scat - ter - ing
3. Scat - ter - ing pre - cious seed, doubt - ing nev - er, Scat - ter - ing

pre - cious seed by the hill - side, Scat - ter - ing pre - cious seed
pre - cious seed, free - ly sow - ing, Scat - ter - ing pre - cious seed
pre - cious seed, trust - ing ev - er, Sow - ing the word with pray'r

o'er the field, wide ; Scat - ter - ing pre - cious seed by the way.
trust - ing, know - ing, Sure - ly the Lord will send it the rain.
and en - deav - or, Trust - ing the Lord for growth and for yield.

REFRAIN.

Sow - ing in the morn - - ing, Sow - - ing
Sow-ing the seed, Sow-ing the pre-cious seed, Sow-ing the seed,

at the noon - - tide, Sow - - ing in the
Sow - ing the pre - cious seed, Sow - ing the seed,

Scattering Precious Seed

pp

eve - - - ning, Sow-ng the precious seed by the way. . . .

Sow-ing the pre-cious seed, by the way.

326 My Lord and I

Sung amid the rocks and caves of France during the fierce Huguenot persecutions 300 years ago.

Arranged by F. S. S.   F. S. SHEPARD

1. I have a friend so pre-cious, So ver-y dear to me, He loves me with such
2. Some-times I'm faint and wea-ry, He knows that I am weak, And, as he bids me
3. I tell him all my sor-rows, I tell him all my joys, I tell him all that
4. He knows how I am long-ing Some precious soul to win Back to the ways of

ten - der love, Loves me so faith-ful - ly; I could not live a - part from him,
lean on him, His help I glad - ly seek; He leads me in the paths of light,
pleas - es me, I tell him what an - noys; He tells me what I ought to do,
right-eous-ness From wea - ry paths of sin; He bids me tell his won-drous love

I long to feel him nigh, And so we dwell to - geth - er, My Lord and I.
Be-neath a sun - ny sky, And so we walk to - geth - er, My Lord and I.
He tells me what to try, And so we talk to - geth - er, My Lord and I.
And why he came to die, And so we work to - geth - er, My Lord and I.

My precious Lord and I.

327 A Call for Help

J. B. SMITH

AMANDA MOTTE

1. At home and a-broad, on life's bat-tle-field, Brave sol-diers are need - ed their
2. Our Cap - tain is call - ing for vol - un-teers now, Let all to his mandates sub-
3. Oh, who then will go in the strength of the Lord, Up- lift - ing his ban - ner, pro-

ser - vice to yield For Je - sus who died that . all might have life. Come
mis - sive - ly bow; Not life and not friends let . . an - y hold dear While
claim - ing his word? Who will help to re-deem dy - ing souls from the grave, In

REFRAIN.

en - ter the bat - tle, be bold in the strife. The trum - pet is sounding, we're
cries of the need - y break out on your ear.
tell - ing of Je - sus the might - y to save?

off to the fray, Im-man - u-el's ban-ner we'll lift up to-day. Then onward, still onward in

his name we go, Till all of his crea-tures the Lord's name will know.

𝔥igher than 𝕴 11s.

Lead me to the Rock that is higher than I. Psalm 61: 2

WM. HUNTER

1. In sea-sons of grief to my God I'll re-pair, When my heart's o-ver-whelmed with sor-row and care; From the end of the earth, un-to thee will I cry, Lead me to the Rock that is high-er than I.

2. When Sa-tan, my foe, com-eth in like a flood, To . . drive my poor soul from the foun-tain of God, I'll . pray to the Sav-iour who kind-ly did die, Lead me to the Rock that is high-er than I.

3. When tempted by Sa-tan the Spir-it to grieve, And the ser-vice of Christ, my Re-deem-er, to leave, I'll . claim my re-la-tion to Je-sus, on high—The Rock of Sal-va-tion, that's high-er than I.

4. O Sav-iour of sin-ners, when faint and de-pressed, With man-i-fold tri-als and sor-rows op-pressed, I'll . bow at thy feet, and with con-fi-dence cry, Lead me to the Rock that is high-er than I.

5. And when I have end-ed my pil-grim-age here, In . . Je-sus' pure right-eous-ness let me ap-pear; In the swell-ing of Jor-dan on thee I'll re-ly, And look to the Rock that is high-er than I.

6. And when the last trum-pet shall sound thro' the skies, And the dead from the dust of the earth shall a-rise; With mil-lions I'll join far a-bove yon-der sky, To praise the kind Rock that is high-er than I.

High-er than I, high-er than I, Lead me to the Rock that is high-er than I.

Missionary Hymn

329

Refrain by L. J. L.

L. Mason

1. From Greenland's i - cy moun - tains, From In - dia's cor - al strand,
2. What though the spi - cy breez - es Blow soft o'er Cey - lon's isle;
3. Can we, whose souls are light - ed With wis - dom from on high,
4. Waft, waft, ye winds, his sto - ry, And you, ye wa - ters, roll,

Where Af - ric's sun - ny foun - tains Roll down their gold - en sand,
Though ev - 'ry pros - pect pleas - es, And on - ly man is vile;
Can we to men be - night - ed The lamp of life de - ny?
Till like a sea of glo - ry It spreads from pole to pole;

From ma - ny an an - cient riv - er, From ma - ny a palm - y plain,
REF. O fill us with thy spir - it, Pre - pare us, Lord, to go,
In vain with lav - ish kind - ness The gifts of God are strewn;
REF. Send! Send! O Lord, thy work - ers, A - cross the dark blue sea,
Sal - va - tion! O Sal - va - tion! The joy - ful sound pro - claim,
REF. 'Twas love that sent the Sav - iour To die on Cal - v'ry's hill;
Till o'er our ran - somed na - ture The Lamb for sin - ners slain,
REF. We're com - ing, yes, we're com - ing, Lord, speed us on our way,

D.S. Refrain.

They call us to de - liv - er Their land from er - ror's chain.
And teach the dark - ened hea - then The love of Christ to know.
The hea - then in his blind - ness Bows down to wood and stone.
To bear the bless - ed mes - sage,—Christ died to ran - som thee.
Till each re - mot - est na - tion Has learnt Mes - si - ah's name.
'Twas love that brought re - demp - tion, 'Tis love that's wait - ing still.
Re - deem - er, King, Cre - a - tor, In bliss re - turns to reign.
That souls now lost in dark - ness, May reign through end - less day.

330 Send the Light

C. H. G.

CHAS. H. GABRIEL

1. There's a call comes ring-ing o'er the rest-less wave, Send the light! . .
2. We have heard the Ma - ce - do - nian call to - day, Send the light! . .
3. Let us pray that grace may ev - 'ry-where a - bound, Send the light! . .
4. Let us not grow wea - ry in the work of love, Send the light!

Send the light!

Send the light! There are souls to res - cue, there are souls to save,
Send the light! And a gold - en of - f'ring at the cross we lay,
Send the light! And a Christ - like spir - it ev - 'ry-where be found,
Send the light! Let us gath - er jew - els for a crown a - bove,

Send the light!

Send the light! . . . . Send the light! . . . .

Send the light! Send the light!

REFRAIN.

Send the light, . . . the bless - ed gos - pel light, Let it
Send the light, . . . and let its ra - diant beams Light the

| 1 | 2 |

shine . . . from shore to shore! . . . .
world . . . for - ev - er — — more. (for-ev - er-more.)

331 Speed Away

W. E. M. HACKLEMAN

Theme from WOODBURY
Har. by W. E. M. H.

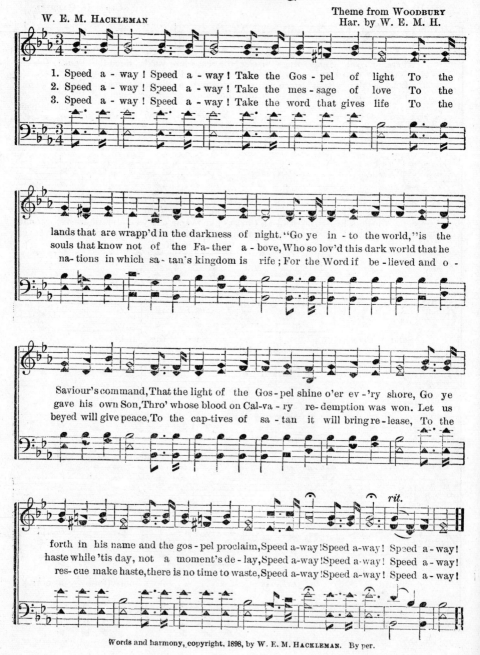

1. Speed a-way! Speed a-way! Take the Gos-pel of light To the
2. Speed a-way! Speed a-way! Take the mes-sage of love To the
3. Speed a-way! Speed a-way! Take the word that gives life To the

lands that are wrapp'd in the darkness of night. "Go ye in-to the world," is the
souls that know not of the Fa-ther a-bove, Who so lov'd this dark world that he
na-tions in which sa-tan's kingdom is rife; For the Word if be-lieved and o-

Saviour's command, That the light of the Gos-pel shine o'er ev-'ry shore, Go ye
gave his own Son, Thro' whose blood on Cal-va-ry re-demption was won. Let us
beyed will give peace, To the cap-tives of sa-tan it will bring re-lease, To the

rit.

forth in his name and the gos-pel proclaim, Speed a-way! Speed a-way! Speed a-way!
haste while 'tis day, not a moment's de-lay, Speed a-way! Speed a-way! Speed a-way!
res-cue make haste, there is no time to waste, Speed a-way! Speed a-way! Speed a-way!

332 Hark! the Voice of Jesus Calling 8s. 7s. D.

"For they are white already to harvest." John 4: 33

DANIEL MARCH   CHAS. EDW. POLLOCK, by per.

1. Hark! the voice of Je - sus call - ing—"Who will go and work to - day?
2. If you can - not cross the o - cean, And the hea - then lands ex - plore,
3. While the souls of men are dy - ing, And the Mas - ter calls for you,

Fields are white, the har - vest wait - ing,—Who will bear the sheaves a - way?"
You can find the hea - then near - er, You can help them at your door;
Let none hear you i - dly say - ing, "There is noth - ing I can do."

Loud and long the Mas - ter call - eth, Rich re - ward he of - fers free;
If you can - not speak like an - gels, If you can - not preach like Paul,
Glad - ly take the task he gives you, Let his work your pleas - ure be;

Who will an - swer, glad - ly say - ing, "Here am I, O Lord, send me?"
You can tell the love of Je - sus, You can say, he died for all.
An - swer quick - ly when he call - eth, "Here am I, O Lord, send me."

R. A. EVILSIZER

J. HENRY SHOWALTER

1. The time of the har-vest is nigh, Al' rip-ened the wait-ing fields lie;
2. The Lord of the har-vest needs *you* — There's work that *you* on-ly can do;
3. Oh, broth-er, the la-bor is blest, And af-ter the toil com-eth rest;

The la-b'rers are few, Christ call-eth for you To glean for his gar-ner on high.
Then do not de-lay, But has-ten a-way And glean where the toil-ers are few.
Your Saviour and Lord Will rich-ly re-ward, If you will but heed his re-quest.

REFRAIN.

The la - b'rers are few; Christ call — eth for you; . Then
The lab'rers, the lab'rers are few, are few, Christ calleth, he call-eth for you, for you; Then

has - ten a - way, . The Lord of the har-vest o - bey. (to-day.)
has-ten, oh, has-ten a - way, a-way, The Lord of the har-vest o - bey. (to-day.)

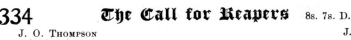

334 The Call for Reapers 8s. 7s. D.

J. O. THOMPSON

J. B. O. CLEMM

Spirited.

1. Far and near the fields are teem-ing, With the waves of rip-ened grain;
2. Send them forth with morn's first beaming, Send them in the noon-tide's glare;
3. O thou, whom thy Lord is send-ing, Gath-er now the sheaves of gold,

Far and near their gold is gleaming, O'er the sun-ny slope and plain.
When the sun's last rays are gleaming, Bid them gath-er ev-'ry-where.
Heavenward then at eve-ning wend-ing, Thou shalt come with joy un-told.

REFRAIN.

Lord of har-vest, send forth reap-ers! Hear us, Lord, to thee we cry;

Send them now the sheaves to gath-er, Ere the har-vest time pass by.

335

Go work in my vineyard. Matt. 21: 28

1 Hark the voice of Jesus crying—
  "Who will go and work to-day?
Fields are white and harvest waiting:
  Who will bear the sheaves away?"
Loud and strong the Master calleth,
  Rich reward he offers thee;
Who will answer, gladly saying,
  "Here am I; send me, send me."

2 Let none hear you idly saying,
  "There is nothing I can do,"
While the souls of men are dying,
  And the Master calls for you.
Take the task he gives you gladly;
  Let his work your pleasure be:
Answer quickly when he calleth,
  "Here am I; send me, send me."

DANIEL MARCH, D.D.

'Tis the Harvest Time

A. Thomas

J. H. Hall

1. 'Tis the har-vest time, 'tis the har-vest time, To the fields I must a - way;
2. 'Tis the har-vest time, 'tis the har-vest time, Oh! who will go a - long?
3. 'Tis the har-vest time, 'tis the har-vest time, There is work for all to - day;

For the Mas-ter now is call-ing me, To go and work to-day.
See the fields for har-vest now are white; I hear the reap-er's song.
If you can-not be a reap-er, You can bear the sheaves a-way.

REFRAIN.

Glean - ing on the hill - side, Glean - ing on the plain,
Glean-ing on the hill-side, hill-side, Gleaning on the sun-ny plain,

Work - ing for the Mas - ter, 'Mong . . . the gold-en grain.
Working, work - ing for the Master, 'Mong the golden grain, 'Mong the golden grain.

337

Gather the Golden Grain

"Put ye in the sickle, for the harvest is ripe." Joel 3: 13

Mrs. E. W. CHAPMAN   FRANK M. DAVIS

1. Go out and gath-er the gold-en grain, The world is your har - vest
2. Go lift the soul from the haunts of sin, The treas-ures of grace dis -
3. Go find some pearl on the o - cean strand, The shell may be rough and

field; Your toil for Je - sus will not be vain For he will the in-crease yield.
play; Your mis - sion here is to work and win, Go show to the lost the way.
brown, But pol - ished by the dear Master's hand, 'Twill shine in his jew - el'd crown.

REFRAIN.

Gath - er, gath - er, Gath - er in the gold - en grain;
Gath - er, gath - er, gath - er, gath - er,

Gath - er, gath - er, Gath - er in the gold - en grain.
Gath - er, gath - er, gath - er, gath - er,

338 Gather Them into the Fold

Words arranged   J. Henry Showalter

1. In from the high-ways and by-ways of sin, In from the storm and cold,
2. Bring them to Je - sus from pal - ace and cot, Waifs from the lane and street;
3. Gath - er them in, jew - els bright for his crown ; Gath-er them in to - day ;

Gath - er the lambs that are go - ing a - stray, In - to the Shepherd's fold.
He will re-ceive them as he did of old, Guid - ing their way-ward feet.
Gath - er the rich and the poor just the same, Show them the nar - row way.

REFRAIN.

Gath - er them in from the by - ways of sin, In from the storm and cold ;

Gath - er the lambs that are go - ing a - stray, In - to the Shepherd's fold.

339 Open the Wells of Salvation

"Spring up, O well." Num. 21: 17

Rev. Elisha A. Hoffman

Chas. Edw. Pollock

Earnestly.

1. Lord, I am fond - ly, ear - nest - ly long - ing In - to thy ho - ly like-ness to grow; Thirsting for more and deep-er com-mun-ion, Yearning thy love more ful - ly to know.

2. Dead to the world would I be, O Fa - ther! Dead un - to sin, a - live un - to thee; Cru - ci - fy all the earth-ly with - in me, Emptied of sin and self may I be.

3. I would be thine, and serve thee for - ev - er, Filled with thy spir - it, lost in thy love; Come to my heart, Lord, come with annointing, Showers of grace send down from a - bove.

REFRAIN.

O - pen the wells of grace and sal - va - tion, Pour the rich streams deep in - to my heart; Cleanse and re - fine my tho't and af - fec-tion, Seal me and make me pure as thou art.

Children's Song of Praise

Arr. by J. Henry Showalter

1. Lord, a lit-tle band, and low-ly, We are come to sing to thee;
2. Fill our hearts with tho'ts of Je-sus, And of heav'n, where he has gone;
3. For we know the Lord of glo-ry Al-ways sees what chil-dren do,
4. Let our sins be all for-giv-en; Make us fear what-e'er is wrong;

FINE.

Thou art great, and high, and ho-ly— Oh, how sol-emn we should be!
And let noth-ing ev-er please us He would grieve to look up-on.
And is writ-ing now the sto-ry Of our thoughts and ac-tions, too.
Lead us on our way to heav-en, There to sing a no-bler song.

D.S. Press-ing on, in the line of du-ty, We shall meet to part no more.

REFRAIN.

D.S.

Far a-way, in the realms of beau-ty, Far-ther on, to the gold-en shore,

341

Ashburn 7s.

E. T. Hildebrand, by per.

1. They who seek the throne of grace, Find that throne in ev-'ry place;
2. In our sick-ness and our health, In our want, or in our wealth,
3. When our earth-ly com-forts fail, When the woes of life pre-vail,
4. Then, my soul, in ev-'ry strait, To thy Fa-ther come, and wait;

If we live a life of pray'r, God is pres - ent ev - 'ry-where.
If we look to God in pray'r, God is pres - ent ev - 'ry-where.
'Tis the time for ear - nest pray'r, God is pres - ent ev - 'ry-where.
He will an - swer ev - 'ry pray'r, God is pres - ent ev - 'ry-where.

342 The Sweet Story of Old

"And he took them up in his arms, put his hands upon them, and blessed them." Mark 10: 16

Mrs. Jemima Luke   J. C. Englebrecht

1. I think when I read that sweet sto - ry of old, When Je - sus was here
2. I wish that his hands had been plac'd on my head, His arms had been thrown
3. Yet still to his foot - stool in pray'r I may go, And ask for a share
4. In that beau - ti - ful place he has gone to pre - pare, For all that are wash'd

a - mong men, How he called lit - tle chil - dren as lambs to his fold, I should
a - round me, And that I might have seen his kind look when he said, "Let the
in his love, And if I now ear - nest - ly seek him be - low, I shall
and for - giv - en; And ma - ny dear chil - dren are gath - er - ing there, "For of

Fine Refrain   *D.S.*

like to have been with them then. I should like to have been with them then.
lit - tle ones come un - to me." "Let the lit - tle ones come un - to me."
see him and hear him a - bove, I shall see him and hear him a - bove.
such is the king-dom of heav'n." "For of such is the king-dom of heaven."

343 Suffer the Children to Come

Dr. I. L. MITCHELL

W. A. OGDEN

1. { Hark ! I hear my Sav-iour say: "Suf-fer the chil-dren to come to me;"
   { Do - not turn the lambs a - way, "Suf-fer the chil-dren to (*Omit.* . . .)
2. { Tell them Je - sus loves them all, "Suf-fer the chil-dren to come to me,"
   { He will guide them lest they fall, "Suf-fer the chil-dren to (*Omit.* . . .)
3. { Take them gen - tly by the hand, "Suf-fer the chil-dren to come to me,"
   { Lead them to the bet - ter - land, "Suf-fer the chil-dren to (*Omit.* . . .)

come." Point them to the Fa - ther's throne, Speak to them in ten-d'rest tone,
come." Oh, for - bid them not, I pray, Let the chil-dren come to - day,
come." Lead them with a will - ing mind, Tell them of a Sav-iour kind;

Je - sus calls them for his own, "Suf - fer the chil - dren to come."
Hear the bless - ed Sav - iour say : "Suf - fer the chil - dren to come."
They e - ter - nal life may find, "Suf - fer the chil - dren to come,"
D.S. *watch and pray,* "*Suf - fer the chil - dren to come.*"

FULL CHORUS.

Do not turn the lambs a-way, Precious in his sight are they; Teach them how to

344 Something I Would Tell You

E. R. LATTA

S. E. DUNCAN

1. I have some-thing I would tell you, That 'tis ver - y sweet to know!
2. I have some-thing I would tell you, That is old, and yet, 'tis new!
3. I have some-thing I would tell you, Of the ag - o - ny he felt,
4. I have some-thing I would tell you, Of the Sav - iour cru - ci - fied!

'Tis a - bout the in - fant Sav - iour, Born to save the world from woe!
How the Sav - iour preached sal - va - tion, When he in - to man-hood grew!
Then he prayed the cup might pass him, As in gar - den drear he knelt!
How, for you and me, he suf-fered—How, for sin - ners lost, he died!

REFRAIN.

I have something I would tell you, Of a crown up - on the brow,

And a place a - mong the an - gels! Do you want to hear it now?

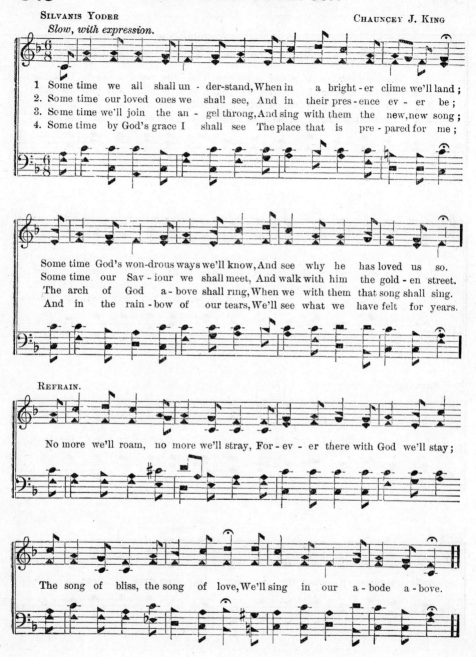

345 Some Time We'll See

Silvanis Yoder

Chauncey J. King

Slow, with expression.

1 Some time we all shall un - der-stand, When in a bright - er clime we'll land;
2. Some time our loved ones we shall see, And in their pres - ence ev - er be;
3. Some time we'll join the an - gel throng, And sing with them the new, new song;
4. Some time by God's grace I shall see The place that is pre - pared for me;

Some time God's won-drous ways we'll know, And see why he has loved us so.
Some time our Sav - iour we shall meet, And walk with him the gold - en street.
The arch of God a - bove shall ring, When we with them that song shall sing.
And in the rain - bow of our tears, We'll see what we have felt for years.

REFRAIN.

No more we'll roam, no more we'll stray, For - ev - er there with God we'll stay;

The song of bliss, the song of love, We'll sing in our a - bode a - bove.

346

I Wonder

"And his name shall be called wonderful." Isa. 9: 6

Rev. Elisha A. Hoffman

Chas. Edw. Pollock

1. I won-der, oft-en won-der, Just how it came to be That there is up in
2. I won-der, oft-en won-der, Just why his ten-der love Brought down the dear Re
3. I won-der, oft-en won-der, That he can bear with me, En-dur-ing all my

heav-en, A man-sion fair for me; And then do I re-mem-ber That
deem-er From his bright home a-bove; And then do I re-mem-ber That
fol-lies, And yet so gra-cious be; And then do I re-mem-ber His

the dear Son of God Once shed for reb-el sin-ners His own a-ton-ing blood.
on the shameful tree The Sav-iour made a-tonement For ten-der love of me.
grace is rich and free, And that he is so pa-tient Be-cause he so loves me.

REFRAIN.

For-ev-er at his feet I'll sit, And won-der at the grace So

large and free it found for me In heav'n a dwell-ing-place.

347 Awake, O Earth

Lucy Randolph Fleming

J. Henry Showalter

1. A-wake, a-wake, O earth! Thy ma-ny voi-ces raise, And let the echo-ing
2. A-wake, a-wake, O earth! For-get the hour of gloom, When in thy shudd'ring
3. Bring treasures of the field, Bring leaf and blos-som sweet, Thy choic-est and thy
4. Lift up thy gates with praise, And robes of joy put on, The Lord of life and

hills Re-peat the note of praise. Let all the isles re-joice, Let seas take
breast Thy Ma-ker claimed a tomb. Put off thy win-try robes For garb of
best, Be-fore his pierc-ed feet. While all thy sons are glad, And tears are
death Hath ris-en to his throne. He hath gone up on high, And giv-eth

up the strain, Christ from the dead hath come, He lives, he lives a-gain.
joy-ous spring, Crown thee with lil-ies fair, To greet the ris-en King.
put a-way, Let youth and age a-like Sing Christ is ris'n to-day.
gifts to men; He lives, no more to die, He lives, he lives a-gain.

D.S. from the dead hath come, He lives, he lives a-gain.

REFRAIN.

He lives . . a-gain! . . Our ris-en Lord, to-day! Christ
He lives! Christ lives! He lives a-gain!

I Love to Tell the Story

7s. 6s. D.

"I will speak of thy wondrous works." Psalm 145: 5

KATE HANKEY

W. K. JACOBS

1. I love to tell the sto - ry Of un - seen things a - bove,
2. I love to tell the sto - ry! More won - der - ful it seems,
3. I love to tell the sto - ry! For those who know it best

Of Je - sus and his glo - ry, Of Je - sus and his love;
Than all the gold - en fan - cies, Of all our gold - en dreams;
Seem hun - ger - ing and thirst - ing To hear it, like the rest;

I love to tell the sto - ry. Be - cause I know it's true;
I love to tell the sto - ry! It did so much for me;
And when, in scenes of glo - ry, I sing the new, new song,

It sat - is - fies my long - ings, As noth - ing else would do.
And that is just the rea - son I tell it now to thee.
'Twill be the old, old sto - ry That I have loved so long.

349 O Everlasting Light

HORATIUS BONAR
Slow.

E. S. HALLMAN

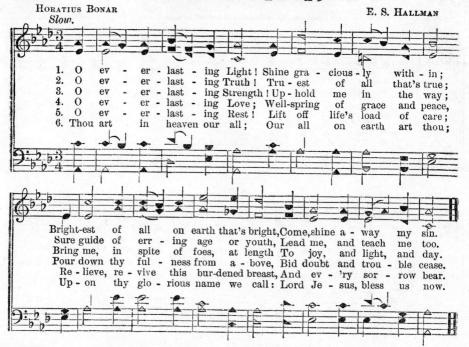

1. O ev - er - last - ing Light! Shine gra - cious - ly with - in;
2. O ev - er - last - ing Truth! Tru - est of all that's true;
3. O ev - er - last - ing Strength! Up - hold me in the way;
4. O ev - er - last - ing Love; Well-spring of grace and peace,
5. O ev - er - last - ing Rest! Lift off life's load of care;
6. Thou art in heaven our all; Our all on earth art thou;

Bright-est of all on earth that's bright, Come, shine a - way my sin.
Sure guide of err - ing age or youth, Lead me, and teach me too.
Bring me, in spite of foes, at length To joy, and light, and day.
Pour down thy ful - ness from a - bove, Bid doubt and trou - ble cease.
Re - lieve, re - vive this bur-dened breast, And ev - 'ry sor - row bear.
Up - on thy glo - rious name we call: Lord Je - sus, bless us now.

350 Come, Ye Disconsolate 11s. 10s. P. M.

"To heal the broken-hearted." Luke 4: 18

THOS. MOORE and THOS. HASTINGS

SAMUEL WEBBE

1. Come, ye dis - con - so-late, wher - e'er ye lan - guish, Come, at the
2. Joy of the des - o-late, light of the stray - ing, Hope of the
3. Here see the bread of life; see wa - ters flow - ing Forth from the

mer - cy-seat fer - vent-ly kneel; Here bring your wounded hearts, here tell your
pen - i - tent, fade - less and pure—Here speaks the Com-fort - er, in mer - cy
throne of God, bound-less in love; Come to the feast pre-pared; come, ev - er

Come, Ye Disconsolate

an - guish; Earth has no sor - row that heav'n can - not heal.
say - ing, "Earth has no sor - row that heav'n can - not cure."
know - ing, Earth has no sor - row but heav'n can re - move.

351   Gently, Lord, Oh, Gently

Thomas Hastings

W. K. Jacobs

DUET.

1. Gen - tly, Lord, oh, gen - tly lead us Through this lone - ly vale of
2. In the hour of pain and an - guish, In the hour when death draws

tears, Thro' the chang - es thou'st de - creed us, Till our last great change ap - pears;
near, Suf - fer not our souls to lan-guish, Suf - fer not our souls to fear;

CHORUS.

When temp-ta - tion's darts as - sail us, When in de - vious paths we
And when mor - tal life is end - ed, Bid us in thine arms to

stray, Let thy good - ness nev - er fail us, Lead us in thy per - fect way.
rest, Till by an - gel bands at-tend - ed We a - wake a - mong the blest.

No, not One

Rev. JOHNSON OATMAN, Jr.

GEO. C. HUGG

Slow, and with great feeling.

1. There's not a friend like the low-ly Je-sus, No, not one! no, not one!
2. No friend like him is so high and ho-ly, No, not one! no, not one!
3. There's not an hour that he is not near us, No, not one! no, not one!
4. Did ev-er saint find this friend for-sake him? No, not one! no, not one!
5. Was e'er a gift like the Sav-iour giv-en? No, not one! no, not one!

None else could heal all our soul's dis-eas-es, No, not one! no, not one!
And yet no friend is so meek and low-ly, No, not one! no, not one!
No night so dark but his love can cheer us, No, not one! no, not one!
Or sin-ner find that he would not take him? No, not one! no, not one!
Will he re-fuse us a home in heav-en? No, not one! no, not one!

REFRAIN.

Je-sus knows all a-bout our struggles, He will guide till the day is done,

There's not a friend like the low-ly Je-sus, No, not one! no, not one!

Anon. Mrs. Harriet Warner, *Re Qua.* Rev. J. W. Dadman

1. I am dwell-ing on the moun-tain, Where the gold-en sun-light gleams
2. I can see far down the moun-tain, Where I wan-dered wea-ry years,
3. I am drink-ing at the foun-tain, Where I ev-er would a-bide;
4. Tell me not of hea-vy cross-es, Nor the bur-dens hard to bear,
5. Oh, the Cross has won-drous glo-ry! Oft I've proved this to be true;

O'er a land whose wondrous beau-ty Far ex-ceeds my fond-est dreams;
Oft-en hin-dered in my jour-ney By the ghosts of doubts and fears,
For I've tast-ed life's pure riv-er, And my soul is sat-is-fied;
For I've found this great sal-va-tion Makes each bur-den light ap-pear;
When I'm in the way so nar-row, I can see a path-way through;

Where the air is pure, ce-les-tial, La-den with the breath of flowers,
Bro-ken vows and dis-ap-pointments Thick-ly sprin-kled all the way,
There's no thirst-ing for life's pleas-ures, Nor a-dorn-ing, rich and gay,
And I love to fol-low Je-sus, Glad-ly count-ing all but dross,
And how sweet-ly Je-sus whis-pers: Take the Cross, thou need'st not fear,

Ref. *Is not this the land of Beu-lah, Bless-ed, bless-ed land of light,*

D.S.

They are bloom-ing by the foun-tain, 'Neath the nev-er-fad-ing bow'rs.
But the Spir-it led, un-er-ring, To the land I hold to-day.
For I've found a rich-er treas-ure, One that fad-eth not a-way.
World-'y hon-ors all for-sak-ing For the glo-ry of the Cross.
For I've tried the way be-fore thee, And the glo-ry lin-gers near.
Where the flow-ers bloom for-ev-er, And the sun is al-ways bright?

In His Name

Isaac Watts

J. Henry Showalter

1. Am I a sol - dier of the cross, A fol - l'wer of the Lamb?
2. Must I be car - ried to the skies On flow - 'ry beds of ease,
3. Are there no foes for me to face? Must I not stem the flood?
4. Sure I must fight if I would reign; In - crease my cour - age, Lord;

And shall I fear to own his cause, Or blush to speak his name?
While oth - ers fought to win the prize, And sailed thro' blood - y seas?
Is this vile world a friend to grace, To help me on to God?
I'll bear the toil, en - dure the pain, Sup - port - ed by thy word.

REFRAIN.

In his name . . . I'll bear the cross, And will ne'er the fight give o'er; . .

In his ev - er blessed name I'll bear, I'll bear the cross, And will ne'er the fight. the fight give o'er;

With his grace . . . . I'll win the crown, And will praise him ev - er - more.

With his freely promised grace I'll win, I'll win the crown, And will praise him ever, ev - er - more.

Copyright, 1900, by J. Henry Showalter. By per.

355 The Story That Never Grows Old

JOHN H. YATES

M. L. McPHAIL

1. How dear to my heart is the sto-ry of old, The sto-ry that
2. It came to my heart when, all fet-tered by sin, I sat in the
3. It comes to my soul when the tempt-er is nigh With snares for my
4. When sor-row is mine, and on pil-lows of stone My ach-ing head
5. When down in the "val-ley and shad-ow of Death," I en-ter the

ev-er is new; The mes-sage that saints of all a-ges have told,
pris-on of doubt; Like an-gel of old, the glad sto-ry came in
way-wea-ry feet; It tells of the Rock that is high-er than I,
seeks for re-pose, This sto-ry brings com-fort and peace from the throne,
gloom of the grave, I'll tell the old sto-ry with life's lat-est breath,

REFRAIN.

The mes-sage so ten-der and true. The sto-ry that nev-er grows
And led me tri-umph-ant-ly out.
And leads to its bliss-ful re-treat.
My des-ert blooms forth like a rose.
Of Christ and his pow-er to save. that

old, ... Though o-ver and o-ver 'tis told; . . . The
nev-er grows old, 'tis told;

sto-ry so dear, bringing heav-en so near, Sweet sto-ry that nev-er grows old.

356

Arlington C. M.

The Lord is risen indeed. Luke 24: 34

Dr. T. A. Arne

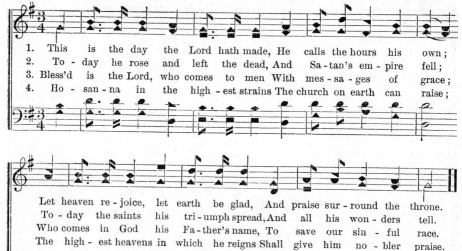

1. This is the day the Lord hath made, He calls the hours his own;
2. To - day he rose and left the dead, And Sa - tan's em - pire fell;
3. Bless'd is the Lord, who comes to men With mes - sa - ges of grace;
4. Ho - san - na in the high - est strains The church on earth can raise;

Let heaven re - joice, let earth be glad, And praise sur - round the throne.
To - day the saints his tri - umph spread, And all his won - ders tell.
Who comes in God his Fa - ther's name, To save our sin - ful race.
The high - est heavens in which he reigns Shall give him no - bler praise.

---

357   *Increase our faith.* Luke 17: 5

1 Oh, for a faith that will not shrink,
  Though pressed by every foe,
That will not tremble on the brink
  Of any earthly woe!

2 That will not murmur nor complain
  Beneath the chastening rod,
But, in the hour of grief or pain,
  Will lean upon its God.

3 A faith that shines more bright and clear
  When tempests rage without;
That, when in danger, knows no fear,
  In darkness, feels no doubt.

4 Lord, give us such a faith as this,
  And then, whate'er may come,
We'll taste, ev'n here, the hallow'd bliss
  Of an eternal home.

W. H. BATHURST, 1831

358   *Love as brethren.* 1 Pet. 3: 8

1 How sweet, how heavenly is the sight,
  When those who love the Lord
In one another's peace delight,
  And so fulfil his word.

2 When each can feel his brother's sigh,
  And with him bear a part;
When sorrow flows from eye to eye,
  And joy from heart to heart.

3 When, free from envy, scorn, and pride,
  Our wishes all above,
Each can his brother's failings hide,
  And show a brother's love.

4 Let love, in one delightful stream,
  Through every bosom flow,
And union sweet, and dear esteem,
  In every action glow.

359 Have Faith in God

E. E. HEWITT   GEO. F. ROSCHE
DUET.

1. "Have faith in God," the Sav-iour said; He saw the path that we must
2. Have faith in God tho' clouds a-rise And o-ver-spread the glow-ing
3. Have faith in God: a fa-ther's heart Would to his child all good im-
4. Have faith in God: his word di-vine By day and night shall bright-ly

tread; The fre-quent thorn, the fad-ing flow'r, The joy or pain of ev-'ry hour.
skies; Tho' sun and stars grow dim and pale, His boundless love shall nev-er fail.
part; Much more will he re-gard the pray'r Of those who cast on him their care.
shine, Un-til we pass the gates of light, And faith shall yield to bliss-ful sight.

Faster.
CHORUS.

O bless-ed faith! Its song of cheer Re-vives our
        O faith!   of cheer
The Shep-herd's staff,   The Shep-herd's rod,   (Omit. . . . .
        the staff,   the rod,

hope, dis-pels our fear;
    our hope,   our fear;
                    Still leads us on; have faith . . in God.
                                                    in God.

Copyright, 1898, by GEO. F. ROSCHE. By per.

360 — **Olive's Brow** — L. M.

Rev. Wm. Bingham Tappan

Wm. B. Bradbury

1. 'Tis mid-night, and on Ol - ive's brow The star is dimm'd that late-ly shone;
2. 'Tis mid-night, and from all re-moved The Sav-iour wres-tles 'lone with fears;
3. 'Tis mid-night, and for oth - er's guilt The Man of Sor-rows weeps in blood;
4. 'Tis mid-night, and from eth - er - plains Is borne the song that an - gels know;

'Tis mid-night in the gar - den now, The suf-f'ring Sav-iour prays a - lone.
E'en that dis - ci - ple whom he lov'd Heeds not his Mas-ter's grief and tears.
Yet he who hath in an-guish knelt, Is not for - sak - en by his God.
Un - heard by mor-tals are the strains That sweet-ly soothe the Saviour's woe.

361 — **Lilies of the Field** — L. M.

"Consider the lilies, how they grow." Luke 12: 27

J. D. Brunk

1. Be - hold the li - lies of the field, That bloom a-round the Mas-ter's feet;
2. Be - hold the spar-rows as they fly; They come at his command and call;
3. Our ver - y hairs he counts with care; He knows our dai - ly hopes and fears;
4. Oh, look up - on the Lord so near! Re-pose be-neath the shel-tered rock;

Their droop-ing leaves new fragrance yield, By Hermon's dew and grate - ful heat.
They seem but specks up - on the sky; And yet he notes them when they fall.
When griefs as - sail and tem-pests scare, He notes the mourner's se - cret tears.
The cross he light - ens by his cheer, The wind he tem-pers to his flock.

362 Ninety=Fifth C. M

ISAAC WATTS

Arr. by J. H. H.

1. When I can read my ti-tle clear To mansions in the skies, I bid farewell to
2. Should earth against my soul engage, And fie-ry darts be hurl'd, Then I can smile at
3. Let cares like a wild deluge come, And storms of sor-row fall! May I but safely
4. There shall I bathe my wea-ry soul In seas of heav'nly rest, And not a wave of

ev-'ry fear, I bid fare-well to ev-'ry fear, And wipe . my weeping eyes.
Satan's rage, Then I can smile at Sa-tan's rage, And face . a frowning world.
reach my home, May I but safe-ly reach my home, My God, . my heav'n, my all.
trou-ble roll, And not a wave of trou-ble roll A - cross . my peaceful breast.

By per. THE RUEBUSH-KIEFFER CO., owners.

363 Siloam C. M.

REGINALD HEBER, 1812

I. B. WOODBURY, 1850

With gentleness.

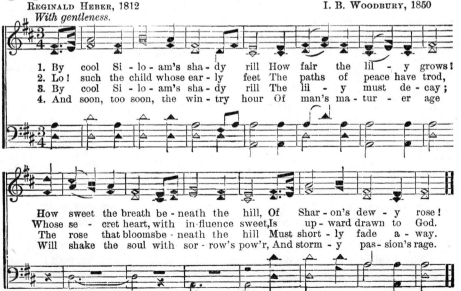

1. By cool Si-lo-am's sha-dy rill How fair the lil-y grows!
2. Lo! such the child whose ear-ly feet The paths of peace have trod,
3. By cool Si-lo-am's sha-dy rill The lil-y must de-cay;
4. And soon, too soon, the win-try hour Of man's ma-tur-er age

How sweet the breath be-neath the hill, Of Shar-on's dew-y rose!
Whose se-cret heart, with in-fluence sweet, Is up-ward drawn to God.
The rose that bloomsbe-neath the hill Must short-ly fade a-way.
Will shake the soul with sor-row's pow'r, And storm-y pas-sion's rage.

Mendota C. M.

Admonish him as a brother. 2 Thess. 3: 15

F. G. Lee

Arr.

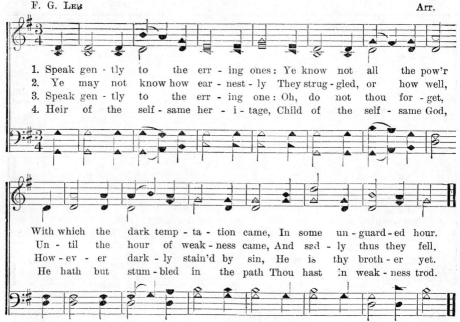

1. Speak gen - tly to the err - ing ones: Ye know not all the pow'r
2. Ye may not know how ear - nest - ly They strug - gled, or how well,
3. Speak gen - tly to the err - ing one: Oh, do not thou for - get,
4. Heir of the self - same her - i - tage, Child of the self - same God,

With which the dark temp - ta - tion came, In some un - guard - ed hour.
Un - til the hour of weak - ness came, And sad - ly thus they fell.
How - ev - er dark - ly stain'd by sin, He is thy broth - er yet.
He hath but stum - bled in the path Thou hast in weak - ness trod.

5 Speak gently to the erring one:
  For is it not enough

That innocence and peace are gone,
  Without our censure rough?

6 It surely is a weary lot
  That sin-crushed heart to bear;
And they who share a happier fate
  Their chidings well may spare.

365 *I will bless the Lord at all times.* Ps. 34: 1

1 Thro' all the changing scenes of life,
  In trouble and in joy,
The praises of my God shall still
  My heart and tongue employ.

2 The hosts of God encamp around
  The dwellings of the just;
Deliverance he affords to all
  Who on his succor trust.

366 *I will be glad and rejoice in thy mercies.* Ps. 31: 7

1 Sweet was the time when first I felt
  The Saviour's pard'ning blood
Applied to cleanse my soul from guilt,
  And bring me home to God.

2 Soon as the morn the light reveals,
  His praises tune my tongue;
And when the evening shade prevails,
  His love is all my song.

3 In prayer my soul draws near the Lord,
  And sees his glory shine;
And when I read his holy word,
  I claim each promise mine.

4 When Satan threatens to prevail,
  And make my soul his prey;
Then, Lord, thy mercies cannot fail,
  Thy help do not delay!

367

Mattie C. M.

Her ways are ways of pleasantness. Prov. 3: 17

MICHAEL BRUCE
Moderato.

L. C. EVERETT

1. Oh, hap-py is the man who hears Re - li-gion's warning voice, And who ce-
2. For she hath treas-ures great-er far Than east and west un - fold ; And her re-
3. In her right hand is length of days For those who heed her voice ; Her left hand
4. She guides the young with in - no-cence In pleasure's paths to tread ; A crown of
5. Ac-cord-ing as her la - bors rise, So her re-wards in-crease ; Her ways are

les - tial wisdom makes His ear-ly, on - ly choice, His ear - ly, on - ly choice.
wards more precious are Than all their stores of gold, Than all their stores of gold.
of - fers wealth and praise To make her sons re - joice, To make her sons re - joice.
glo - ry she be-stows Up-on the hoar - y head, Up - on the hoar-y head.
ways of pleasantness, And all her paths are peace, And all her paths are peace.

368

Golden Hills S. M.

PHILIP DODDRIDGE, 1740

A. CHAPIN, 1832

1. Grace ! 'tis a charm - ing sound, Har - mo - nious to mine ear ;
2. Grace first con - trived the way To save re - bel - lious man;
3. Grace led my rov - ing feet To tread the heav'n - ly road;
4. Grace all the work shall crown, Thro' ev - er - last - ing days;

Heav'n with the ech - o shall re - sound, And all the earth shall hear.
And all the steps that grace dis - play First drew the won - drous plan.
And new sup - plies each hour I meet, While press-ing on to God.
It lays in heav'n the top - most-stone, And well de - serves the praise.

369 Tell the Sweet Old Story

8s. 7s.

Geo. W. Lyon

J. Henry Showalter

1. Go and tell the sweet old sto - ry Of the Sav - iour's pre - cious love,
2. Tell how great is his com - pas - sion, How he died up - on the tree,
3. Shout a - loud, O ye re - deemed ones, Tell it o'er and o'er a - gain,

How he came to earth from heav - en, That he might his good - ness prove.
To re - deem the lost and dy - ing, And to set the cap - tive free.
Till the dis - tant hea - then na - tions Shall a - dore and praise his name.

REFRAIN.

Tell it o'er . . . . . and keep on tell - ing, 'Tis so won - - drous
Tell it o'er and o'er a - gain, and keep on tell - ing, 'Tis so wondrous, 'tis so wondrous,

and so sweet, ... Tell it till . . . . . un - num - bered
'tis so won - drous and so sweet, Tell it till the hosts, the great un - num - bered

Tell the Sweet Old Story

mil - lions Lay their tro - phies at his feet. . . .
mil - lions Lay their tro - phies down at Je - sus' pierc - ed feet, his feet.

370   Let Them Come to Me

E. T. HILDEBRAND, by per.

Moderato.

1. Je - sus loves a lit - tle child, Smil-ing in its child-ish glee; Says of such in
2. In the bless-ed Sun-day school, They are taught to fear the Lord; Here they find his
3. When life's toilsome work is done, When the stormy strife is o'er, Then a - round his

accents mild, "Let them come to me." Let them come, forbid them not, They will sing a -
ho - ly way, Learn to love his word. Armed with this they may go forth, Triumph o - ver
shining throne, On the bliss-ful shore, Shall his hap-py children meet, Sing and shout, their

round the throne; Mil - lions now are sing - ing there, Mil - lions more may come.
ev - 'ry foe, Spread-ing joy o'er all the earth, Sooth-ing hu - man woe.
suf-f'rings o'er, Cast their crowns at Je - sus' feet, Praise him ev - er - more.

371 Is My Name Written There

Mrs. Mary A. Kidder

Frank M. Davis

1. Lord, I care not for rich-es, Neither sil-ver nor gold; I would make sure of heav-en, I would en-ter the fold. In the book of thy king-dom, With its pa-ges so fair, Tell me, Je-sus, my Sav-iour, Is my name writ-ten there?

2. Lord, my sins they are man-y, Like the sands of the sea, But thy blood, oh, my Sav-iour, Is suf-fi-cient for me; For thy prom-ise is writ-ten, In bright let-ters that glow, "Tho' your sins be as scar-let, I will make them like snow."

3. Oh! that beau-ti-ful cit-y, With its man-sions of light, With its glo-ri-fied be-ings, In pure gar-ments of white; Where no e-vil thing com-eth, To de-spoil what is fair; Where the an-gels are watch-ing, Yes, my name's written there.

REFRAIN.

Is my name writ-ten there, On the page white and fair?
In the book of thy king-dom, Is my name writ-ten there?

Ref. for 2d & 3d Stanzas.

Yes, my name's writ-ten there, On the page white and fair,
In the book of thy king-dom, Yes, my name's writ-ten there.

372 𝕰𝖋𝖋𝖎𝖊 8s. 7s.

"*God is light, and in him is no darkness.*" 1 John 1: 5

J. Allen   D. M. Click

1. God is love, his mer-cy bright-ens All the path in which we move;
2. Chance and change are bu-sy ev-er; Worlds de-cay, and a-ges move;
3. E'en the hour that dark-est seem-eth Will his change-less good-ness prove;
4. He with earth-ly cares en-twin-eth Hope and com-fort from a-bove;

Bliss he forms, and woe he light-ens; God is light, and God is love.
But his mer-cy wan-eth nev-er; God is light, and God is love.
From the mist his bright-ness stream-eth; God is light, and God is love.
Ev-'ry-where his glo-ry shin-eth; God is light, and God is love.

373 𝖂𝖎𝖑𝖒𝖔𝖙 8s. 7s.

"*Now is the day of salvation.*" 2 Cor. 6: 2

Jas. Montgomery   C. M. von Weber

1. Lis-ten to the gen-tle promptings Of the Spir-it's warn-ing voice;
2. Sweet-ly call-ing on the err-ing, Par-dons of-fered with-out price;
3. Joy and hope the trou-bled conscience Will al-lay with sooth-ing peace;
4. Hes-i-tate no lon-ger, sin-ner, Lest the Spir-it, sad and grieved,

Will ye heed his sol-emn warnings? Can ye slight his won-drous love?
Come, ac-cept the in-vi-ta-tion, And re-ceive the of-fered grace.
Press ye then to realms of glo-ry, Run with joy the of-fered race.
Should for-sake thee, now and ev-er, Nev-er-more to be de-ceived.

5 Broken hearts and contrite spirits,
   These the Lord will not despise;
 Trust in Christ's atoning merits,
   In his precious sacrifice.

6 Time is short, and life is flying;
   You must perish if you stay;
 Christ is coming, men are dying,
   Halt no longer, come to-day.

374 Knocking at the Door

"Behold, I stand at the door and knock." Rev. iii: 20

Mrs. M. B. C. Slade

Dr. A. B. Everett

1. Who at my door is stand - ing, Pa - tient - ly draw - ing near,
2. Lone - ly with-out he's stay - ing, Lone - ly with - in am I,
3. All thro' the dark hours drear - y, Knock - ing a - gain is he;
4. Door of my heart, I has - ten! Thee will I o - pen wide,

En - trance with-in de - mand - ing? Whose is the voice I hear?
While I am still de - lay - ing, Will he not pass me by?
Je - sus, art thou not wea - ry, Wait - ing so long for me?
Tho' he re-buke and chas - ten, He shall with me a - bide.

REFRAIN.

Sweet - ly the tones are fall - ing:—"O - pen the door for me!

If thou wilt heed my call - ing, I will a - bide with thee."

By per. R. M. McIntosh

375

Jesus Knows

GEO. C. HUGG

GEO. C HUGG

1. When this poor heart is burdened with grief. No - bod - y knows like Je - sus!
2. When on the mount of joy and de - light, No - bod - y knows like Je - sus!
3. All that I am, or ev - er shall be, No - bod - y knows like Je - sus!

When at the Cross I cry for re - lief, No - bod - y knows like Je - sus!
When faith up - lifts to man-sions so bright, No - bod - y knows like Je - sus!
All there re - mains in glo - ry for me, No - bod - y knows like Je - sus!

REFRAIN.

No - bod - y knows like Je - sus! No - bod - y knows like Je - sus!

Pre - cious Re - deem - er, Broth - er and Friend, No - bod - y knows like Je - sus!

376 Sweet Day S. M.

B. C. UNSELD

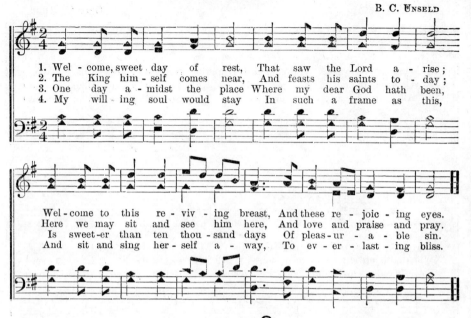

1. Wel - come, sweet day of rest, That saw the Lord a - rise;
2. The King him - self comes near, And feasts his saints to - day;
3. One day a - midst the place Where my dear God hath been,
4. My will - ing soul would stay In such a frame as this,

Wel - come to this re - viv - ing breast, And these re - joic - ing eyes.
Here we may sit and see him here, And love and praise and pray.
Is sweet-er than ten thou - sand days Of pleas - ur - a - ble sin.
And sit and sing her - self a - way, To ev - er - last - ing bliss.

---

377 *God who is rich in mercy.* Eph. 2: 4

1 And are we yet alive,
　And see each other's face?
Glory and praise to Jesus give
　For his redeeming grace.

2 Preserved by power divine
　To full salvation here,
Again in Jesus' praise we join
　And in his sight appear.

3 What troubles have we seen;
　What conflicts have we passed;
Fightings without and fears within,
　Since we assembled last.

4 But out of all, the Lord
　Hath brought us by his love;
And still he doth his help afford,
　And hides our life above.

5 Let us take up the cross
　Till we the crown obtain,
And gladly reckon all things loss,
　So we may Jesus gain.

378 *One body in Christ.* Rom. 12: 5

1 And let our bodies part,
　To different climes repair,—
Inseparably joined in heart
　The friends of Jesus are.

2 Jesus, the Corner-stone,
　Did first our hearts unite,
And still he keeps our spirits one,
　Who walk with him in white.

3 The vineyard of their Lord
　Before his laborers lies;
And lo! we see the vast reward
　Reserved in paradise.

4 There all our toils are o'er,
　Our suffering and our pain:—
Who meet on that eternal shore,
　Shall never part again.

5 To gather home his own
　God shall his angels send,
And bid our bliss on earth begun,
　In deathless triumph end.

CHARLES WESLEY, 1749

379 Grateful Submission

Daniel Kauffman

A. B. Kolb

1. We bow to thee, O Lord, on high; To thee our hearts in-cline; Sub-
2. The high-est sta-tion here on earth Is at our Sav-iour's feet; 'Tis
3. Our Sav-iour, tho' our Mas-ter, Lord, In true hu-mil-i-ty. By
4. A pat-tern he did kind-ly give To His dis-ci-ples true: He
5. Then af-ter-wards he said to them, "Go forth (I go with you), And
6. Then teach us, Lord, to do thy will, What-ev-er that may be: May

mit-ting to thy word, we pray, Thy will be done, not mine.
there we learn our Mas-ter's will, We find the mer-cy-seat.
ac-tion taught that we might see The great must ser-vants be.
washed their feet, then said to them, "Do as I've done to you."
teach all na-tions ev-'ry-thing I've command-ed you to do."
thy free grace at-tend us here, And in e-ter-ni-ty.

REFRAIN.

Lord, as this sol-emn rite we keep, With joy we wor-ship thee; May

we with hum-ble hearts, O Lord, Thy faith-ful ser-vants be. . . .

Bealoth S. M. D.

Timothy Dwight, 1800

1. I love thy king-dom, Lord, The house of thine a-bode—
2. For her my tears shall fall, For her my pray'rs as-cend;
3. Je-sus, thou Friend di-vine, Our Sav-iour and our King,

The church our blest Re-deem-er sav'd With his own pre-cious blood.
To her my cares and toils be giv'n Till toils and cares shall end.
Thy hand from ev-'ry snare and foe Shall great de-liv-'rance bring.

I love thy church, O God, Her walls be-fore thee stand.
Be-yond my high-est joy I prize her heav'n-ly ways,
Sure as thy truth shall last, To Zi-on shall be giv'n

Dear as the ap-ple of thine eye, And gra-ven on thy hand.
Her sweet com-mun-ion, sol-emn vows, Her hymns of love and praise.
The bright-est glo-ries earth can yield, And bright-er bliss of heav'n.

381

Steiner S. M. D

Isaac Watts, 1709

A. B. Kolb

1. How beau - teous are their feet, Who stand on Zi - on's hill,
2. How hap - py are our ears, That hear this joy - ful sound,
3. The watch - men join their voice, And tune - ful notes em - ploy,

Who bring sal - va - tion on their tongues, And words of peace re - veal.
Which kings and pro - phets wait - ed for, And sought but nev - er found.
Je - ru - sa - lem breaks forth in songs, And des - erts learn the joy.

How charm - ing is their voice, How sweet their ti - dings are,
How bless - ed are our eyes, That see this heav'n - ly light,
The Lord makes bare his arm, Thro' all the earth a - broad,

Zi - on be - hold thy Sav - iour King, He reigns and tri - umphs here.
Pro - phets and kings de - sired it long, But died with - out the sight.
Let ev - 'ry na - tion now be - hold Their Sav - iour and their God.

The Light of the World

"Ye are the light of the world." Matt. 5: 14

Rev. R. J. Craig

J. D. Brunk, by per.

1. Ye are the light of the world, Driv-ing the dark-ness a-way,
2. Ye are the light of the world, Caus-ing the clouds to de-part,
3. Ye are the light of the world; Thro' you the true light must shine,

Shed-ding your beams on the lost, Chang-ing their night in-to day.
Throw-ing the sun-shine of peace Down on the poor burdened heart.
Call-ing the lost sons of men Home to the Fa-ther di-vine.

Then let your light ev-er shine, Show-ing the right way to go;
Then let your light ev-er shine, Loved ones are pant-ing for rest;
Then let your light ev-er shine, Hal-low the name that is love;

Glad-ly the lost ones will see— God's bound-less love they will know.
Sun-shine their souls will re-vive, Lift-ing them up to the blest.
You will each shine as a star, Fixed in the or-bit a-bove.

W. K. J.

W. K. JACOBS, by per.

1. When the trump shall sound and time shall be no more, And
2. On that morn - ing when the dead in Christ shall rise E -
3. Let us la - bor on un - til our race is run, And

morn - ing breaks, ev - er - last - ing, fair, When the saved, up - on the
ter - nal glo - ry with him to share, When his cho - sen ones, be -
tell to all of his love and care; Then when all the toils of

REFRAIN.

oth - er shore Shall meet with the Sav - iour there:Then we'll be hap - py with
yond the skies Shall meet with the Sav - iour there:
earth are done We'll meet with our Sav - iour there.   be

Christ,   Yes, We'll be hap - py with those gone   be - fore, And
hap - py with Christ,   those gone be - fore,

with the ransomed ones who do his will So hap - py for ev - er - more.

384 Rest Over Jordan

Geo. B. Holsinger, by per.

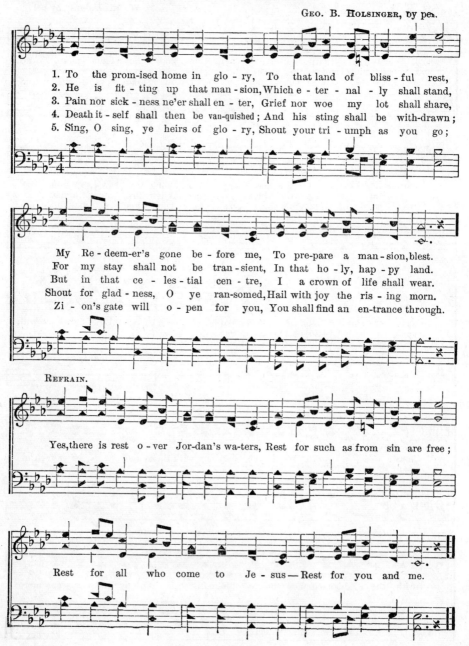

1. To the prom-ised home in glo-ry, To that land of bliss-ful rest,
2. He is fit-ting up that man-sion, Which e-ter-nal-ly shall stand,
3. Pain nor sick-ness ne'er shall en-ter, Grief nor woe my lot shall share,
4. Death it-self shall then be van-quished; And his sting shall be with-drawn;
5. Sing, O sing, ye heirs of glo-ry, Shout your tri-umph as you go;

My Re-deem-er's gone be-fore me, To pre-pare a man-sion, blest.
For my stay shall not be tran-sient, In that ho-ly, hap-py land.
But in that ce-les-tial cen-tre, I a crown of life shall wear.
Shout for glad-ness, O ye ran-somed, Hail with joy the ris-ing morn.
Zi-on's gate will o-pen for you, You shall find an en-trance through.

Refrain.

Yes, there is rest o-ver Jor-dan's wa-ters, Rest for such as from sin are free;

Rest for all who come to Je-sus—Rest for you and me.

385 Love Not the World

GERTRUDE A. FLORY

GEO. B. HOLSINGER, by per.

1. Love not the world! Its daz-zling show Con-ceals a snare of death;
2. Love not the world! Its wealth, re-nown, The blood-bought soul en-slaves;
3. Love not the world! Its sin and strife Ex-ceed the good and true;
4. Love not the world! Pure joys a-bove All earth-ly things tran-scend;
5. Love not the world! O Chris-tian, hear, In shin-ing words im-pearled,

The sweet-est joy earth can be-stow, Dies as a wast-ed breath.
Oh, strive to win a heav'n-ly crown, Which plumes of glo-ry wave.
Oh, con-se-crate to Christ your life! He drained death's cup for you.
In Je-sus lose each i-dol love, And ev-er up-ward tend.
Shall on your ho-ly brow ap-pear, "He did not love the world."

REFRAIN.

Love not the world is Je-sus' plea, Sweet life to you he brought;

A-lone with death on Cal-va-ry, Your sin-lost soul he sought.

Be not Afraid

A. Metzler

From "Temple Star," by per.

1. When tri - als and temp - ta - tions A - round thee dark - ly flow, When
2. When wa - ters of af - flic - tion May seem to o - ver - flow, Or
3. The soul that Je - sus lov - eth He'll chas - ten and re - fine, That
4. "Let not your heart be trou - bled, Oh, hear the Sav - iour speak, God

storms and griefs as - sail thee To bring thy cour - age low, Be not dis -
through some fi - ery tri - al You may be called to go, Keep up your
like a gold - en lus - tre It may the bright - er shine; The dross a -
com - forts you in sor - rows, When sad you feel and weak; He leads you

cour - aged, broth - er, But firm - ly stand and wait; The clouds a - gain will
faith and cour - age, The Lord will dis - si - pate The waves that dash a -
lone will per - ish, The gold is bright - er made; Be not dis - cour - aged,
through the riv - er Which sin - ners can - not wade, And death shall lose its

Refrain.

van - ish, Oh, be thou not a - fraid ! There is sweet rest in heav'n, There is sweet rest in
gainst thee, Fear not, be not a - fraid !
broth - er, Fear not, be not a - fraid !
ter - rors, Fear not, be not a - fraid !

heav'n, There is sweet rest, there is sweet rest, There is sweet rest in heav'n.

Arr.

1. The war in which the sol-dier fights Is not the war for me; By
2. The sword the crest-ed war-rior wields, Is not the sword for me; While
3. The fame that's gained by men of blood, Is not the fame for me; By
4. The wreath that finds the vic-tor's brow, Is not the wreath for me, For,

it are crush'd all fond delights, And sad-ness here I see; But there's a war, a
march-ing o - ver tent-ed fields, To death or vic-to-ry; But there's a sword that
drench-ing earth in go-ry flood, Of friend and en-e-my; But oh, the fame, the
to re-ceive it who would vow, Save that thro' pride it be; But there's a wreath,—a

ho-ly strife, In which is gain'd a bliss-ful life, Thro' all e-ter-ni-ty. Oh,
pierc-es deep, And of-ten makes the sin-ner weep; And to the Sav-iour flee; Oh,
glo-ry bright, The Christian sol-dier has in sight, As on-ward marches he; Oh,
shin-ing crown For him, who gains (O great renown,) O'er sin the vic-to-ry; Oh,

that's the war for me! Oh, that's the war for me! Oh, that's the war for me!
that's the sword for me! Oh, that's the sword for me! Oh, that's the sword for me!
that's the fame for me! Oh, that's the fame for me! Oh, that's the fame for me!
that's the wreath for me! Oh, that's the wreath for me! Oh, that's the wreath for me!

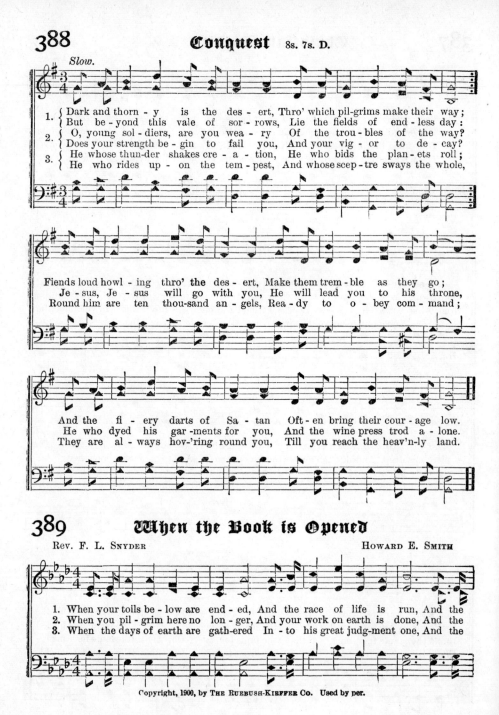

388 Conquest 8s. 7s. D.

Slow.

1. { Dark and thorn - y is the des - ert, Thro' which pil-grims make their way;
  { But be - yond this vale of sor - rows, Lie the fields of end - less day :
2. { O, young sol - diers, are you wea - ry Of the trou - bles of the way?
  { Does your strength be - gin to fail you, And your vig - or to de - cay?
3. { He whose thun-der shakes cre - a - tion, He who bids the plan - ets roll;
  { He who rides up - on the tem - pest, And whose scep - tre sways the whole,

Fiends loud howl - ing thro' the des - ert, Make them trem - ble as they go;
Je - sus, Je - sus will go with you, He will lead you to his throne,
Round him are ten thou-sand an - gels, Rea - dy to o - bey com - mand;

And the fi - ery darts of Sa - tan Oft - en bring their cour - age low.
He who dyed his gar -ments for you, And the wine press trod a - lone.
They are al - ways hov-'ring round you, Till you reach the heav'n-ly land.

389 When the Book is Opened

Rev. F. L. Snyder   Howard E. Smith

1. When your toils be - low are end - ed, And the race of life is run, And the
2. When you pil - grim here no lon - ger, And your work on earth is done, And the
3. When the days of earth are gath-ered In - to his great judg-ment one, And the

REFRAIN.

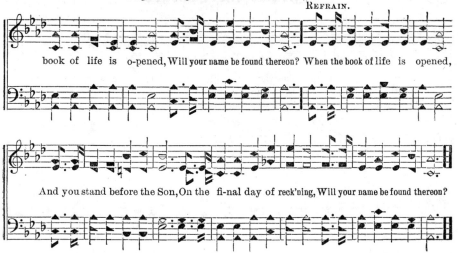

book of life is o-pened, Will your name be found thereon? When the book of life is opened,

And you stand before the Son, On the fi-nal day of reck'ning, Will your name be found thereon?

390   No Abiding City Here   8s. 7s.

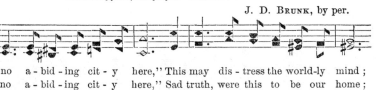

" We walk by faith, not by sight." 2 Cor. 5: 7

J. D. BRUNK, by per.

1. "We've no a-bid-ing cit-y here," This may dis-tress the world-ly mind;
2. "We've no a-bid-ing cit-y here," Sad truth, were this to be our home;
3. "We've no a-bid-ing cit-y here," Then let us live as pil-grims do;
4. "We've no a-bid-ing cit-y here," We seek a cit-y out of sight;

But should not cost the saint a tear, Who hopes a bet-ter rest to find.
But let this tho't our spir-its cheer, "We seek a cit-y yet to come."
Let not the world our rest ap-pear, But let us haste from all be-low.
Zi-on its name — the Lord is there, It shines with ev-er-last-ing light.

R. A. Van Pelt

J. D. Brunk

1. Our Sav-iour in his earth-ly life Taught peace, and how we should for-give;
2. He taught us when by man op-pressed, To of-fer e'en the oth-er cheek;
3. When at the last he was betrayed,—Dis-hon-ored by the trai-tor's kiss,—

He taught us to re-frain from strife, And showed us how in love to live.
To pray in spir-it, faith pos-sessed, And his for-giv-ing love to seek.
He gave command to sheathe the blade : Nor need-ed he such arm as this.

No bit-ter tone, no an-gry blow, No weap-on save his pre-cious word;
For an-gry word has nev-er yet A heart-ache healed—a will sub-dued,
All lamb-like to the slaugh-ter led, While nails and spear his life-blood drew,

No emp-ty pomp, no gau-dy show : He gen-tly leads us by his love.
Nor made a sin-ner turn and set His heart on God, with faith en-dued.
This crowning pray'r its glo-ry shed : "For-give ! they know not what they do."

W. K. JACOBS

W. K. JACOBS, by per.

In majestic style.

1. Won - der - ful Sav - iour, Re - deem - er, Thou in ten - d'rest love
2. Thou hast in great - est com - pas - sion Died our souls to save:
3. O - pen my heart e'er to hear thee, Quick to hear thy voice;

Watch - est o'er ev - 'ry be - liev - er, From thy throne a - bove.
Pur - chased for us our re - demp - tion, Hope be - yond the grave.
Fill thou my soul with thy prais - es, Let my heart re - joice.

REFRAIN.

Won - der - ful Sav - iour! Mer - ci - ful Sav - iour!
Je - sus, wonder-ful Sav - iour, Je - sus, mer - ci - ful Sav - iour,

My hope and Re - deem - er, Who shed his blood for me.
shed his blood for me. (for me.)

393 Home, Sweet Home

"They desire a better country." Heb. 11: 16

DAVID DENHAM

H. R. BISHOP

1. 'Mid scenes of con-fu-sion and crea—ture com-plaints, How
2. Sweet bonds that u—nite all the chil—dren of peace ! And
3. While here in the val—ley of con—flict I stay, Oh,
4. I long, dear—est Lord, in thy beau—ty to shine, No

sweet to my soul is com-mun—ion with saints ! To
thrice, bless—ed Je—sus, whose love . . can—not cease ! Though
give me sub-mis—sion and strength as my day, In
more as an ex—ile in sor—row to pine, And

find . . at the ban—quet of mer—cy there's room, And
oft from thy pres—ence in sad—ness I roam, I
all my af-flic—tions to thee would I come, Rein . . thy dear im-age a—rise from the tomb, With

REFRAIN.

feel in the pres-ence of Je—sus at home. Home, home,
long to be-hold thee, in glo—ry at home.
joic—ing in hope of my glo—ri-ous home.
glo—ri-fied mil-lions to praise thee at home.

sweet, sweet home, Pre-pare me, dear Sav-iour, for glo—ry, my home.

394

Windham L. M.

The broad and narrow way. Matt. 7: 13, 14

I. Watts

Daniel Read, 1785

1. Broad is the road that leads to death, And thou-sands walk to-geth-er there,
2. "De-ny thy-self, and take thy cross," Is the Re-deem-er's great com-mand;
3. The fear-ful soul that tires and faints, And walks the ways of God no more,
4. Lord, let not all my hopes be vain; Cre-ate my heart en-tire-ly new,

But wis-dom shows a nar-row path, With here and there a trav-el-er.
Na-ture must count her gold but dross, If she would gain this heav'n-ly land.
Is but es-teemed al-most a saint, And makes his own de-struc-tion sure.
Which hyp-o-crites could ne'er at-tain, Which false a-pos-tates nev-er knew.

395

Come to Me L. M.

"Him that cometh to me I will in no wise cast out." John 6: 37

J. D. Brunk

1. With tear-ful eyes I look a-round, Life seems a dark and storm-y sea;
2. It tells me of a place of rest, It tells me where my soul may flee;
3. When na-ture shud-ders, loth to part From all I love, en-joy, and see;
4. Come, for all else must fail and die; Earth is no rest-ing, place for thee;
5. O voice of mer-cy! voice of love! In con-flict, grief, and ag-o-ny,

Yet, 'midst the gloom, I hear a sound, A heav'n-ly whis-per, "Come to me."
Oh! to the wea-ry, faint, op-press'd, How sweet the bid-ding, "Come to me."
When a faint chill steals o'er my heart A sweet voice ut-ters, "Come to me."
Heav'n-ward di-rect thy weep-ing eye, I am thy por-tion, "Come to me."
Sup-port me, cheer me from a-bove! And gen-tly whis-per, "Come to me;"

396 Little Ones Like Me

Geo. B. Holsinger, by per.

1. Je-sus, when he left the sky, And for sin-ners came to die, In his mer-cy
2. Moth-ers then the Sav-iour sought, In the pla-ces where he taught, Un-to him their
3. Did the Sav-iour say them nay? No, he kind-ly bade them stay; Suffer'd none to
4. Chil-dren, then, should love him now, Strive his ho-ly will to do, Pray to him, and

Fine. Refrain. D. S.

passed not by Lit-tle ones like me. Lit-tle ones like me, Lit-tle ones like me;
chil-dren bro't, Lit-tle ones like me.
turn a-way Lit-tle ones like me.
praise him too, Lit-tle ones like me.

397 Sweet Day S. M.

B. C. Unseld

1. Once more, be-fore we part, Oh, bless the Sav-iour's name!
2. Lord, in thy grace we came, That bless-ing still im-part,
3. Still on thy ho-ly word We'll live, and feed, and grow;
4. Now, Lord, be-fore we part, Help us to bless thy name;

Let ev-'ry tongue and ev-'ry heart A-dore and praise the same.
We met in Je-sus' sa-cred name, In Je-sus' name we part.
And still go on to know the Lord, And prac-tice what we know.
Let ev-'ry tongue and ev-'ry heart A-dore and praise the same.

398 Parting Hymn C. M. D

1. How pleas-ant thus to dwell be-low, In fel-low-ship of love;
2. Yes, hap-py tho't when we are free From earth-ly grief and pain,
3. Then let us walk in strength di-vine, Still walk in wis-dom's ways;

And though we part, 'tis bliss to know The good shall meet a-bove;
In heav'n we shall each oth-er see, And nev-er part a-gain;
That we, with those who love, may join In nev-er-end-ing praise;

D.S. *To meet to part no more,*

The good shall meet a-bove, . . . The good shall meet a-bove, . .
And nev-er part a-gain, . . . And nev-er part a-gain, . .
In nev-er-end-ing praise, . . . In nev-er-end-ing praise. .

To meet to part no more, .. On Ca-naan's hap-py shore,
FINE.

And though we part, 'tis bliss to know The good shall meet a-bove.
In heav'n we shall each oth-er see, And nev-er part a-gain.
That we, with those who love, may join In nev-er-end-ing praise.

And sing the ev-er-last-ing song With those who've gone be-fore.

REFRAIN.   D.S.

Oh! that will be joy-ful, joy-ful, joy-ful, Oh! that will be joy-ful,

399

Dennis S. M.

"Being knit together in love." Col. 2: 2

John Fawcett

From H. G. Nageli

1. Blest be the tie that binds Our hearts in Chris-tian love;
2. Be-fore our Fa-ther's throne, We pour our ar-dent pray'rs;
3. We share our mu-tual woes, Our mu-tual bur-dens bear;
4. When we a-sun-der part, It gives us in-ward pain;

The fel-low-ship of kin-dred minds Is like to that a-bove.
Our fears, our hopes, our aims are one, Our com-forts and our cares.
And oft-en for each oth-er flows The sym-pa-thiz-ing tear.
But we shall still be joined in heart, And hope to meet a-gain.

400 *"Wherein he had made us accepted in the beloved."* Eph. 1: 6

1 My soul, with joy attend,
   While Jesus silence breaks;
No angel's harp such music yields,
   As what my shepherd speaks.

2 "I know my sheep," he cries,
   "My soul approves them well:
Vain is the treach'rous world's disguise,
   And vain the rage of hell.

3 I freely feed them now
   With tokens of my love;
But richer pastures I prepare,
   And sweeter streams above.

4 Unnumbered years of bliss
   I to my sheep will give;
And while my throne unshaken stands,
   Shall all my chosen live.

5 This tried Almighty Hand,
   Is raised for their defense: [there?
Where is the power shall reach them
   Or what shall force them thence?

6 Enough, my gracious Lord,
   Let faith triumphant cry;
My heart can on this promise live,
   Can on this promise die.

401 *"His commandments are not grievous."*

1 How gentle God's commands!
   How kind his precepts are!
Come, cast your burdens on the Lord,
   And trust his constant care.

2 Beneath his watchful eye
   His saints securely dwell,
That hand which bears all nature up,
   Shall guard his children well.

3 Why should this anxious load
   Press down your weary mind?
Haste to your heav'nly Father's throne,
   And sweet refreshment find.

4 His goodness stands approved,
   Unchanged from day to day;
Come, drop your burden at his feet,
   And bear a song away.

DODDRIDGE

Newark 7s. 6s. D.

1. Oh, when shall I see Je - sus, And dwell with him a - bove?
2. But now I am a sol - dier, My Cap - tain's gone be - fore;
3. Through grace I am de - ter - min'd To con - quer though I die;

To drink the flow - ing foun - tains Of ev - er - last - ing love?
He's giv - en me my or - ders, And tells me not to fear.
And then a - way to Je - sus On wings of love I'll fly.

When shall I be de - liv - ered From this vain world of sin,
And if I hold out faith - ful, A crown of life he'll give,
Fare - well to sin and sor - row, I bid them both a - dieu;

And with my bless - ed Je - sus Drink end - less pleas - ures in?
And all his val - iant sol - diers E - ter - nal life shall have.
And you, my friends, prove faith - ful, And on your way pur - sue.

403 Beautiful Homeland

(EFFECTIVE AS A SOLO)

Laura E. Newell   Geo. B. Holsinger, by per.

1. A cit-y a-waits us we soon shall be-hold, Whose walls are of jas-per, whose
2. The friends that we love who have gone on be-fore Now wait for our com-ing on
3. O home-land! dear homeland, tho' eye hath not seen, And sometimes the shadow-y

streets are of gold; Not half of its glo-ries have ev-er been told,
yon-der bright shore, Where day nev-er fades, tears may fall nev-er more,
clouds in-ter-vene, Thy light we'll be-hold, and thy pas-tures so green.

Fine. Refrain.

rit.

Bless-ed homeland, dear homeland, sweet home of the soul. Oh, I long, yes, I

long there to dwell (there to dwell), 'Mid the pleas-ures no mor-tal can
no

D.S.

tell, ... In the place our dear Sav-iour has gone to pre-pare,
mor-tal can tell,

404

Good=bye
(PARTING HYMN)

Rev. Johnson Oatman, Jr.

Geo. C. Hugg

1. These scenes, so bright, now take their flight As birds in sum-mer seem to fly ;
2. As oft we meet, and dear ones greet, Heart speaks to heart and eye to eye ;
3. Some-time we'll meet, some-time we'll greet Each oth - er in that land on high ;

A - gain we stand with part - ing hand, Good-bye, good bye, good - bye.
Time speeds a - way, and soon we say, Good-bye, good - bye, good - bye.
There we will stay, and nev - er say, Good-bye, good - bye, good - bye.

REFRAIN.

Good - bye, good-bye, we breathe a sigh, We say fare - well with tear-dimmed eye ;

God bless you all, God keep you all, Good - bye, good - bye, good - bye.

God be with You

" The grace of our Lord Jesus Christ be with you." **Romans 16: 20**

J. E. Rankin, D.D.

W. G. Tomer, by per.

1. God be with you till we meet a - gain, By his coun-sels guide, up-hold you,
2. God be with you till we meet a - gain, 'Neath his wings se - cure - ly hide you,
3. God be with you till we meet a - gain, When life's per - ils thick confound you,
4. God be with you till we meet a - gain, Keep love's banner float - ing o'er you,

With his sheep se - cure - ly fold you, God be with you till we meet a - gain.
Dai - ly man - na still pro - vide you, God be with you till we meet a - gain.
Put his arms un - fail - ing round you, God be with you till we meet a - gain.
Smite death's threat'ning wave be - fore you, God be with you till we meet a - gain.

REFRAIN.

Till we meet, . . . till we meet, . . Till we
Till we meet, till we meet,

meet at Je - sus' feet; Till we meet, . . . till we
till we meet; Till we meet,

meet, . God be with you till we meet a - gain.
till we meet,

Used by per. J. E. Rankin, owner of copyright

Parting Hand L. M. D.

"He that loveth his brother abideth in the light." 1 John 2: 10

JEREMIAH INGALS, 1863

1. My dear-est friends, in bonds of love, Our hearts in sweet-est un-ion prove,
2. How sweet the hours have passed a-way, When we have met to sing and pray,
3. And since it is God's ho-ly will, We must be part-ed for a-while,
4. How oft I've seen the flow-ing tears, And heard you tell your hopes and fears;

Your friendship's like a draw-ing band, Yet we must take the part-ing hand.
How loath I've been to leave the place Where Je-sus shows his smil-ing face.
In sweet sub-mis-sion all in one, We'll say, "Our Fa-ther's will be done."
Your hearts with love have seemed to flame, Which makes me hope we'll meet a-gain.

Your pres-ence sweet, your un-ion dear, Your words de-light-ful to my ear;
Oh, could I stay with friends so kind, How would it cheer my strug-gling mind!
Dear fel-low-youth in chris-tian ties, Who seek for man-sions in the skies,
Ye mourn-ing souls, in sad sur-prise, Je-sus re-mem-bers all your cries;

And when I see that we must part, You draw like chords a-round my heart.
But du-ty makes me un-der-stand That we must take the part-ing hand.
Fight on, you'll win the hap-py shore, Where part-ing hands are known no more.
Oh, taste his grace, in all that land We'll no more take the part-ing hand.

407 **Expostulation** 11s.

"Pray for one another." James 5: 16

Josiah Hopkins

1. Fare-well, my dear breth-ren, the time is at hand, That we must be part-ed from this so-cial band; Our sev-'ral en-gage-ments now call us a-way; Our part-ing is need-ful, and we must o-bey.

2. Fare-well, my dear breth-ren, fare-well for a while, We'll soon meet a-gain, if kind Prov-i-dence smile; And while we are part-ed and scat-tered a-broad, We'll pray for each oth-er, and trust in the Lord.

3. Fare-well, faith-ful sol-diers, you'll soon be dis-charged, The war will be end-ed, your boun-ty en-larged; With shout-ing and sing-ing, though Jor-dan may roar, We'll en-ter fair Ca-naan, and rest on the shore.

4. Fare-well, young-er breth-ren, just list-ed for war, Sore tri-als a-wait you, but Je-sus is near: Al-though you must trav-el the dark wil-der-ness, Your Cap-tain's be-fore you, he'll lead you in peace.

408 **Josie** 7s.

"He sendeth out his word." Psalm 147: 18

T. Kelly

A. S. Kieffer

1. Sav-iour, bless thy word to all; Quick and pow'r-ful let it prove;

2. Thine own gra-cious mes-sage bless; Fol-low it with pow'r di-vine;

Josie

Oh, may sin-ners hear thy call; Let thy peo-ple grow in love.
Give the gos-pel great suc-cess; Thine the work, the glo-ry thine.

409 — Fair Haven

SUTTON

Scotch Air

Slow.

1. Hail! sweet-est, dear-est tie that binds Our glow-ing hearts in one;
2. No lin-g'ring hope, no part-ing sigh, Our fu-ture meet-ing knows;

FINE.

Hail! sa-cred hope, that tunes our minds To har-mo-ny di-vine:
The friend-ship beams from ev-'ry eye, And hope im-mor-tal grows.

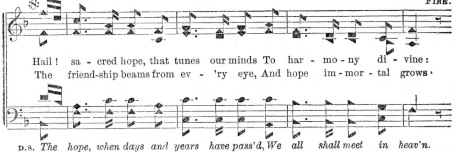

D.S. *The hope, when days and years have pass'd, We all shall meet in heav'n.*

D.S.

It is the hope, the bliss-ful hope Which Je-sus' grace has giv'n;
Oh, sa-cred hope, oh, bliss-ful hope Which Je-sus' grace has giv'n;

Old Hundred L. M

GUILLAUME FRANC, 1549

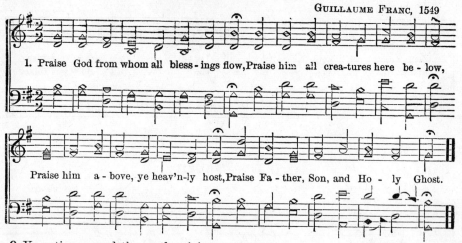

1. Praise God from whom all bless-ings flow, Praise him all crea-tures here be-low,

Praise him a-bove, ye heav'n-ly host, Praise Fa-ther, Son, and Ho-ly Ghost.

2 Ye nations round the earth rejoice
Before the Lord your Sovereign King;
Serve him with cheerful heart and voice;
With all your tongues his glory sing.

3 The Lord is God : 'Tis he alone
Doth life, and breath, and being give :
We are his work, and not our own;
The sheep that on his pasture live.

411 *" The Lord shall command the blessing."* Deut. 28:8

1 Dismiss us with thy blessing, Lord —
Help us to feed upon thy word;
All that has been amiss forgive,
And let thy truth within us live.

2 Though we are guilty, thou art good —
Wash all our works in Jesus' blood;
Give every fettered soul release,
And bid us all depart in peace.

JAS. HART

412 ## Benediction

J. D. BRUNK

The grace of our Lord Je-sus Christ, and the love of God, .. And the com-

mun-ion of the Ho-ly Ghost, be with you all, Now and ev-er-more. A-MEN.

METRICAL INDEX OF TUNES.

TOPICAL INDEX.

Topical Index.

Topical Index.

Topical Index.

GENERAL INDEX

Titles in Roman, First Lines in Italics, When Titles and First Lines are alike, Capitals.

GENERAL INDEX

GENERAL INDEX

GENERAL INDEX

GENERAL INDEX

GENERAL INDEX

GENERAL INDEX

Church and Sunday School Hymnal
Supplement

*A Collection of Hymns and Sacred Songs, Arranged
as a Supplement to Church and Sunday
School Hymnal*

———o———

COMPILED BY THE FOLLOWING COMMITTEE, APPOINTED
BY THE MENNONITE GENERAL CONFERENCE

C. Z. YODER, *Chairman*
J. D. BRUNK, *Musical Editor*
S. F. COFFMAN, *Hymn Editor*
J. B. SMITH
S. S. YODER

Mennonite Publishing House

SCOTTDALE   **PENNA.**

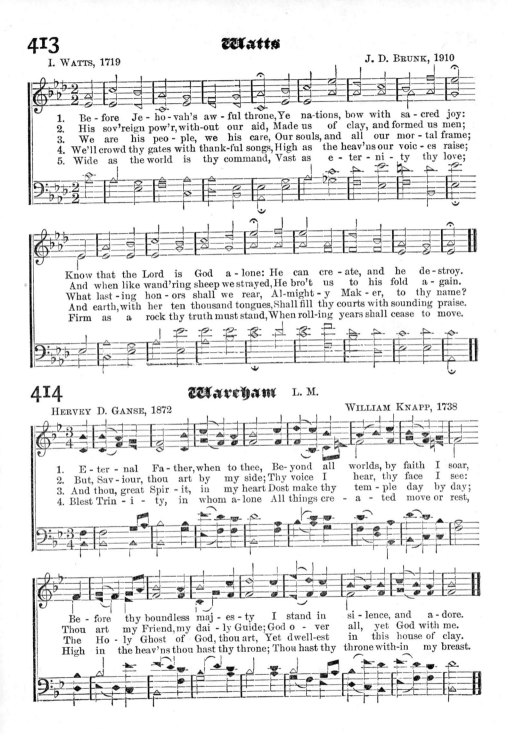

413

Watts

I. WATTS, 1719

J. D. BRUNK, 1910

1. Be - fore Je - ho - vah's aw - ful throne, Ye na - tions, bow with sa - cred joy:
2. His sov'reign pow'r, with-out our aid, Made us of clay, and formed us men;
3. We are his peo - ple, we his care, Our souls, and all our mor - tal frame;
4. We'll crowd thy gates with thank-ful songs, High as the heav'ns our voic - es raise;
5. Wide as the world is thy command, Vast as e - ter - ni - ty thy love;

Know that the Lord is God a - lone: He can cre - ate, and he de - stroy.
And when like wand'ring sheep we strayed, He bro't us to his fold a - gain.
What last - ing hon - ors shall we rear, Al - might - y Mak - er, to thy name?
And earth, with her ten thousand tongues, Shall fill thy courts with sounding praise.
Firm as a rock thy truth must stand, When roll-ing years shall cease to move.

414

Wareham L. M.

HERVEY D. GANSE, 1872

WILLIAM KNAPP, 1738

1. E - ter - nal Fa - ther, when to thee, Be - yond all worlds, by faith I soar,
2. But, Sav - iour, thou art by my side; Thy voice I hear, thy face I see:
3. And thou, great Spir - it, in my heart Dost make thy tem - ple day by day;
4. Blest Trin - i - ty, in whom a - lone All things cre - a - ted move or rest,

Be - fore thy boundless maj - es - ty I stand in si - lence, and a - dore.
Thou art my Friend, my dai - ly Guide; God o - ver all, yet God with me.
The Ho - ly Ghost of God, thou art, Yet dwell-est in this house of clay.
High in the heav'ns thou hast thy throne; Thou hast thy throne with-in my breast.

415 **Sefton** L. M.

GEORG WEISSEL, 1642 Tr.   J. BAPTISTE CALKIN, 1872

1. Lift up your heads, ye might-y gates; Be-hold, the King of Glo-ry waits;
2. O blest the land, the cit-y blest, Where Christ the Rul-er is confessed!
3. Fling wide the por-tals of your heart; Make it a tem-ple set a-part
4. Re-deem-er, come! I o-pen wide My heart to thee; here, Lord, a-bide.

The King of kings is draw-ing near, The Sav-iour of the world is here.
O hap-py hearts and hap-py homes, To whom this King in tri-umph comes!
From earth-ly use for heav'n's em-ploy, Adorned with pray'r, and love, and joy.
Let me thy in-ner pres-ence feel; Thy grace and love in me re-veal.

416 **Beatitudo** C. M.

TATE and BRADY'S New Version, 1696, 1698   JOHN B. DYKES, 1875

1. As pants the hart for cool-ing streams When heat-ed in the chase,
2. For thee, my God, the liv-ing God, My thirst-y soul doth pine;
3. Why rest-less, why cast down, my soul? Trust God; and he'll em-ploy
4. Why rest-less, why cast down, my soul? Hope still; and thou shalt sing

So longs my soul, O God, for thee, And thy re-fresh-ing grace.
O when shall I be-hold thy Face, Thou Maj-es-ty Di-vine!
His aid for thee, and change these sighs To thank-ful hymns of joy.
The praise of him who is thy God, Thy health's e-ter-nal Spring.

417 St. Agnes C. M.

E. Caswall Tr.

John B. Dykes

1. Je - sus, the ver - y tho't of thee, With sweet-ness fills my breast;
2. Nor voice can sing, nor heart can frame, Nor can the mem - 'ry find
3. Oh, hope of ev - 'ry con - trite heart! Oh, joy of all the meek!
4. And those who find thee, find a bliss Nor tongue nor pen can show;
5. Je - sus! our on - ly joy be thou, As thou our prize wilt be;

But sweet - er far thy face to see, And in thy pres - ence rest.
A sweet - er sound than thy blest name, O Sav - iour of man - kind!
To those who fall, how kind thou art! How good to those who seek!
The love of Je - sus, what it is None but his loved ones know.
Je - sus! be thou our glo - ry now, And thro' e - ter - ni - ty.

418 St. Martin's C. M.

Isaac Watts, 1706

William Tans'ur, 1735

1. Be - hold the glo - ries of the Lamb, A - mid the Fa-ther's throne;
2. Let el - ders wor - ship at his feet, The church a - dore a - round,
3. Those are the prayers of all the saints, And these the hymns they raise;
4. Now, to the Lamb that once was slain Be end - less bless-ings paid;
5. Thou hast re - deemed our souls with blood, Hast set the pris - 'ners free;

Pre - pare new hon - ors for his name, And songs be - fore un-known.
With vi - als full of o - dors sweet, And harps of sweet-er sound.
Je - sus is kind to our com-plaints, He loves to hear our praise.
Sal - va - tion, glo - ry, joy, re - main For-ev - er on thy head.
Hast made us kings and priests to God, And we shall reign with thee.

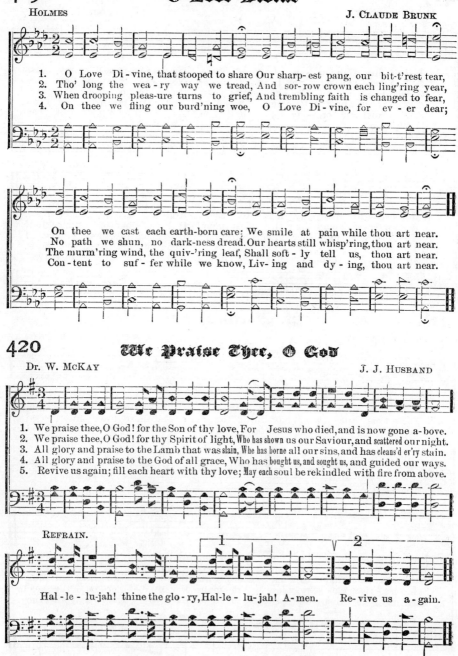

419 O Love Divine

HOLMES

J. CLAUDE BRUNK

1. O Love Divine, that stooped to share Our sharp-est pang, our bit-t'rest tear,
2. Tho' long the wea-ry way we tread, And sor-row crown each ling'ring year,
3. When drooping pleas-ure turns to grief, And trembling faith is changed to fear,
4. On thee we fling our burd'ning woe, O Love Di-vine, for ev-er dear;

On thee we cast each earth-born care; We smile at pain while thou art near.
No path we shun, no dark-ness dread. Our hearts still whisp'ring, thou art near.
The murm'ring wind, the quiv'ring leaf, Shall soft-ly tell us, thou art near.
Con-tent to suf-fer while we know, Liv-ing and dy-ing, thou art near.

420 We Praise Thee, O God

Dr. W. McKAY

J. J. HUSBAND

1. We praise thee, O God! for the Son of thy love, For Jesus who died, and is now gone a-bove.
2. We praise thee, O God! for thy Spirit of light, Who has shown us our Saviour, and scattered our night.
3. All glory and praise to the Lamb that was slain, Who has borne all our sins, and has cleans'd ev'ry stain.
4. All glory and praise to the God of all grace, Who has bought us, and sought us, and guided our ways.
5. Revive us again; fill each heart with thy love; May each soul be rekindled with fire from above.

REFRAIN.

Hal-le-lu-jah! thine the glo-ry, Hal-le-lu-jah! A-men. Re-vive us a-gain.

Lingham C. M.

Joseph Funk   Arr. by F. L. A.

1. O for.......... a thou - sand tongues to sing My great Re -
2. My gra - cious Mas - ter and my God, As - sist me
3. Je - sus,......... the name........ that calms our fears, That bids our
4. He breaks...... the pow'r........ of can - cell'd sin, He sets the

deem - er's praise, My great........... Re - deem - er's praise; The glo - ries
to pro - claim, As - sist........... me to pro - claim, To spread thro'
sor - rows cease, That bids.......... our sor - rows cease, 'Tis mu - sic
pris - 'ner free, He sets........... the pris - 'ner free; His blood can

of......... my God...... and King, The tri-umphs of, the triumphs of his grace,
all........ the earth..... a - broad, The hon - ors of, the hon - ors of thy name,
in.......... the sin - ner's ears, 'Tis life and health, 'tis life and health and peace,
make..... the foul - est clean, His blood a- vails, his blood a- vails for me,

The tri-umphs of his grace,...... The tri - umphs of his grace.
The hon - ors of thy name,...... The hon - ors of thy name.
'Tis life and health and peace,......'Tis life......... and health and peace.
His blood a - vails for me,......... His blood...... a - vails for me.

422 Creation L. M.

JOSIAH CONDER, 1824   Arr. from JOSEPH HAYDN

1. The Lord is King! lift up your voice, O earth; and all ye heav'ns, re-joice:
2. The Lord is King! who then shall dare Re-sist his will, dis-trust his care,
3. The Lord is King! Child of the dust, The Judge of all the earth is just;
4. One Lord, one em-pire, all se-cures; He reigns, and life and death are yours:

From world to world the joy shall ring, "The Lord Om-nip-o-tent is King!"
Or mur-mur at his wise de-crees, Or doubt his roy-al prom-is-es?
Ho-ly and true are all his ways: Let ev-'ry crea-ture speak his praise.
Thro' earth and heav'n one song shall ring, "The Lord Om-nip-o-tent is King!"

423 Lyons

R. GRANT, 1833   Arr. from MICHAEL HAYDN

1. Oh, wor-ship the King all glo-rious a-bove, And grate-ful-ly
2. Oh, tell of his might and sing of his grace, Whose robe is the
3. Thy boun-ti-ful care what tongue can re-cite? It breathes in the
4. Frail chil-dren of dust, and feeb-le as frail, In Thee do we

sing his won-der-ful love; Our Shield and De-fend-er, the
light, whose can-o-py space; His char-iots of wrath the deep
air, it shines in the light, It streams from the hills, it de-
trust, nor find thee to fail; Thy mer-cies how ten-der! how

Lyons

An - cient of days, Pa - vil - ioned in splen - dor, and gird - ed with praise.
thun - der - clouds form, And dark is his path on the wings of the storm.
scends to the plain, And sweet - ly dis - tils in the dew and the rain.
firm to the end, Our Mak - er, De - fend - er, Re - deem - er and Friend.

424 **Benedic Anima**

HENRY F. LYTE, 1834

Sir JOHN GOSS, 1867

1. Praise, my soul, the King of heav - en; To his feet thy trib - ute bring;
2. Praise him for his grace and fav - or To our fa - thers in dis - tress;
3. Fa - ther - like, he tends and spares us; Well our feeb - le frame he knows;
4. An - gels, help us to a - dore him; Ye be - hold him face to face;

Ransomed, healed, re - stored, for - giv - en, Who, like me, his praise should sing?
Praise him, still the same for ev - er, Slow to chide, and swift to bless;
In his hands he gen - tly bears us, Res - cues us from all our foes;
Sun and moon, bow down be - fore him; Dwell - ers all in time and space,

Praise him, praise him, praise him, praise him, Praise the Ev - er - last - ing King.
Praise him, praise him, praise him, praise him, Glo - rious in his faith - ful - ness.
Praise him, praise him, praise him, praise him, Wide - ly as his mer - cy goes.
Praise him, praise him, praise him, praise him, Praise with us the God of grace.

425 Harwell

T. Kelly, 1804

L. Mason, 1792-1872

FINE.

1. { Hark! ten thou - sand harps and voic - es Sound the note of praise a - bove; }
   { Je - sus reigns, and heav'n re - joic - es; Je - sus reigns, the God of love: }
2. { King of glo - ry! reign for ev - er—Thine an ev - er - last-ing crown; }
   { Noth - ing, from thy love, shall sev - er Those whom thou hast made thine own; }
3. { Sav - iour! hast - en thine ap - pear - ing; Bring, oh, bring the glo-rious day, }
   { When, the aw - ful sum-mons hear - ing, Heav'n and earth shall pass a - way; }

D.C.—Al - le - lu - ia, al - le - lu - ia, Al - le - lu - ia. A - men.

D.C.

See, he sits on yon - der throne; Je - sus rules the world a - lone.
Hap - py ob - jects of thy grace, Des - tined to be-hold thy face.
Then, with gold-en harps we'll sing,— "Glo - ry, glo-ry to our King!"

1. See, he sits on yon - der throne; Je - sus rules the world a - lone.

426 Duke Street L. M.

Isaac Watts, 1719

John Hatton, c. 1793

1. Je - sus shall reign wher - e'er the sun Does his suc - cess - ive jour - neys run;
2. For him shall end - less pray'r be made, And prais - es throng to crown his head;
3. Blessings a - bound wher - e'er he reigns; The prisoner leaps to lose his chains,
4. Let ev - 'ry crea - ture rise and bring Pe - cul - iar hon - ors to our King,

His kingdom stretch from shore to shore, Till moons shall wax and wane no more.
His name, like sweet per - fume, shall rise With ev - 'ry morn - ing sac - ri - fice;
The wea - ry find e - ter - nal rest, And all the sons of want are blest.
An - gels de - scend with songs a - gain, And earth re - peat the loud A - men.

God Is Good

ELSIE BYLER

SYLVIA BONTRAGER

1. O, thou the great e - ter - nal One, Whose goodness ev - 'ry age hath stood,
2. Teach me to know thy ten - der care, Thy matchless grace, th'a - ton - ing blood;
3. When doubts, un - rest and fears as - sail, When grief comes o'er me like a flood,
4. When hu - man friendships shall de - cay, And earth af - firm its fin - i - tude,

Thou art ex - alt - ed o - ver all, For thou art great and thou art good.
Thy sovereign pow'r up - hold - ing all, But more and more that thou art good.
My brightest day be turned to night, — I rest se - cure, for God is good.
When time wanes to e - ter - ni - ty, One thing re - mains, — our God is good.

428

Thatcher S. M.

STEPHEN G. BULFINCH

Arr. from GEORGE F. HANDEL

1. Hail to the sab - bath day! The day di - vine - ly giv'n,
2. Lord, in this sa - cred hour, With - in thy courts we bend,
3. But thou art not a - lone In courts by mor - tals trod;
4. Thy tem - ple is the arch Of yon un - meas - ured sky;
5. Lord, may that ho - lier day Dawn on thy serv - ants' sight;

When men to God their hom - age pay, And earth draws near to heav'n.
And bless thy love, and own thy pow'r, Our Fa - ther and our Friend.
Nor on - ly is the day thine own When man draws near to God:
Thy sab - bath, the stu - pen - dous march Of vast e - ter - ni - ty.
And pur - er wor - ship may we pay In heav - en's un - clouded light.

429 St. Anne C. M.

A. C. Coxe, 1839

W. Croft, 1708

1. Oh, where are kings and em-pires now Of old that went and came?
2. We mark her good-ly bat-tle-ments, And her foun-da-tions strong;
3. For not like king-doms of the world Thy ho-ly church, O God!
4. Un-shak-en as e-ter-nal hills, Im-mov-a-ble she stands,

But, Lord, thy Church is pray-ing yet, A thou-sand years the same.
We hear with-in the sol-emn voice Of her un-end-ing song.
Though earth-quake shocks are threat'ning her, And tem-pest are a-broad;
A moun-tain that shall fill the earth, A house not made by hands.

430 'Tis the Blessed Hour of Prayer.

F. J. Crosby

W. H. Doane

1. 'Tis the bless-ed hour of pray'r, when our hearts low-ly bend, And we
2. 'Tis the bless-ed hour of pray'r, when the Sav-iour draws near, With a
3. 'Tis the bless-ed hour of pray'r, when the tempt-ed and tried To the
4. At the bless-ed hour of pray'r, trust-ing him we be-lieve That the

gath-er to Je-sus, our Sav-iour and Friend; If we come to him in
ten-der com-pas-sion his chil-dren to hear; When he tells us we may
Sav-iour who loves them their sor-row con-fide; With a sym-pa-thiz-ing
bless-ings we're need-ing we'll sure-ly re-ceive, In the ful-ness of this

'Tis the Blessed Hour of Prayer

faith, his pro - tec - tion to share; *(D.S.)*
cast at his feet ev - 'ry care;
heart he re - moves ev - 'ry care;
trust we shall lose ev - 'ry care;

What a balm for the wea - ry! O how

FINE. REFRAIN.   D.S.

sweet to be there! Bless - ed hour of pray'r, Bless - ed hour of pray'r;

431 **Corinth**

JAMES EDMESTON, 1821   SAMUEL WEBBE'S Collection, 1792

1. Lead us, heav'n-ly Fa - ther, lead us O'er the world's tem - pest-uous sea;
2. Sav-iour, breathe for - give - ness o'er us; All our weak-ness thou dost know;
3. Spir - it of our God, de - scend-ing, Fill our hearts with heav'n-ly joy,

Guard us, guide us, keep us, feed us, For we have no help but thee;
Thou didst tread this earth be - fore us, Thou didst feel its keen - est woe;
Love with ev - 'ry pas - sion blend-ing, Pleas-ure that can nev - er cloy;

Yet pos - sess - ing ev - 'ry bless - ing, If our God our Fa - ther be.
Lone and drea - ry, faint and wear - y, Thro' the des - ert thou didst go.
Thus pro - vid - ed, par-doned, guid-ed, Noth-ing can our peace de - stroy.

Dedham C. M.

"Be perfectly joined together." 1 Cor. 1: 10.

C. Wesley

Wm. Gardiner

1. All praise to our re-deem-ing Lord, Who joins us by his grace,
2. He bids us build each oth-er up; And, gath-ered in-to one,
3. The kiss of peace to each we give— A pledge of Chris-tian love;
4. Love is the gold-en chain that binds Be-liev-ers all in one;

And bids us, each to each re-stored, To-geth-er seek his face.
To our high call-ing's glo-rious hope, We hand in hand go on.
In love, while here on earth, we'll live, In love we'll dwell a-bove.
And he's an heir of heav'n that finds His bos-om glow with love.

433 Morecambe

Anon.

1. Draw nigh and take the bod-y of the Lord, And drink sal-va-tion's cup for you out pour'd,
2. Sal-va-tion's giv-er, Christ, the on-ly Son, By his dear cross and blood the victory won.
3. He, that his saints in this world rules and shields, To all be-liev-ers life e-ternal yields,

Saved by that bod-y and a-toning blood, With souls refreshed, we render thanks to God.
Of-fered was he for great-est and for least, Him-self the vic-tim, and him-self the priest.
With heav'nly bread makes them that hunger whole, Gives living wa-ters to the thirsting soul.

434 In Thy Holy Place

S. F. COFFMAN

J. D. BRUNK

1. In thy ho-ly place we bow, Per-fumes sweet to heav-en rise,
2. Ho-ly light doth fill this place; Spir-it light our way to guide.
3. On thy ho-ly bread we feed, Hun-ger nev-er more to know.

While our gold-en cen-sers glow With the fire of sac-ri-fice.
In the pres-ence of his face Sin and dark-ness ne'er can hide.
Thou sup-pli-est all our need. Fa-ther, whith-er shall we go?

Saints low bend-ing, pray'rs as-cend-ing, Ho-ly lips and hands im-plore;—
Heav-en's gleaming, ful-ness stream-ing, Life and truth for man is found.
Ne'er for-sak-ing, here par-tak-ing Bread our souls to sat-is-fy.

Faith be-liev-ing and re-ceiv-ing Grace from him whom we a-dore.
Light per-vad-ing, nev-er fad-ing, Light-ing all the world a-round.
Here a-bid-ing and con-fid-ing, We shall nev-er want nor die.

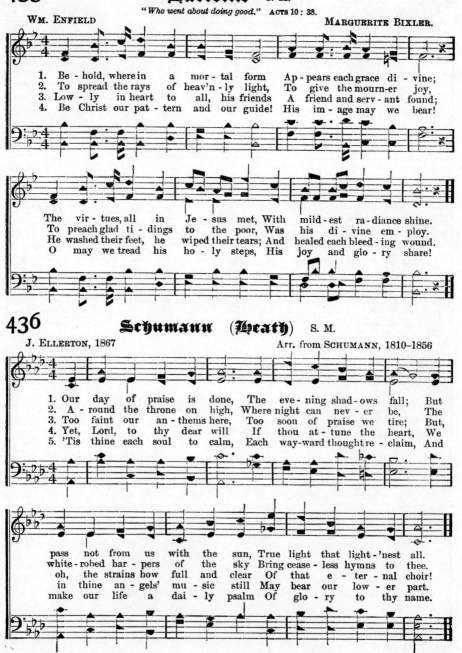

435 **Hartville** C. M.

"Who went about doing good." ACTS 10 : 38.

WM. ENFIELD

MARGUERITE BIXLER.

1. Be - hold, where in a mor - tal form Ap - pears each grace di - vine;
2. To spread the rays of heav'n - ly light, To give the mourn-er joy,
3. Low - ly in heart to all, his friends A friend and serv - ant found;
4. Be Christ our pat - tern and our guide! His im - age may we bear!

The vir - tues, all in Je - sus met, With mild - est ra - diance shine.
To preach glad ti - dings to the poor, Was his di - vine em - ploy.
He washed their feet, he wiped their tears; And healed each bleed - ing wound.
O may we tread his ho - ly steps, His joy and glo - ry share!

436 **Schumann (Heath)** S. M.

J. ELLERTON, 1867

Arr. from SCHUMANN, 1810–1856

1. Our day of praise is done, The eve - ning shad - ows fall; But
2. A - round the throne on high, Where night can nev - er be, The
3. Too faint our an - thems here, Too soon of praise we tire; But,
4. Yet, Lord, to thy dear will If thou at - tune the heart, We
5. 'Tis thine each soul to calm, Each way-ward thought re - claim, And

pass not from us with the sun, True light that light - 'nest all.
white - robed har - pers of the sky Bring cease - less hymns to thee.
oh, the strains how full and clear Of that e - ter - nal choir!
in thine an - gels' mu - sic still May bear our low - er part.
make our life a dai - ly psalm Of glo - ry to thy name.

437

Holley L. M.

J. Montgomery, 1825

G. Hews, 1835

1. Pour out thy Spir-it from on high; Lord, thine or-dain-ed serv-ants bless;
2. With-in thy tem-ple when they stand To teach the truth as taught by thee,
3. Wisdom and zeal and faith im-part, Firmness with meekness, from a-bove,
4. To watch and pray, and nev-er faint; By day and night strict guard to keep;
5. Then, while their work is fin-ished here, In hum-ble hope their charge re-sign,

Grac-es and gifts to each sup-ply, And clothe them with thy righteous-ness.
Sav-iour, like stars in thy right hand The an-gels of the churches be.
To bear thy peo-ple on their heart, And love the souls whom thou dost love;
To warn the sin-ner, cheer the saint, Nour-ish thy lambs, and feed thy sheep;
When the Chief Shepherd shall ap-pear, O God, may they and we be thine.

438

Seymour

H. W. Baker, 1861

Arr. from Carl von Weber, 1826

1. Praise, O praise our God and King! Hymns of ad-o-ra-tion sing;
2. Praise him that he made the sun Day by day his course to run;
3. Praise him that he gave the rain To ma-ture the swell-ing grain;
4. Praise him for our har-vest-store, He hath filled the gar-ner-floor;
5. Glo-ry to our bounteous King; Glo-ry let cre-a-tion sing;

For his mer-cies still en-dure, Ev-er faith-ful, ev-er sure.
And the sil-ver moon by night, Shin-ing with her gen-tle light.
And hath bid the fer-tile field Of its pre-cious fruits to yield.
And for rich-er food than this, Pledge of ev-er-last-ing bliss.
Glo-ry to the Fa-ther, Son, And blest Spir-it, Three in One.

11

439 Break Thou the Bread of Life

MARY A. LATHBURY

W. F. SHERWIN

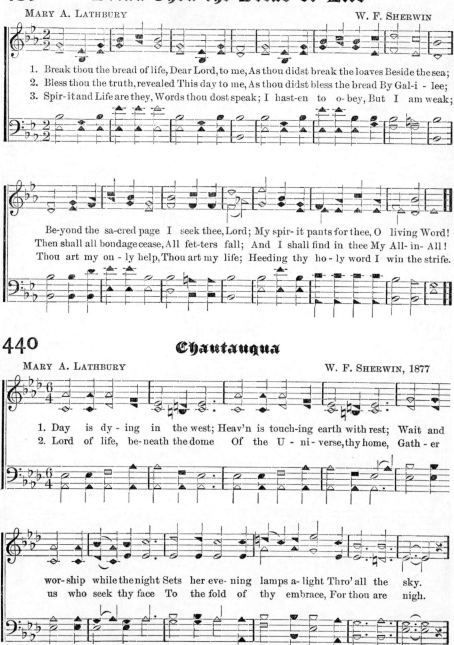

1. Break thou the bread of life, Dear Lord, to me, As thou didst break the loaves Beside the sea;
2. Bless thou the truth, revealed This day to me, As thou didst bless the bread By Gal-i - lee;
3. Spir-it and Life are they, Words thou dost speak; I hast-en to o- bey, But I am weak;

Be-yond the sa-cred page I seek thee, Lord; My spir- it pants for thee, O living Word!
Then shall all bondage cease, All fet-ters fall; And I shall find in thee My All- in- All!
Thou art my on - ly help, Thou art my life; Heeding thy ho - ly word I win the strife.

440 Chautauqua

MARY A. LATHBURY

W. F. SHERWIN, 1877

1. Day is dy - ing in the west; Heav'n is touch-ing earth with rest; Wait and
2. Lord of life, be- neath the dome Of the U - ni- verse, thy home, Gath - er

wor-ship while the night Sets her eve- ning lamps a- light Thro' all the sky.
us who seek thy face To the fold of thy embrace, For thou are nigh.

Chautauqua

p REFRAIN.

Ho-ly, ho-ly, ho-ly, Lord God of Hosts! Heav'n and earth are

cres.

full of thee! Heav'n and earth are prais-ing thee, O Lord most high!

441 Eventide

HENRY F. LYTE, 1847   WILLIAM H. MONK, 1861

1. A-bide with me: fast falls the e-ven-tide; The darkness deepens; Lord, with me abide:
2. Swift to its close ebbs out life's lit-tle day; Earth's joys grow dim, its glories pass away;
3. I need thy presence ev'ry passing hour; What but thy grace can foil the tempter's pow'r?
4. I fear no foe, with thee at hand to bless: Ills have no weight, and tears no bitterness.
5. Hold thou thy cross before my closing eyes; Shine thro' the gloom, and point me to the skies:

When oth-er help-ers fail, and comforts flee, Help of the helpless, O a-bide with me.
Change and de-cay in all around I see; O thou who changest not, a-bide with me.
Who like thy-self my guide and stay can be? Thro' cloud and sunshine, O a-bide with me.
Where is death's sting? where, grave, thy victory? I triumph still, if thou a-bide with me.
Heav'n's morning breaks, and earth's vain shadows flee: In life, in death, O Lord, abide with me.

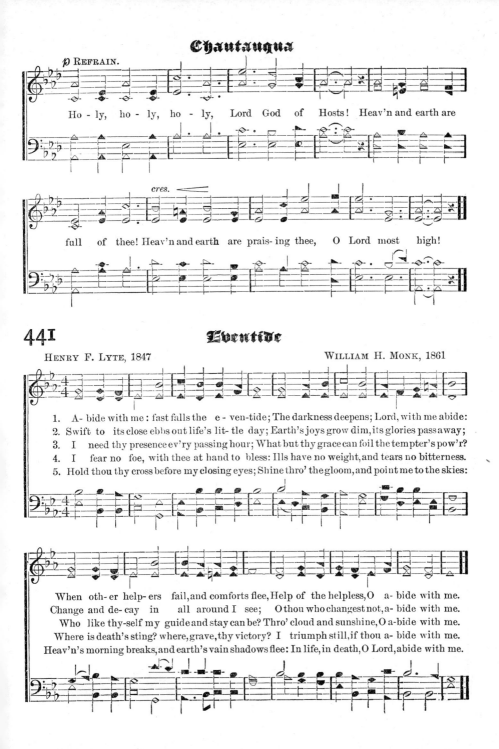

1. When Christ be - held, in sin - ful night, His bride, deceived, en - slaved and lost;
2. Thy plighted faith to him, thy Lord, Thy bri - dal veil doth ev - er show.
3. Ex - alt - ed by such heav -'nly grace, The church in pa - tience doth a - bide,

Com - pas-sion brought a sav - ing light, And paid the ransom's aw - ful cost.
Thy husband, he; thy law his word; None oth - er law or serv - ice know.
And waits to see his glo - rious face When Christ shall come to own his bride.

Oh, bride, he gave his life for thee, His blood thy cleans-ing hath se - cured.
Thy mod - est ways are his de - light; By hum - ble grac - es art thou known.
O won-drous love! yet all for me. My love in him will I con - fide.

Let ho - li - ness thy gar - ments be; Thy pure heart nev - er be al - lured.
An heir of glo - ry, this thy right, To share with Christ a roy - al throne.
My heart is long - ing, Christ, for thee; Where thou art, there would I a - bide.

J. S. B. Monsell, 1862

J. B. Dykes, 1872

1. O love di - vine and gold - en, Mys - te - rious depth and height,
2. God bless these hands u - nit - ed; God bless these hearts made one!
3. Here in earth's home pre - par - ing For the bright home a - bove,

To thee the world be - hold - en, Looks up for life and light;
Un - sev - ered and un - blight - ed May they through life go on,—
And there for ev - er shar - ing Its joy where "God is love."

REFRAIN.

O love di - vine and gen - tle, The bless - er and the blest,

Be - neath thy care pa - ren - tal The world lies down in rest.

444 Love at Home

Arr. by J. D. Brunk

Tenderly.

1. There is beau-ty all a-round, When there's love at home; There is joy in
2. In the cot-tage there is joy, When there's love at home; Hate and en-vy
3. Kind-ly heav-en smiles a-bove, When there's love at home; All the earth is
4. Je-sus, show thy mer-cy mine, *Then* there's love at home; Sweet-ly whis-per,

ev'ry sound, When there's love at home; Peace and plenty here a-bide, Smiling sweet on
ne'er annoy, When there's love at home; Ros-es blossom 'neath our feet, All the earth's a
filled with love, When there's love at home; Sweeter sings the brooklet by, Brighter beams the
"I am thine," *Then* there's love at home; Source of love, thy cheering light Far exceeds the

ev-'ry side, Time doth soft-ly, sweet-ly glide, When there's love at home, Love at
gar-den sweet, Mak-ing life a bliss complete, When there's love at home, Love at
az-ure sky; Oh, there's One who smiles on high When there's love at home, Love at
sun so bright—Can dis-pell the gloom of night; *Then* there's love at home, Love at

Love at home, yes,

at home,

home, love at home; Time doth softly, sweetly glide, When there's love at home.
home, love at home; Mak-ing life a bliss complete When there's love at home.
home, love at home; Oh, there's One who smiles on high, When there's love at home.
home, love at home; Can dispel the gloom of night, *Then* there's love at home.

love at home, Love at home, oh, love at home,

445 Yield Not to Temptation

H. R. PALMER

H. R. PALMER

1. Yield not to temp-ta-tion, For yield-ing is sin; Each vic-t'ry will
2. Shun e-vil com-pan-ions, Bad language dis-dain, God's name hold in
3. To him that o'er-com-eth God giv-eth a crown; Thro' faith we shall

help you Some oth-er to win; Fight man-ful-ly on-ward,
rev-'rence Nor take it in vain; Be thoughtful and earn-est,
con-quer, Though oft-en cast down; He who is our Sav-iour,

Dark pas-sions sub-due, Look ev-er to Je-sus, He'll car-ry you through.
Kind-heart-ed and true, Look ev-er to Je-sus, He'll car-ry you through.
Our strength will re-new, Look ev-er to Je-sus, He'll car-ry you through.

CHORUS.

Ask the Sav-iour to help you, Com-fort, strengthen and keep you;

He is will-ing to aid you, He will car-ry you through.

446 Bullinger

JOHN M. NEALE, 1862

Rev. ETHELBERT W. BULLINGER, 1877

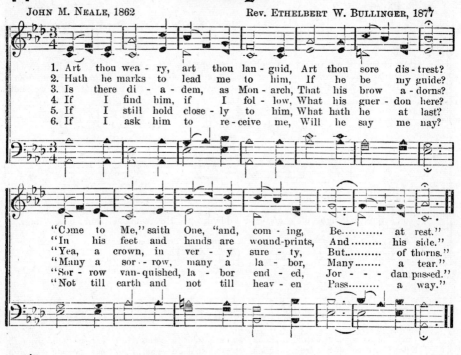

1. Art thou wea - ry, art thou lan - guid, Art thou sore dis - trest?
2. Hath he marks to lead me to him, If he be my guide?
3. Is there di - a - dem, as Mon - arch, That his brow a - dorns?
4. If I find him, if I fol - low, What his guer - don here?
5. If I still hold close - ly to him, What hath he at last?
6. If I ask him to re - ceive me, Will he say me nay?

"Come to Me," saith One, "and, com - ing, Be......... at rest."
"In his feet and hands are wound-prints, And......... his side."
"Yea, a crown, in ver - y sure - ty, But......... of thorns."
"Many a sor - row, many a la - bor, Many......... a tear."
"Sor - row van - quished, la - bor end - ed, Jor - - - dan passed."
"Not till earth and not till heav - en Pass......... a way."

447 The Cleft of the Rock

S. E. GOOD

S. E. GOOD

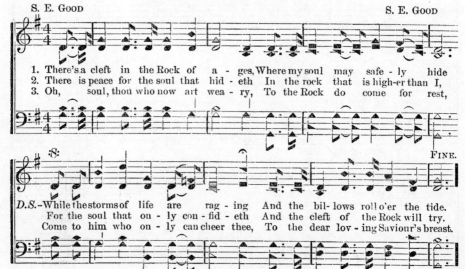

1. There's a cleft in the Rock of a - ges, Where my soul may safe - ly hide
2. There is peace for the soul that hid - eth In the rock that is high-er than I,
3. Oh, soul, thou who now art wea - ry, To the Rock do come for rest,

FINE.

D.S. — While the storms of life are rag - ing And the bil - lows roll o'er the tide.
For the soul that on - ly con - fid - eth And the cleft of the Rock will try.
Come to him who on - ly can cheer thee, To the dear lov - ing Saviour's breast.

The Cleft of the Rock

REFRAIN.

Oh, the cleft of the Rock Where my soul may hide

Oh, the cleft of the Rock, Oh, the cleft of the Rock Where my soul may securely, may se-cure-ly hide.

448 Tread Softly

(SOLO AND QUARTET.)

FANNY J. CROSBY

W. H. DOANE

Gently.

1. Be si-lent, be si-lent, A whis-per is heard, Be si-lent, and
2. Be si-lent, be si-lent, For ho-ly this place, This al-tar that
3. Be si-lent, be si-lent, Breathe hum-bly our pray'r, A fore-taste of
4. Be si-lent, be si-lent, His mer-cy re-cord; Be si-lent, be

REFRAIN.

list-en, Oh, treas-ure each word.
ech-oes The mess-age of grace.
E-den This mo-ment we share.
si-lent, And wait on the Lord.

Tread soft-ly, tread soft-ly, The

Tread soft-ly here, tread soft-ly here,

Mas-ter is here; Tread soft-ly, tread soft-ly, He bids us draw near.

Tread soft-ly here, tread soft-ly here,

Copyright, 1903, by W. H. DOANE. Used by per.

I Must Tell Jesus

MATT. 14 : 12.

Rev. ELISHA A. HOFFMAN   Rev. ELISHA A. HOFFMAN

1. I must tell Je - sus all of my tri - als; I can - not bear these
2. I must tell Je - sus all of my troub - les; He is a kind, com -
3. Tempted and tried I need a great Sav - iour, One who can help my
4. O how the world to e - vil al - lures me! O how my heart is

:S:

bur - dens a - lone; In my dis - tress he kind - ly will help me;
pas - sion - ate Friend; If I but ask him, he will de - liv - er,
bur - dens to bear; I must tell Je - sus, I must tell Je - sus,
tempt - ed to sin! I must tell Je - sus, and he will help me

D.S.—I must tell Je - sus, I must tell Je - sus,

FINE. REFRAIN.

He ev - er loves and cares for his own.
Make of my troub - les quick - ly an end.
He all my cares and sor - rows will share.
O - ver the world the vic - t'ry to win.

I must tell Je - sus!

Je - sus can help me, Je - sus a - lone.

D.S.

I must tell Je - sus! I can - not bear my bur - dens a - lone;

450 "But for a Moment"

A. A. P.

GEO. C. STEBBINS

1. "But for a mo-ment"—this val-ley of sor-rows, Darken'd with shad-ows and heav-y with sighs; Bright dawns the mor-row, the glo-ri-ous mor-row! Faint not! The sun shall with heal-ing a-rise!

2. "Far more ex-ceed-ing," the heav-en-ly glo-ry— Suf-fer-ings here with it can-not com-pare. Glo-ry e-ter-nal the guer-don for an-guish— Ra-di-ant crowns, for the thorns, o-ver there!

3. Tem-po-ral things like a va-por shall van-ish. High-er than earth lies the land of our choice. Up-ward we press to the king-dom e-ter-nal; Je-sus, our King, we be-hold and re-joice!

REFRAIN.

"But for a moment!" On-ly a moment! Light our affliction—'twill soon pass a-way.

"But for a moment!" On-ly a moment! Then comes the glory, for-ev-er and aye!

451 Holy Ghost, with Light Divine

"Lead me in thy truth, and teach me." Ps. 25 : 5.

ANDREW REED L. M. GOTTSCHALK Arr. by H. P. M.

1. Ho - ly Ghost, with light di - vine, Shine up - on this heart of mine;
2. Ho - ly Ghost, with pow'r di - vine, Cleanse this guilt - y heart of mine;
3. Ho - ly Ghost, with joy di - vine, Cheer this sad-dened heart of mine;
4. Ho - ly Spir - it, all di - vine, Dwell with - in this heart of mine;

Chase the shades of night a - way, Turn my dark-ness in - to day.
Long hath sin, with - out con - trol, Held do - min - ion o'er my soul.
Bid my ma - ny woes de - part, Heal my wounded, bleed - ing heart.
Cast down ev - 'ry i - dol - throne, Reign su - preme—and reign a - lone.

452 It is Well with My Soul

H. G. SPAFFORD P. P. BLISS

1. When peace, like a riv - er, at - tend-eth my way, When sorrow like sea billows roll;
2. Tho' Sa tan should buf - fet, tho' tri-als should come, Let this blest assurance con-trol,
3. My sin—oh, the bliss of this glo - ri-ous tho't—My sin—not in part but the whole,
4. And, Lord, haste the day When the faith shall be sight, The clouds be roll'd back as a scroll,

What-ev - er my lot, thou hast taught me to say, It is well, it is well with my soul.
That Christ hath regard-ed my help-less es - tate, And hath shed his own blood for my soul.
Is nailed to his cross and I bear it no more; Praise the Lord, praise the Lord, oh, my soul!
The trump shall resound, and the Lord shall descend; "Even so"—it is well with my soul.

It is Well with My Soul

REFRAIN.

It is well............ with my soul,........ It is well, it is well with my soul!

It is well .... with my soul,

---

453   # Sweetly Resting

MARY D. JAMES   W. WARREN BENTLY

1. In the rift - ed Rock I'm rest - ing, Safe - ly shel - tered, I a - bide;
2. Long pur-sued by sin and Sa - tan, Wea - ry, sad, I longed for rest;
3. Peace, which pass - eth un - der-stand - ing, Joy, the world can nev - er give,
4. In the rift - ed Rock I'll hide me, Till the storms of life are past;

There no foes nor storms mo-lest me, While with-in the cleft I hide.
Then I found this heav'n-ly shel - ter, O-pened in my Saviour's breast.
Now in Je - sus, I am find - ing; In his smiles of love I live.
All se - cure in this blest ref - uge, Heed-ing not the fierc - est blast.

REFRAIN.

Now I'm rest - ing, sweet-ly rest - ing, In the cleft once made for me:

Je - sus, bless - ed Rock of A - ges, I will hide my-self in thee.

THE EVANGELICAL PUB. CO., Chicago, owners of copyright. Used by permission.

454

Trust and Obey

Rev. J. H. SAMMIS

D. B. TOWNER

1. When we walk with the Lord In the light of his word, What a glo - ry he
2. Not a shad - ow can rise, Not a cloud in the skies, But his smile quick-ly
3. Not a bur - den we bear, Not a sor - row we share, But our toil he doth
4. But we nev - er can prove The de-lights of his love, Un - til all on the
5. Then in fel - low - ship sweet We will sit at his feet, Or we'll walk by his

sheds on our way! While we do his good will, He a - bides with us still,
drives it a - way; Not a doubt nor a fear, Not a sigh nor a tear,
rich - ly re - pay; Not a grief nor a loss, Not a frown nor a cross,
al - tar we lay; For the fa - vor he shows, And the joy he be - stows,
side in the way; What he says we will do, Where he sends we will go,

REFRAIN.

And with all who will trust and o - bey.
Can a - bide while we trust and o - bey.
But is blest if we trust and o - bey. Trust and o - bey, For there's
Are for them who will trust and o - bey.
Nev - er fear, on - ly trust and o - bey.

no oth - er way To be hap - py in Je - sus, but to trust and o - bey.

455 Lean on His Arms

Edgar Lewis

L. E. Jones

1. Just lean up-on the arms of Je - sus, He'll help you a - long,
2. Just lean up-on the arms of Je - sus, He'll bright-en the way,
3. Just lean up-on the arms of Je - sus, O bring ev - 'ry care,
4. Just lean up-on the arms of Je - sus, Then leave all to him,

help you a - long; If you will trust His love un - fail - ing, He'll
bright-en the way; Just fol - low glad-ly where he lead - eth, His
bring ev - 'ry care! The bur - den that has seemed so heav - y, Take
leave all to him; His heart is full of love and mer - cy, His

REFRAIN.

fill your heart with song.
gen - tle voice o - bey.
to the Lord in pray'r.
eyes are nev - er dim.

Lean on his arms, trust-ing in his love;
Lean up - on his arms, ful - ly trust-ing in his love;

Lean on his arms, all his mer - cies prove; Lean on his
Lean up - on his arms and all his mer - cies prove; Lean up - on his

arms, look-ing home a - bove, Just lean on the Sav - iour's arms!
arms, ev - er

456 Canonbury L. M.

H. W. Baker

R. Schumann

1. Al-might-y God, whose on - ly Son O'er sin and death the tri-umph won,
2. In his dear name to thee we pray For all who err and go a-stray,
3. And some with-in thy sa-cred fold, To ho-ly things are dead and cold,
4. And ma-ny a quickened soul with-in There lurks the se-cret love of sin,
5. O give re-pent-ance true and deep To all thy lost and wandering sheep!
6. That so from an-gel hosts a-bove May rise a sweet-er song of love,

And ev - er lives to in - ter- cede For souls who thy sweet mer - cy need;
For sin - ner's, where-so - e'er they be, Who do not serve and hon - or thee.
And waste the pre - cious hours of life In self - ish ease, or toil, or strife;
A way-ward will, or anx - ious fears, Or lingering taint of by - gone years.
And kin - dle in their hearts the fire Of ho - ly love and pure de - sire:
And we, with all the blest, a - dore Thy name, O God, for ev - er-more.

457 Pass Me Not

Fanny J. Crosby

W. H. Doane

1. Pass me not, O gen - tle Sav - iour, Hear my hum - ble cry;
2. Let me at a throne of mer - cy Find a sweet re - lief;
3. Trust - ing on - ly in thy mer - it, Would I seek thy face;
4. Thou the spring of all my com - fort More than life to me,

REFRAIN.

While on oth - ers thou art smil - ing, Do not pass me by.
Kneel-ing there in deep con - tri - tion, Help my un - be - lief: } Sav - iour, Sav - iour,
Heal my wounded, broken spir - it, Save me by thy grace.
Whom have I on earth be-side thee? Whom in heav'n but thee?

Pass Me Not

hear my hum-ble cry, While on oth-ers thou art call-ing, Do not pass me by.

458 The Solid Rock

EDWARD MOTE   W. B. BRADBURY

1. My hope is built on noth-ing less Than Je-sus' blood and
2. When dark-ness seems to veil his face, I rest on his un-
3. His oath, his cov-e-nant, and blood, Sup-port me in the
4. When he shall come with trum-pet sound, O, may I then in

right-eous-ness; I dare not trust the sweet-est frame, But whol-ly
chang-ing grace; In ev-'ry high and storm-y gale, My anch-or
whelm-ing flood; When all a-round my soul gives way, He then is
him be found; Clad in his right-eous-ness a-lone, Fault-less to

REFRAIN.

lean on Je-sus' name. }
holds with-in the vail. } On Christ, the sol-id Rock, I stand; All
all my hope and stay. }
stand be-fore the throne. }

oth-er ground is sink-ing sand, All oth-er ground is sink-ing sand.

2 TIM. 1 : 12.

EL. NATHAN

JAMES McGRANAHAN

Moderato.

1. I know not why God's won-drous grace To me he hath made known,
2. I know not how this sav - ing faith To me he did im - part,
3. I know not how the Spir - it moves, Con - vinc - ing men of sin.
4. I know not what of good or ill May be re - served for me,
5. I know not when my Lord may come, At night or noon - day fair.

Nor why— un - wor - thy—Christ in love Re - deemed me for his own.
Nor how be - liev - ing in his word Wrought peace with-in my heart.
Re - veal - ing Je - sus through the word, Cre - at - ing faith in him.
Of wea - ry ways or gol - den days, Be - fore his face I see.
Nor if I'll walk the vale with him, Or "meet him in the air."

REFRAIN.

But "I know whom I have be - liev - ed, And am per-suad - ed that he is a - ble

To keep that which I've com - mit - ted un - to him a-gainst that day."

Copyright, 1883 and 1887, by JAMES McGRANAHAN.

The Precious Name

"And blessed be His glorious name for ever." PSA. 72: 19.

Mrs. LYDIA BAXTER   W. H. DOANE, by per

1. Take the name of Je - sus with you, Child of sor - row and of woe—
2. Take the name of Je - sus ev - er, As a shield from ev - 'ry snare;
3. Oh! the pre-cious name of Je - sus; How it thrills our souls with joy,
4. At the name of Je - sus bow - ing, Fall - ing pros-trate at his feet,

It will joy and com-fort give you, Take it then where'er you go.
If temp - ta - tions 'round you gath - er, Breathe that ho - ly name in pray'r.
When his lov - ing arms re - ceive us, And his songs our tongues employ!
King of kings in heav'n we'll crown him, When our jour - ney is com-plete.

REFRAIN.

Pre - cious name, O how sweet! Hope of earth and joy of
Pre-cious name, O how sweet!

heav'n, Precious name, O how sweet— Hope of earth and joy of heav'n.
Precious name, O how sweet, how sweet,

461 Be Ye Strong in the Lord

"Be strong in the Lord, and in the power of his might." EPH. 6 : 10.

EL. NATHAN

IRA D. SANKEY

1. "Be ye strong in the Lord and the pow-er of his might," Firmly
2. "Be ye strong in the Lord and the pow-er of his might," Nev-er
3. "Be ye strong in the Lord and the pow-er of his might," For his

stand-ing for the truth of his word; He shall lead you safe-ly through the
turn-ing from the face of the foe; He will sure-ly by you stand, as you
prom-is-es shall nev-er, nev-er fail; By thy right hand he'll hold thee while

thick-est of the fight, You shall con-quer in the name of the Lord.
bat-tle for the right, In the pow-er of his might on-ward go.
bat-tling for the right, Trust-ing him thou shalt for ev-er-more pre-vail.

REFRAIN.

Firm-ly stand for the right, On to
Firm-ly stand for the right,

vic-t'ry at the King's command; For the hon-or of the Lord, and the

Be Ye Strong in the Lord

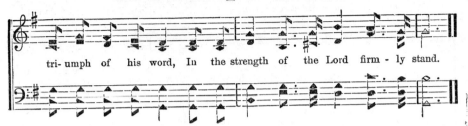

tri - umph of his word, In the strength of the Lord firm - ly stand.

462

Higher Ground

"The high calling of God in Christ Jesus." PHIL. 3: 14.

JOHNSON OATMAN, JR.   CHAS. H. GABRIEL

1. I'm press-ing on the up-ward way, New heights I'm gain - ing ev - 'ry day;
2. My heart has no de - sire to stay Where doubts a - rise and fears dis - may;
3. I want to live a - bove the world, Tho' Sa-tan's darts at me are hurled;
4. I want to scale the utmost height, And catch a gleam of glo - ry bright;

FINE.

Still pray - ing as I'm onward bound, "Lord, plant my feet on high - er ground."
Tho' some may dwell where these a - bound, My pray'r, my aim is high - er ground.
For faith has caught the joy - ful sound, The song of saints on high - er ground.
But still I'll pray till heav'n I've found, "Lord, lead me on to high - er ground."

D.S.—than I have found; Lord, plant my feet on high - er ground.

REFRAIN.   D.S.

Lord, lift me up and let me stand, By faith, on heav-en's ta - ble-land,—A higher plane

463 The Cross is Not Greater

May be sung as a Solo and Chorus.

Com. BALLINGTON BOOTH

1. The cross that he gave may be heav-y, But it ne'er out-weighs his grace,
2. The thorns in my path are not sharp-er Than com-posed his crown for me,
3. The light of his love shin-eth bright-er, As it falls on paths of woe,
4. His will I have joy in ful-fill-ing, As I'm walk-ing in his sight,

The storm that I feared may sur-round me, But it ne'er ex-cludes his face.
The cup that I drink not more bit-ter Than he drank in Geth-sem-a-ne.
The toil of my work groweth light-er, As I stoop to raise the low.
My all to the blood I am bring-ing, It a-lone can keep me right.

REFRAIN.

The cross is not great-er than his grace, The storm can-not hide his bless-ed face; I am sat-is-fied to know That with Je-sus here be-low, I can con-quer ev-'ry foe.

Does Jesus Care

"The very hairs of your head are all numbered." MATT. 10: 30.

Rev. FRANK E. GRAFF   J. LINCOLN HALL

1. Does Je - sus care when my heart is pained Too deep - ly for mirth or song;
2. Does Je - sus care when my way is dark With a name - less dread and fear?
3. Does Je - sus care when I've tried and fail'd To re - sist some temp-ta-tion strong?
4. Does Je - sus care when I've said "good-bye" To the dearest on earth to me,

As the burdens press, And the cares distress, And the way grows weary and long?
As the daylight fades Into deep night shades, Does he care e-nough to be near?
When in my deep grief I find no re - lief, Tho' my tears flow all the night long?
And my sad heart aches 'Till it near-ly breaks—Is this aught to him? does he see?

REFRAIN.

O yes, he cares, I know he cares, His heart is touched with my grief;......

When the days are wea - ry, The long nights dreary, I know my Sav - iour cares.
he cares.

465

Lux Benigna

J. H. NEWMAN, 1832

J. B. DYKES, 1823–1876

1. Lead, kind-ly Light, a-mid th'en-cir-cling gloom, Lead thou me on;
2. I was not ev-er thus, nor prayed that thou Shouldst lead me on;
3. So long thy pow'r has blest me, sure it still Will lead me on;

The night is dark, and I am far from home; Lead thou me on:
I loved to choose and see my path; but now Lead thou me on.
O'er moor and fen, o'er crag and tor-rent, till The night is gone;

cres.

Keep thou my feet; I do not ask to see............
I loved the gar-ish day, and, spite of fears,.........
And with the morn those an-gel-fac-es smile,.........

dim.   *p*

The dis-tant scene,— one step e-nough for me.
Pride ruled my will: re-mem-ber not past years.
Which I have loved long since, and lost a-while.

466 Blessed Quietness

Mrs. M. P. Ferguson, alt.

Arr. by J. H. F.

1. Joys are flow - ing like a riv - er, Since the Com - fort - er has come;
2. Ev - 'ry-thing is turned to glad - ness, All a-round this glo - rious Guest;
3. Like the rain that falls from heav - en, Like the sun - light from the sky,
4. What a won - der - ful sal - va - tion Where we al - ways see his face!

He a - bides with us for - ev - er, Makes the trust- ing heart his home.
Ban-ished un - be - lief and sad - ness, All is per - fect peace and rest.
So the Ho - ly Spir - it giv - en, Falls up - on us from on high.
What a peace - ful hab - i - ta - tion! What a qui - et rest - ing place!

REFRAIN.

Bless - ed qui - et-ness, ho - ly qui - et-ness, Blest as - sur - ance in my soul!

On the storm-y sea Je - sus speaks to me, And the bil-lows cease to roll.

467 Maryton L. M.

W. GLADDEN, 1880

H. P. SMITH, 1874

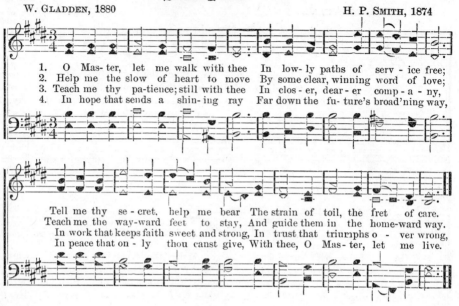

1. O Mas- ter, let me walk with thee In low- ly paths of serv - ice free;
2. Help me the slow of heart to move By some clear, winning word of love;
3. Teach me thy pa-tience; still with thee In clos - er, dear - er comp - a - ny,
4. In hope that sends a shin- ing ray Far down the fu - ture's broad'ning way,

Tell me thy se - cret, help me bear The strain of toil, the fret of care.
Teach me the way-ward feet to stay, And guide them in the home-ward way.
In work that keeps faith sweet and strong, In trust that triumphs o - ver wrong,
In peace that on - ly thou canst give, With thee, O Mas- ter, let me live.

468 Love That Will Not Let Me Go

GEORGE MATHESON

ALBERT L. PEACE

1. O love that will not let me go, I rest my wea - ry
2. O light that fol - lowest all my way, I yield my flick'ring
3. O joy that seek- est me thro' pain, I can - not close my
4. O cross that lift - est up my head, I dare not ask to

soul in thee; I give thee back the life I owe, That
torch to thee; My heart re - stores its bor- rowed ray, That
heart to thee; I trace the rain - bow thro' the rain, And
hide from thee; I lay in dust life's glo - ry dead, And

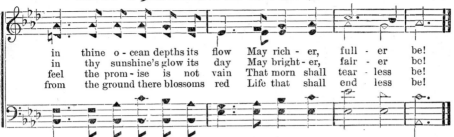

Love That Will Not Let Me Go

in	thine o-cean depths its	flow	May rich-er,	full - er	be!
in	thy sunshine's glow its	day	May bright-er,	fair - er	be!
feel	the prom-ise is not	vain	That morn shall	tear - less	be!
from	the ground there blossoms	red	Life that shall	end - less	be!

469 Turn Your Faces Toward the Morning

JESSIE BROWN POUNDS   J. H. FILLMORE

Allegretto.

1. Turn your fac - es toward the morn-ing, Wea - ry watch-ers of the night;
2. Turn your fac - es toward the morn-ing, Long the joy - less hours have been;
3. Turn your fac - es toward the morn-ing, Weeping pass - es with the night;

Fling your east - ward win-dows o - pen, Look a - broad and seek the light!
Yet God's prom-ise nev - er fails us, Let the ear - ly day-beams in!
Lo! the day in glo - ry break-ing, Turn your fac - es toward the light!

REFRAIN.

Turn your fac - es toward the morning, Wea - ry watch-ers of the night;

Turn your fac - es toward the morn-ing, Look a - broad and seek the light.

470 Near the Cross

F. J. CROSBY

W. H. DOANE

1. Je - sus, keep me near the Cross, There a pre-cious fount-ain
2. Near the Cross, a tremb-ling soul, Love and mer-cy found me;
3. Near the Cross! O Lamb of God, Bring its scenes be-fore me;
4. Near the Cross I'll watch and wait, Hop-ing, trust-ing ev - er,

Free to all— a heal-ing stream, Flows from Cal-vary's mount-ain.
There the bright and Morn-ing Star Shed its beams a-round me.
Help me walk from day to day, With its shad-ows o'er me.
Till I reach the gold-en strand, Just be-yond the riv - er.

REFRAIN.

In the Cross, in the Cross, Be my glo-ry ev - er;

Till my rap-tured soul shall find Rest be-yond the riv - er.

Heavenly Sunlight

H. J. ZELLEY

G. H. COOK

1. Walk-ing in sun - light, all of my jour - ney; O - ver the mount-ains,
2. Shad- ows a - round me, shad- ows a - bove me, Nev - er con - ceal my
3. In the bright sun - light, ev - er re - joic - ing, Press-ing my way to

through the deep vale; Je - sus has said I'll nev - er for - sake thee,
Sav - iour and Guide; He is the Light, in him is no dark - ness,
man-sions a - bove; Sing-ing his prais - es, glad - ly I'm walk - ing,

REFRAIN.

Prom - ise di - vine that nev - er can fail.
Ev - er I'm walk-ing close to his side.
Walk - ing in sun - light, sun-light of love.
Heav - en - ly sun - light,

heav-en - ly sun - light: Flooding my soul with glo - ry di - vine: Hal - le -

lu - jah, I am re - joic - ing, Sing-ing his prais - es, Je - sus is mine.

472 I Heard the Voice of Jesus Say

BONAR   J. D. BRUNK

1. I heard the voice of Je-sus say, "Come un-to me and rest;
2. I heard the voice of Je-sus say, "Be-hold, I free-ly give
3. I heard the voice of Je-sus say, "I am this dark world's Light;

Lay down, thou wea-ry one, lay down Thy head up-on my breast!"
The liv-ing wa-ter; thirst-y one, Stoop down and drink and live!"
Look un-to me, thy morn shall rise And all thy day be bright!"

I came to Je-sus as I was, Wea-ry and worn and sad;
I came to Je-sus, and I drank Of that life-giv-ing stream:
I looked to Je-sus, and I found In him my Star, my Sun;

I found in him a rest-ing place, And he has made me glad.
My thirst was quenched, my soul re-vived, And now I live in him.
And in that light of life I'll walk Till all my jour-ney's done.

473 I am Thine, O Lord

F. J. Crosby

W. H. Doane

1. I am Thine, O Lord, I have heard thy voice, And it told thy love to me;
2. Con-se-crate me now to thy serv-ice, Lord, By the pow'r of grace di - vine;
3. O the pure de-light of a sin-gle hour That be-fore thy throne I spend,
4. There are depths of love that I can-not know Till I cross the nar - row sea,

But I long to rise in the arms of faith, And be clos - er drawn to thee.
Let my soul look up with a stead-fast hope, And my will be lost in thine.
When I kneel in pray'r, and with thee my God, I commune as friend with friend.
There are heights of joy that I may not reach Till I rest in peace with thee.

REFRAIN.

Draw me near - er, near-er, bless-ed Lord, To the cross where thou hast died;
near - er, near - er,

Draw me near - er, near- er, near-er, bless-ed Lord, To thy precious, bleeding side.

474

Jesus Calls Us

Mrs. Cecil F. Alexander

William H. Jude

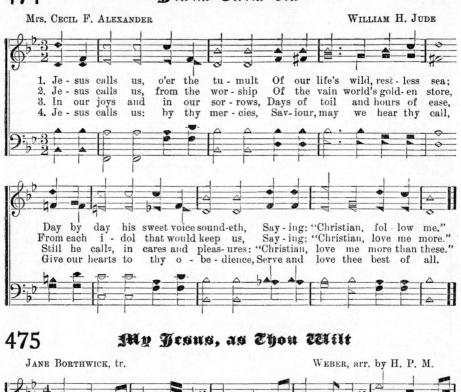

1. Je - sus calls us, o'er the tu - mult Of our life's wild, rest - less sea;
2. Je - sus calls us, from the wor - ship Of the vain world's gold - en store,
3. In our joys and in our sor - rows, Days of toil and hours of ease,
4. Je - sus calls us: by thy mer - cies, Sav - iour, may we hear thy call,

Day by day his sweet voice sound-eth, Say - ing: "Christian, fol - low me."
From each i - dol that would keep us, Say - ing: "Christian, love me more."
Still he calls, in cares and pleas - ures: "Christian, love me more than these."
Give our hearts to thy o - be - dience, Serve and love thee best of all.

475

My Jesus, as Thou Wilt

Jane Borthwick, tr.

Weber, arr. by H. P. M.

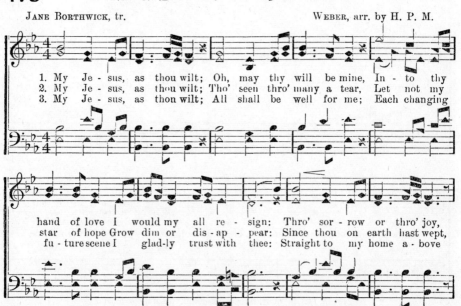

1. My Je - sus, as thou wilt; Oh, may thy will be mine, In - to thy
2. My Je - sus, as thou wilt; Tho' seen thro' many a tear, Let not my
3. My Je - sus, as thou wilt; All shall be well for me; Each changing

hand of love I would my all re - sign: Thro' sor - row or thro' joy,
star of hope Grow dim or dis - ap - pear: Since thou on earth hast wept,
fu - ture scene I glad-ly trust with thee: Straight to my home a - bove

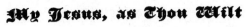

My Jesus, as Thou Wilt

rit.

Con- duct me as thine own, And help me still to say, My Lord, thy will be done.
And sorrowed oft a- lone, If I must weep with thee, My Lord, thy will be done.
I trav- el calm- ly on, And sing, in life or death,—My Lord, thy will be done.

476   **Felix (Raynolds)**

ANNA B. WARNER, 1858   F. MENDELSSOHN, 1809–1847

1. We would see Je - sus; for the shad- ows length - en A - cross this
2. We would see Je - sus, the great rock foun - da - tion Where- on our
3. We would see Je - sus: oth - er lights are pal - ing, Which for long
4. We would see Je - sus: this is all we're need - ing; Strength, joy, and

lit - tle land-scape of our life; We would see Je - sus, our weak
feet were set by sove-reign grace: Nor life nor death, with all their
years we have re-joiced to see; The bless-ings of our pil - grim -
will - ing - ness come with the sight; We would see Je - sus, dy - ing,

faith to strength - en, For the last wea - ri - ness, the fi - nal strife.
ag - i - ta - tion, Can thence re - move us, if we see his face.
age are fail - ing; We would not mourn them, for we go to thee.
ris - en, plead - ing; Then wel - come day, and fare - well mor - tal night.

12

477 Penitence

James Montgomery, 1834

Spencer Lane, 1879

1. In the hour of tri - al, Je - sus, plead for me;
2. With its witch - ing pleas - ures Would this vain world charm,
3. If with sore af - flic - tion Thou in love chas - tise,
4. When in dust and ash - es To the grave I sink,

Lest by base de - ni - al I de - part from thee:
Or its sor - did treas - ures Spread to work me harm,
Pour thy ben - e - dic - tion On the sac - ri - fice;
While heaven's glo - ry flash - es O'er the shelv - ing brink,

When thou seest me wav - er, With a look re - call,......
Bring to my re - mem - brance Sad Geth - sem - a - ne,.........
Then, up - on thine al - tar Free - ly of - fered up,.........
On thy truth re - ly - ing Through that mor - tal strife,......

Nor for fear or fa - vor Suf - fer me to fall.
Or, in dark - er sem - blance, Cross-crowned Cal - va - ry.
Though the flesh may fal - ter, Faith shall drink the cup.
Lord, re - ceive me, dy - ing, To e - ter - nal life.

478 Thy Will be Done

"Thy will be done in earth, as it is in heaven" MATT. 6: 10.

CHARLOTTE ELLIOTT

JAMES McGRANAHAN

1. My God and Fa - ther, while I stray Far from my home, on
2. What tho' in lone - ly grief I sigh For friends be - loved, no
3. Let but my faint- ing heart be blest With thy sweet Spir - it
4. Re - new my will from day to day; Blend it with thine; and
5. Then when on earth I breathe no more The prayer oft mixed with

life's rough way, Oh, teach me from my heart to say, "Thy will be done!"
lon - ger nigh, Sub- mis- sive still would I re - ply, "Thy will be done!"
for its guest, My God, to thee I leave the rest, "Thy will be done!"
take a - way All now that makes it hard to say, "Thy will be done!"
tears be - fore, I'll sing up - on a hap - pier shore, "Thy will be done!"

REFRAIN.

Thy will be done! Thy will be done!
Thy will— thy will be done!— Thy will— thy will be done!

Oh, teach me from my heart to say, "Thy will be done!"
Sub - mis - sive still would I re - ply, "Thy will be done!"
My God, to thee I leave the rest, "Thy will be done!"
All now that makes it hard to say, "Thy will be done!"
I'll sing up - on a hap - pier shore, "Thy will be done!"

Walking in the Sunshine

"And he saith unto them, Follow me." MATT. 4 : 19.

W. ROBERT LINDSAY

IRA D. SANKEY

1. Walk-ing in the sun-shine, beau-ti-ful and bright, In the ros-y morn-ing,
2. In the brightest sun-shine, or the dark-est gloom, In the love-ly springtime,
3. In the gold-en sun-shine, or the shad-ows deep, When the storm is rag-ing,

or the dew-y night; Stead-i-ly ad-vanc-ing on-ward day by day,
or the sum-mer's bloom; Hear the Sav-iour call-ing, has-ten to o-bey,
when it sinks to sleep; Trust-ing in his mer-cy till the clos-ing day,

REFRAIN.

Fol-low Je-sus all the way. Fol-low, we will fol-low Je-sus;
Fol-low, fol-low,

Fol - low, fol-low day by day; On - ward
Fol-low, fol-low On-ward, on-ward

where-so-e'er he leads us, We will fol-low Je-sus all the way.

480

Sweetest Hosannas

" Sing forth the honor of his name ; make his praise glorious." Ps. 66 : 2.

G. P. Hott

J. D. Brunk

Lively. m

1. In from the high - way, in from the by - way, Gath-er the chil - dren se -
2. Go where the ma - ny wan der from Je - sus, Lov-ing-ly whis - per - ing
3. Brighter and bet - ter, gems of the king-dom, Hap-py the chil - dren in

cure-ly from sin; Je-sus has blest them, sweet-ly ca-ressed them, Lov-ing-ly
"Come un - to me;" Sweetly re - call them, for like the chil - dren, Ev - er the
seek-ing the fold; Lov-ing-ly find them, put your arms round them, Just as the

f   **Refrain.**

bid - den us wel-come them in.
king - dom of heav-en shall be. } Help us to win them, help us to
Sav - iour once blest them of old.

cres.   *f*   *m*

gath - er, Help us the jew - els of heav-en to bring; Je - sus has

f

bid - den, "Suffer the chil-dren;" Sweetest ho - san - nas to Je-sus they sing.

481 We Are Little Gleaners

J. H. FILLMORE

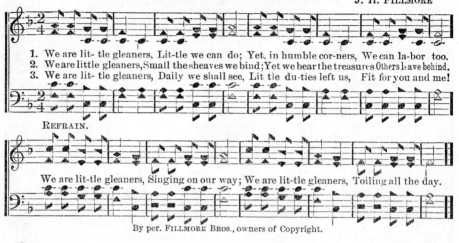

1. We are lit-tle gleaners, Lit-tle we can do; Yet, in humble cor-ners, We can la-bor too.
2. We are little gleaners, Small the sheaves we bind; Yet we bear the treasures Others leave behind.
3. We are lit- tle gleaners, Daily we shall see, Lit-tle du-ties left us, Fit for you and me!

REFRAIN.

We are lit-tle gleaners, Singing on our way; We are lit-tle gleaners, Toiling all the day.

By per. FILLMORE BROS., owners of Copyright.

482 The Christmas Manger Hymn

MARTIN LUTHER

J. E. SPILMAN

1. A - way in a man - ger, no crib for his bed, The lit - tle Lord
2. The cat - tle are low - ing, the poor ba - by wakes, But lit - tle Lord

Je - sus laid down his sweet head; The stars in the sky they looked
Je - sus, no cry - ing he makes. I love thee, Lord Je - sus, look

down where he lay, The lit - tle Lord Je - sus a - sleep in the hay.
down from the sky, And stay by my crib side, watch my lul - la - by.

483

Little Reapers

Arr. by H. T. WARTMANN

1. We are lit-tle reap-ers, toil-ing all the day, Lab-'ring in the har-vest, o'er the ston-y way; Glean-ing 'mong the this-tles, search-ing through the rain, Gath-'ring for the gar-ner, bright and gold-en grain.

2. We are lit-tle reap-ers, in the fields of sin, Striv-ing for the Mas-ter, pre-cious souls to win; Point-ing them to Je-sus, to the Lamb of God, Fol-low-ing his foot-steps in the path he trod.

3. We are lit-tle reap-ers, in the har-vest field; Truth and Right the sick-les that our arms shall wield; And we la-bor ev-er, 'neath our Fa-ther's eye, Gath-'ring for the gar-ner of the throne on high.

REFRAIN.

Toil-ing, toil-ing, toil-ing all the day, Reap-ing for the Mas-ter, we are Paus-ing not for shad-ows that be-cloud our way.

484   Jesus Loves Even Me

"God is love." 1 John iv, 8.

P. P. BLISS   P. P. BLISS

1. I am so glad that our Fa-ther in heav'n Tells of his love in the
2. Tho' I for-get him and wan-der a-way, Still he doth love me wher-
3. Oh, if there's on-ly one song I can sing, When in his beau-ty I

Book he has giv'n, Won-der-ful things in the Bi-ble I see;
ev-er I stray; Back to his dear lov-ing arms would I flee,
see the Great King, This shall my song in e-ter-ni-ty be:

This is the dear-est, that Je-sus loves me.
When I re-mem-ber, that Je-sus loves me.
"Oh, what a won-der that Je-sus loves me."

REFRAIN.

I am so glad that Je-sus loves me, Je-sus loves me, Je-sus loves me,

I am so glad that Je-sus loves me, Je-sus loves e-ven me.

485 Song of the Saviour

Dr. S. Fillmore Bennett

Chas. H. Gabriel

1. Sing we a song of the Sav-iour, Gen-tle, and lov-ing, and true,
2. Born in the Beth-le-hem man-ger, An-gels at-tend-ed his birth,
3. Bear-ing his bur-den of sor-rows, Still did he love us the same;
4. Now to the heav-ens as-cend-ed, Him by the Fa-ther be-hold,

Walk-ing the val-ley of shad-ows, Dy-ing for me and for you.
And from the heav-ens de-scend-ed Songs of re-joic-ing to earth.
All that re-viled him for-giv-ing, Bear-ing the cross and its shame.
Plead-ing the cause of his chil-dren, Lov-ing us just as of old.

REFRAIN.

Praise him, praise him, Gen-tle, and lov-ing and true;

Praise him, praise him, Dy-ing for me and for you.

Copyright, 1893, by Chas. H. Gabriel. Used by per.

486 Beulah

The following tune was improvised and sung by Beulah Smith before she was five years old.

J. B. SMITH

1. In the ear - ly days of child-hood, We will give our hearts to thee,
2. Take our hands that we may use them In kind acts and deeds of love;
3. Take our eyes that we may lift them Up to heav - en all our days;
4. Take our bod - ies— ev - 'ry mem - ber— May they be thy dwell-ing place;

For the Ho - ly Bi - ble tells us, Let the chil - dren come to me.
Take our feet, and keep them safe - ly In the way that leads a - bove.
Take our lips and may they o - pen Ev - er - more to sing thy praise.
Keep them ho - ly, keep them ev - er, Till at last we see thy face.

REFRAIN.

Bless - ed Je - sus, we will love thee, For thou art the children's friend;

Keep us near thee, take us to thee When this earth - ly life shall end.

487 Zion's Glad Morning

REGINALD HEBER, 1811   Arr. from Harmonia Sacra

1. Hail the blest morn when the great Me - di - a - tor, Down from the
2. Bright-est and best of the sons of the morn - ing, Dawn on our
3. Cold on his cra - dle the dew-drops are shin - ing, Low lies his
4. Say shall we yield him, in cost - ly de - vo - tion, O - dors of
5. Vain - ly we of - fer each am - ple ob - la - tion, Vain - ly with

re - gions of glo - ry des - cends. Shep - herds, go wor - ship the
dark - ness and lend us thine aid; Star of the East, the hor -
bed with the beasts of the stall; An - gels a - dore him in
E - dom and off - 'rings di - vine— Gems of the mount - ain and
gold would his fa - vor se - cure; Rich - er by far is the

Zion's Glad Morning

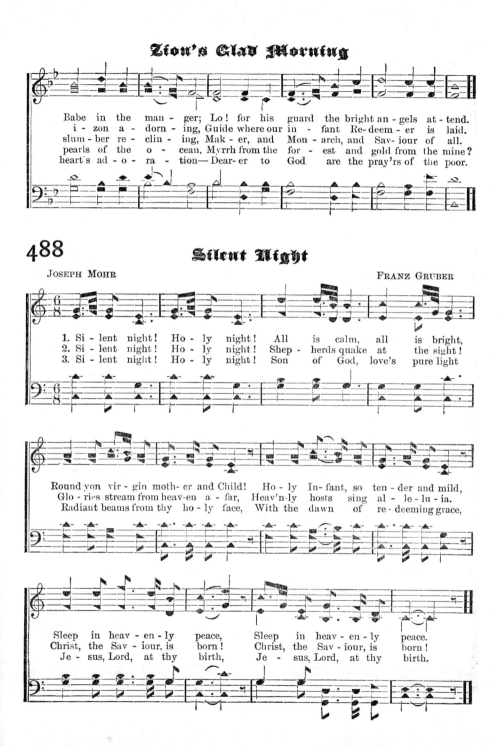

Babe in the man - ger; Lo! for his guard the bright an - gels at - tend.
i - zon a - dorn - ing, Guide where our in - fant Re - deem - er is laid.
slum - ber re - clin - ing, Mak - er, and Mon - arch, and Sav - iour of all.
pearls of the o - cean, Myrrh from the for - est and gold from the mine?
heart's ad - o - ra - tion—Dear - er to God are the pray'rs of the poor.

488 Silent Night

JOSEPH MOHR

FRANZ GRUBER

1. Si - lent night! Ho - ly night! All is calm, all is bright,
2. Si - lent night! Ho - ly night! Shep - herds quake at the sight!
3. Si - lent night! Ho - ly night! Son of God, love's pure light

Round yon vir - gin moth - er and Child! Ho - ly In - fant, so ten - der and mild,
Glo - ries stream from heav - en a - far, Heav'n - ly hosts sing al - le - lu - ia.
Radiant beams from thy ho - ly face, With the dawn of re - deeming grace,

Sleep in heav - en - ly peace, Sleep in heav - en - ly peace.
Christ, the Sav - iour, is born! Christ, the Sav - iour, is born!
Je - sus, Lord, at thy birth, Je - sus, Lord, at thy birth.

489 Carol C. M. D.

NAHUM TATE, 1702   RICHARD S. WILLIS, 1850

1. While shep-herds watched their flocks by night, All seat-ed on the ground,
2. "To you, in Da-vid's town this day, Is born of Da-vid's line,
3. Thus spake the ser-aph, and forth-with Ap-peared a shin-ing throng

The an-gel of the Lord came down, And glo-ry shone a-round.
A Sav-iour, who is Christ the Lord, And this shall be the sign:
Of an-gels prais-ing God, and thus Ad-dressed their joy-ful song:

"Fear not," said he,— for might-y dread Had seized their troub-led mind,—
The heav'n-ly Babe you there shall find To hu-man view dis-played,
"All glo-ry be to God on high, And to the earth be peace:

"Glad ti-dings of great joy I bring To you and all man-kind."
All mean-ly wrapt in swath-ing bands, And in a man-ger laid."
Good-will hence-forth, from heav'n to men, Be-gin and nev-er cease."

Passion Chorale

Ascribed to BERNARD of CLAIRVAUX, 1091–1153, Tr. HANS LEO HASSLER, 1601
Harmonized by J. S. BACH, 1729

1. O sa-cred Head, now wound-ed, With grief and shame weighed down!
2. O no-blest brow and dear-est, In oth-er days the world
3. What thou, my Lord, hast suf-fered Was all for sin-ners' gain:
4. What lan-guage shall I bor-row To thank thee, dear-est Friend,
5. Be near when I am dy-ing, O show thy cross to me;

Now scorn-ful-ly sur-round-ed With thorns, thine on-ly crown:
All feared when thou ap-pear-edst; What shame on thee is hurled!
Mine, mine was the trans-gres-sion, But thine the dead-ly pain.
For this thy dy-ing sor-row, Thy pit-y with-out end?
And for my suc-cor fly-ing, Come, Lord, to set me free:

O sa-cred Head, what glo-ry, What bliss till now was thine!
How art thou pale with an-guish, With sore a-buse and scorn;
Lo, here I fall, my Sav-iour! 'Tis I de-serve thy place;
O make me thine for ev-er; And should I faint-ing be,
These eyes, new faith re-ceiv-ing, From Je-sus shall not move;

Yet, though de-spised and go-ry, I joy to call thee mine.
How does that vis-age lan-guish Which once was bright as morn!
Look on me with thy fav-or, Vouch-safe to me thy grace.
Lord, let me nev-er, nev-er Out-live my love to thee.
For he who dies be-liev-ing, Dies safe-ly, through thy love.

491 I Know That My Redeemer

Jessie Brown Pounds   J. H. Fillmore

1. I know that my Re-deem-er liv - eth, And that on earth............ a -
2. I know his promise nev - er fail - eth, The word he speaks,........... it
3. I know my mansion he pre - par - eth, That where he is................. there

And on the earth

gain shall stand; I know e - ter - nal life he giv - eth, That grace and
can-not die; Tho' cru - el death my flesh as - sail - eth, Yet, I shall
I may be; O won - drous tho't, for me he car - eth, And he at

again shall stand;

Refrain.

pow'r........ are in his hand.
see............... him by and by. } I know, I know............ that Je - sus
last............... will come for me.

I know, I know

That grace and pow'r

liv - eth, And on the earth......... again shall stand; I know, I know........that

And on the earth   I know, I know

rit.

life he giv - eth, That grace and pow'r............ are in his hand.

That grace and pow'r   are in his hand.

492

As the Dawn was Breaking

R. B.

RUFUS BUZZARD

1. As the dawn was calm-ly break-ing, On that glo-rious Eas-ter day, The great
2. Hark! the ver-dant earth is quak-ing, Under heav'n's po-ten-tial sway; For Je-
3. As they left in fear and trembling, There was one who lin-gered long, And she
4. Hal-le-lu-jah! Christ has ris-en, Vic-tor o'er that dark do-main. Earth-ly

truth in mys-t'ry shrouded, Proved a blest re-al-i-ty. Je-sus Christ the
ho-vah's faith-ful an-gel Came and rolled the stone a-way. "He is ris-en,"
stood and wept for sor-row Close be-side that va-cant tomb. But her tears to
foes could not sub-due him, Tho' his bod-y they had slain. "I'm the life and

won-drous Prophet Who had died up-on the tree, Now had vanquished death—vic-
was the mes-sage, And a-gain the an-gel said, "Why come ye to see the
glad fru-i-tion Changed, when Je-sus met her there, For his lov-ing voice so
res-ur-rec-tion," Was the say-ing that he kept; For from death he rose vic-

to-rious, And thus set the cap-tive free.
liv-ing, Here a-mong the si-lent dead."
gen-tle, Soon subdued her vain de-spair.
to-rious, The first fruits of them that slept.

REFRAIN.

Oh, spread the message far and wide:

Yes, spread the joyful news,

Je-sus lives............... and reigns on high, He has vanquished his last foe
Je-sus lives a-gain,

In his earth-life here be-low And is com-ing soon, but nev-er more to die.

Easter Anthem

Arr. from Harmonia Sacra

The Lord is ris'n in-deed! Hal - le-lu-jah!

The Lord is ris'n in-deed! Hal - le-lu - jah!

Now is Christ ris-en from the dead, and be-come the first fruits of

them that slept, Now is Christ ris-en from the dead and be-

come the first fruits of them that slept. Hal - le - lu - jah! Hal - le-

Easter Anthem

lu - jah! Hal - le - lu - jah! And did he rise? And did he

And did he rise?............

rise? And did he rise, did he rise? Hear it, ye na - tions,

And did he rise?............

hear it, O ye dead; He rose, He rose, He rose, He rose, He

burst the bars of death, He burst the bars of death, He burst the bars of

death, And tri - umphed o'er the grave. Then, then, then I rose,

Easter Anthem

Then I rose, Then I rose, Then I rose; Then first hu -

man - i - ty tri - umph-ant passed the crys - tal ports of light, And

seized e - ter - nal youth. Man, all im - mor - tal, hail! Hail!

Heav - en, all lav - ish of strange gifts to man; Thine all the glo - ry,

Man's the boundless bliss; Thine all the glo - ry, Man's the boundless bliss.

Saved by Grace

"By grace are ye saved through faith; and that not of yourselves; it is the gift of God." EPH. 2: 8.

FANNY J. CROSBY

GEO. C. STEBBINS.

SOLO OR DUET.

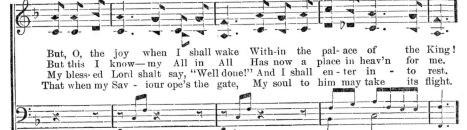

1. Some day the sil - ver cord will break, And I no more as now shall sing;
2. Some day my earth - ly house will fall, I can-not tell how soon 'twill be,
3. Some day, when fades the gold-en sun Beneath the ro - sy tint - ed west,
4. Some day; till then I'll watch and wait, My lamp all trimmed and burning bright,

But, O, the joy when I shall wake With-in the pal- ace of the King!
But this I know—my All in All Has now a place in heav'n for me.
My bless- ed Lord shalt say, "Well done!" And I shall en - ter in - to rest.
That when my Sav - iour ope's the gate, My soul to him may take its flight.

CHORUS.

And I shall see him face to face, And tell the sto- ry—Saved by grace;
shall see to face,

rit.

And I shall see him face to face, And tell the sto- ry—Saved by grace.
shall see to face,

495 My Saviour First of All

FANNY J. CROSBY

JNO. R. SWENEY

1. When my life work is end-ed, and I cross the swelling tide, When the
2. Oh, the soul-thrill-ing rap-ture when I view his bless-ed face, And the
3. Oh, the dear ones in glo-ry, how they beck-on me to come; And our
4. Thro' the gates to the cit-y in a robe of spot-less white He will

bright and glorious morning I shall see, I shall know my Re-deem-er when I
lus-ter of his kind-ly beam-ing eye; How my full heart will praise him for the
part-ing at the riv-er I re-call; To the sweet vales of E-den they will
lead me where no tears will ev-er fall; In the glad song of a-ges I shall

reach the oth-er side, And his smile will be the first to wel-come me.
mer-cy, love and grace That pre-pared for me a man-sion in the sky.
sing my wel-come home; But I long to see my Sav-iour first of all.
min-gle with de-light; But I long to see my Sav-iour first of all.

REFRAIN.

I shall know him, I shall know him, And redeem'd by his side I shall stand,
I shall know him,

I shall know him, I shall know him By the prints of the nails in his hand.
I shall know him,

496 We Are Going Down the Valley

"Yea, though I walk through the valley of the shadow of death, I will fear no evil." PSA. 23: 4.

JESSIE H. BROWN

J. H. FILLMORE

Doloroso.

1. We are go-ing down the val-ley, one by one, With our fa-ces tow'rd the
2. We are go-ing down the val-ley, one by one, When the la-bors of the
3. We are go-ing down the val-ley, one by one, Hu-man comrade you or

set-ting of the sun; Down the val-ley where the mourn-ful cy-press grows,
wea-ry day are done; One by one, the cares of earth for-ev-er past,
I will there have none; But a ten-der hand will guide us lest we fall,

REFRAIN.

Where the stream of death in si-lence on-ward flows. ⎫
We shall stand up-on the riv-er bank at last. ⎬ We are go-ing down the val-ley,
Christ is go-ing down the valley with us all. ⎭

go-ing down the val-ley, Go-ing tow'rd the set-ting of the sun; We are

rit.

going down the valley, go-ing down the valley, Go-ing down the valley, one by one.

497 Crossing the Bar

ALFRED TENNYSON, arr.

B. T. WORDEN

1. Sun - set and ev'n - ing star, And one clear call for me! And
2. Twi - light and ev'n - ing bell, And aft - er that the dark! And
3. For tho' from time and place The flood may bear me far, I

may there be no moan - ing bar When I put out to sea, And
may there be no sad fare-well When I at last em - bark, And
hope to see my Pi - lot's face When I have crossed the bar, I

may there be no moan-ing bar When I put out to sea.
may there be no sad fare-well When I at last em - bark.
hope to see my Pi - lot's face When I have crossed the bar.

Copyright, 1905, by DANIEL B. TOWNER. English Copyright. Used by per.

498 Some Sweet Day

'Sorrow and mourning shall flee away.'' ISAIAH 51: 11.

S. H. C.

S. H. CHORD

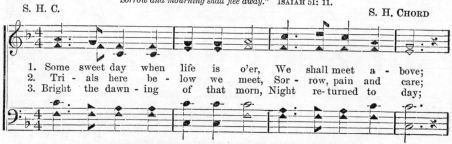

1. Some sweet day when life is o'er, We shall meet a - bove;
2. Tri - als here be - low we meet, Sor - row, pain and care;
3. Bright the dawn - ing of that morn, Night re-turned to day;

By permission THE HOME MUSIC CO., Logansport, Ind. Used by per.

Some Sweet Day

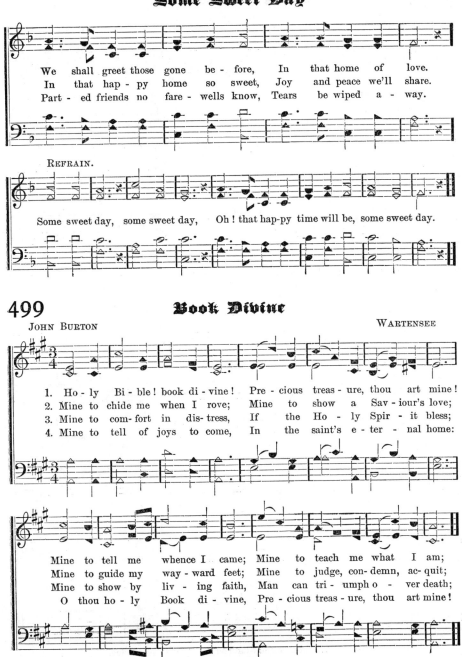

We shall greet those gone be - fore, In that home of love.
In that hap - py home so sweet, Joy and peace we'll share.
Part - ed friends no fare - wells know, Tears be wiped a - way.

REFRAIN.

Some sweet day, some sweet day, Oh! that hap-py time will be, some sweet day.

499 Book Divine

JOHN BURTON

WARTENSEE

1. Ho - ly Bi - ble! book di - vine! Pre - cious treas - ure, thou art mine!
2. Mine to chide me when I rove; Mine to show a Sav - iour's love;
3. Mine to com - fort in dis- tress, If the Ho - ly Spir - it bless;
4. Mine to tell of joys to come, In the saint's e - ter - nal home:

Mine to tell me whence I came; Mine to teach me what I am;
Mine to guide my way - ward feet; Mine to judge, con- demn, ac- quit;
Mine to show by liv - ing faith, Man can tri - umph o - ver death;
O thou ho - ly Book di - vine, Pre - cious treas - ure, thou art mine!

500 Cling to the Bible

Ps. 119 : 110.

M. J. SMITH

J. R. MURRAY

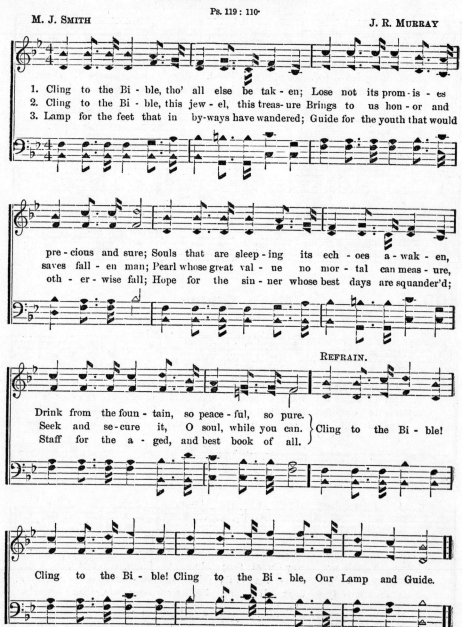

1. Cling to the Bi-ble, tho' all else be tak-en; Lose not its prom-is-es
2. Cling to the Bi-ble, this jew-el, this treas-ure Brings to us hon-or and
3. Lamp for the feet that in by-ways have wandered; Guide for the youth that would

pre-cious and sure; Souls that are sleep-ing its ech-oes a-wak-en,
saves fall-en man; Pearl whose great val-ue no mor-tal can meas-ure,
oth-er-wise fall; Hope for the sin-ner whose best days are squander'd;

REFRAIN.

Drink from the foun-tain, so peace-ful, so pure.
Seek and se-cure it, O soul, while you can. }Cling to the Bi-ble!
Staff for the a-ged, and best book of all.

Cling to the Bi-ble! Cling to the Bi-ble, Our Lamp and Guide.

501 The Ninety and Nine

E. C. Clephane

(To be sung only as a Solo)

Ira D. Sankey

1. There were nine-ty and nine that safe - ly lay In the shel - ter of the
2. "Lord, thou hast here thy nine-ty and nine; Are they not e - nough for
3. But none of the ransomed ev - er knew How deep were the wa - ters
4. "Lord, whence are those blood-drops all the way That mark out the mountain's
5. But all thro' the mountains, thun - der-riv'n, And up from the rock - y

fold, But one was out on the hills a-way, Far off from the
thee?" But the Shepherd made an - swer; "This of mine Has wan-dered a-
cross'd; Nor how dark was the night that the Lord pass'd thro' Ere he found his
track?" "They were shed for one who had gone a-stray Ere the Shep-herd could
steep, There a - rose a glad cry to the gate of heav'n, "Re - joice! I have

gates of gold— A - way on the mountains wild and bare, A-
way from me, And, although the road be rough and steep I
sheep that was lost: Out in the des - ert he heard its cry—
bring him back:" "Lord, whence are thy hands so rent and torn?" "They are
found my sheep!" And the An - gels echoed a - round the throne, "Re -

rit.

way from the ten-der Shepherd's care. A - way from the ten-der Shepherd's care.
go to the desert to find my sheep," "I go to the desert to find my sheep."
Sick and helpless, and ready to die, Sick and helpless, and ready to die.
pierc-ed to-night by many a thorn," "They are pierc-ed to-night by many a thorn."
joice! for the Lord brings back his own!" "Re - joice! for the Lord brings back his own!"

502 Softly and Tenderly

W. L. T.

WILL L. THOMPSON

Very slow

1. Soft-ly and ten-der-ly Je-sus is call-ing, Call-ing for you and for me;
2. Why should we tarry when Je-sus is pleading, Pleading for you and for me?
3. Time is now fleeting, the moments are passing, Pass-ing from you and from me;
4. O for the won-der-ful love he has promised, Promised for you and for me,

See, on the por-tals he's waiting and watching, Watching for you and for me.
Why should we linger and heed not his mer-cies, Mer-cies for you and for me?
Shadows are gath-er-ing, death warnings coming, Com-ing for you and for me.
Tho' we have sinned, He has mer-cy and par-don, Par-don for you and for me.

REFRAIN.

Come home, come home,...... Ye who are wea-ry, come home,.........
come home, come home,

Ear-nest-ly, tender-ly, Je-sus is call-ing, Call-ing, O sinner, come home!

503
Only a Step to Jesus

"Then come thou, for there is peace." 1 Sam. 20 : 21.

FANNY J. CROSBY

W. H. DOANE, by per.

1. On - ly a step to Je - sus! Then why not take it now?
2. On - ly a step to Je - sus! Be - lieve, and thou shalt live;
3. On - ly a step to Je - sus! A step from sin to grace;
4. On - ly a step to Je - sus! O why not come, and say,

Come, and, thy sin con - fess - ing, To him thy Sav - iour bow.
Lov - ing - ly now he's wait - ing, And read - y to for - give.
What hast thy heart de - cid - ed? The mo - ments fly a - pace.
Glad - ly to thee, my Sav - iour, I give my - self a - way.

REFRAIN.

On - ly a step, On - ly a step; Come, he waits for thee;

Come, and, thy sin con - fess - ing, Thou shalt re - ceive a bless - ing;

Do not re - ject the mer - cy He free - ly of - fers thee.

Meet Mother in the Skies

Arr. by W. S. NICKLE

1. In a lone-ly grave-yard, ma-ny miles a-way, Lies your dear old
2. Now the old home, va-cant, has no charms for you; One dear form is
3. Now in true re-pent-ance to the Sav-iour flee; He who par-doned

moth-er, 'neath the cold, cold clay; Mem-'ries oft re-turn-ing
ab-sent,—moth-er, kind and true; Ev-er-more she dwells where
moth-er, mer-cy has for thee; Now he waits to com-fort,

of her tears and sighs; If you love your moth-er, meet her in the skies.
pleas-ure nev-er dies; If you love your moth-er, meet her in the skies.
he will not de-spise; If you love your moth-er, meet her in the skies.

REFRAIN.

Lis-ten to her plead-ing, "Wand'ring boy, come home," Lov-ing-ly en-

treat-ing, do not lon-ger roam; Let your man-hood wak-en,

Meet Mother in the Skies

heaven-ward lift your eyes; If you love your moth-er, meet her in the skies.

505 Open Wide Thy Heart

H. H. PIERSON

R. T. OWEN

1. O - pen wide thy heart to - day At Je - sus' call;
2. O - pen wide thy heart to - day To him who pleads;
3. O - pen wide thy heart to - day To love di - vine,
4. O - pen wide thy heart to - day With all its need,

Bid him en - ter and a - bide, Thy life, thy all.
Heed his voice and fol - low on Wher - e'er he leads.
And a wealth of grace un - told May all be thine.
And the hun - ger of the soul His love will feed.

REFRAIN.

On - ly trust him, and be still; Let him work in thee his will,
be still, his will,

For the heart that's o - pen'd wide......... His love shall fill.
o - pen'd wide His love, his love shall fill.

506 Almost Persuaded

P. P. Bliss   P. P. Bliss

1. "Al - most per - suad - ed," now to be - lieve; "Al - most per - suad - ed,"
2. "Al - most per - suad - ed," come, come to - day; "Al - most per - suad - ed."
3. "Al - most per - suad - ed," har - vest is past! "Al - most per - suad - ed,"

Christ to re - ceive; Seems now some soul to say, "Go, Spir - it,
turn not a - way; Je - sus in - vites you here, An - gels are
doom comes at last! "Al - most" can not a - vail; "Al - most" is

go thy way, Some more con - ven - ient day On thee I'll call."
ling - 'ring near, Pray'rs rise from hearts so dear, O wand - 'rer, come.
but to fail! sad, sad, that bit - ter wail— "Al - most—but lost!"

Copyright, 1902, by The John Church Company. Used by per.

507 My Lord, I'll Go

J. W. Shank   Olive Nafziger

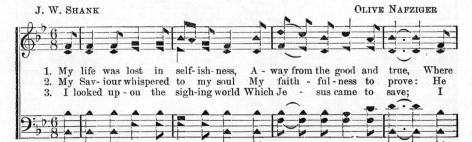

1. My life was lost in self - ish - ness, A - way from the good and true, Where
2. My Sav - iour whispered to my soul My faith - ful - ness to prove: He
3. I looked up - on the sigh - ing world Which Je - sus came to save; I

My Lord, I'll Go

cru - el sin enthralled my heart, Where gloom and darkness grew; But peace and love have
spoke of bit - ter hu - man woe, Which love a - lone can soothe. I saw the sor - row
saw the hung'ring souls of men For whom his life he gave: The mes-sage sank in -

found my soul, And now my heart is free; I've lost the gloom of self - ish-ness,
in his face, I heard his anx-ious plea, Which came in gen - tle pleading tones,
to my soul, Un-moved I could not be; Then came the an-swer from my heart,

REFRAIN.

For Je - sus came to me.
"Wilt thou not go for me?" Out of the gloom and darkness, In - to the az-ure light;
"My Lord, I'll go for thee."

Out of a bar - ren coun-try, Un-to my Lord and right. Father I come to serve thee,

Heeding my Master's call; Out of a life of self-ish-ness, In - to a life for all.

Will There Be Any Stars?

E. E. HEWITT   JNO. R. SWENEY

1. I am thinking to-day of that beautiful land I shall reach when the sun goeth down; When thro' wonderful grace by my Saviour I stand,
2. In the strength of the Lord let me labor and pray, Let me watch as a winner of souls, That bright stars may be mine in the glorious day
3. O what joy it will be when his face I behold, Living gems at his feet to lay down! It would sweeten my bliss in the city of gold,

REFRAIN.

Will there be any stars in my crown?
When his praise like the sea billow rolls.
Should there be any stars in my crown.
Will there be any stars, any stars in my crown, When at ev'ning the sun goeth down?...... When I wake with the go-eth down?

blest in the mansions of rest, Will there be any stars in my crown?......
any stars in my crown!

509 Ye Must be Born Again

"Except a man be born again, he cannot see the kingdom of God." JOHN 3 : 3.

W. T. SLEEPER   GEO. C. STEBBINS

1. A rul - er once came to Je - sus by night, To
2. Ye chil - dren of men, at - tend to the word So
3. O ye who would en - ter that glo - rious rest, And

ask him the way of sal - va - tion and light; The Mas - ter made
sol - emn - ly ut - tered by Je - sus the Lord, And let not this
sing with the ran - som'd the song of the blest, The life ev - er -

an - swer in words true and plain, "Ye must be born a - gain."......
mes - sage to you be in vain, "Ye must be born a - gain."......
last - ing if you would ob - tain, "Ye must be born a - gain."......
a - gain.

REFRAIN.

"Ye must be born a - gain,...... Ye must be born a - gain,...... I
a - gain,   a - gain,

ver - i - ly, ver - i - ly, say un - to thee, Ye must be born a - gain......
a - gain.

John S. B. Monsell, 1863

1. My sins, my sins, my Sav - iour! They take such hold on me,
2. My sins, my sins, my Sav - iour! How sad on thee they fall;
3. My sins, my sins, my Sav - iour! Their guilt I nev - er knew
4. There- fore my songs my Sav - iour! E'en in this time of woe,

I am not a - ble to look up, Save on - ly Christ, to thee;
Seen through thy gen - tle pa - tience, I ten - fold feel them all;
Till with thee in the des - ert I near thy pas - sion drew;
Shall tell of all thy good - ness To suf - f'ring man be - low;

In thee is all for - give - ness, In thee a - bun - dant grace;
I know they are for - giv - en, But still, their pain to me
Till with thee in the gard - en I heard thy plead - ing pray'r,
Thy good - ness and thy fav - or, Whose pres - ence from a - bove

My shad - ow and my sun - shine The brightness of thy face.
Is all the grief and an - guish They laid, my Lord, on thee.
And saw the sweat-drops blood - y, That told thy sor - row there.
Re - joice those hearts, my Sav - iour, That live in thee and love.

Nothing But the Blood

R. L.

Rev. Robert Lowry

1. What can wash a - way my sin? Noth-ing but the blood of Je - sus;
2. For my cleans-ing this I see— Noth-ing but the blood of Je - sus;
3. Noth-ing can for sin a - tone— Noth-ing but the blood of Je - sus;
4. This is all my hope and peace—Noth-ing but the blood of Je - sus;
5. Glo - ry! glo - ry! thus I sing— Noth-ing but the blood of Je - sus;

What can make me pure with - in? Noth-ing but the blood of Je - sus.
For my par - don this my plea—Noth-ing but the blood of Je - sus.
Naught of good that I have done—Noth-ing but the blood of Je - sus.
This is all my right-eous - ness—Noth-ing but the blood of Je - sus.
All my praise for this I bring—Noth-ing but the blood of Je - sus.

REFRAIN.

Oh, pre - cious is the flow That makes me white as snow;

No oth - er fount I know, Noth-ing but the blood of Je - sus.

512 The Hand That was Wounded for Me

HATTIE H. PIERSON   D. B. TOWNER

1. The hand that was nailed to the cross of woe, In love reach-es
2. E'en now I can see, thro' a mist of tears, That hand still out-
3. The hand that wrought won-ders in days of old, Holds treas-ure more

down to the world be-low; 'Tis beck-on-ing now to the souls that roam,
stretched o'er the gulf of years, With heal-ing and hope for my sin-sick soul,—
pre-cious than gems or gold, The price of re-demp-tion from sin and shame,

REFRAIN.

And point-ing the way to the heav'n-ly home.
One touch of its fin-ger will make me whole! ⎬ The hand of my Sav-iour
The gift of sal-va-tion thro' Je-sus' name.

I see,............ The hand that was wounded for me;............ 'Twill lead me in
my Sav-iour I see,   was wounded for me;
I see, I see,   for me;

rall.

love to the man-sions a-bove, The hand that was wound-ed for me!............
                                        was wound-ed for me!

513 At Calvary

WM. R. NEWELL

D. B. TOWNER

1. Years I spent in van-i-ty and pride, Car-ing not my Lord was
2. By God's word at last my sin I learned; Then I trem-bled at the
3. Now I've giv'n to Je-sus ev-'ry-thing, Now I glad-ly own him
4. Oh! the love that drew sal-va-tion's plan, Oh! the grace that brought it

cru-ci-fied, Know-ing not it was for me he died On Cal-va-ry.
law I'd spurned, Till my guilt-y soul im-plor-ing, turned To Cal-va-ry.
as my King, Now my rap-tured soul can on-ly sing Of Cal-va-ry.
down to man, Oh! the might-y gulf that God did span At Cal-va-ry.

REFRAIN.

Mer-cy there was great and grace was free, Par-don there was mul-ti-

plied to me, There my burdened soul found lib-er-ty, At Cal-va-ry.

514

Redeemed

"Let the redeemed of the Lord say so." Ps. 107 : 2.

EL. NATHAN   JAMES McGRANAHAN

1. "Re-deemed!" "re-deemed!" Oh, sing the joy- ful strain! Give praise; give
2. What grace! what grace! That he who calmed the wave, Should stoop, my
3. "Re-deemed!" "re-deemed!" The word has brought repose, And joy, and
4. "Re-deemed!" "re-deemed!" O joy, that I should be In Christ, in

1. "Redeemed!" "redeemed!"   Give praise!

praise and glo-ry to his name; Who gave his blood our souls to save, And
soul, my guilt-y soul to save! That he the curse should bear for me, A
joy that each redeemed one knows, Who sees his sins on Je - sus laid, And
Christ, from sin for - ev - er free! For - ev - er free to praise his name, Who

give praise !

purchased freedom for the slave! And pur - chased free - dom for the slave!
sin - ful wretch, his en - e - my ! A sin - ful wretch his en - e - my !
knows his blood the ran-som paid, And knows his blood the ran - som paid.
bore for me the guilt and shame, Who bore for me the guilt and shame!

And purchased freedom, purchased freedom for the slave!
A sinful wretch, his en - e - my, his en - e - my!
And knows his blood the ran-som paid, the ran - som paid.
Who bore for me the guilt and shame, the guilt and shame !

REFRAIN.

* "Redeemed!" "redeemed!" from sin and all its woe! "Re-deemed!" "re-

Redeemed

deemed" e - ter - nal life to know! "Re - deemed!" "re - deemed!" by

Je - sus' blood, "Re - deemed!" "re - deemed!" Oh, praise the Lord!

515 Brookfield L. M.

Anne Steele

T. B. Southgate, 1814, 1868

1. He lives! the great Re - deem - er lives! What joy the blest as - sur - ance gives!
2. Re - peat - ed crimes a - wake our fears, And jus - tice armed with frowns appears;
3. In ev'ry dark, dis - tress - ful hour, When sin and Sa - tan join their pow'r,
4. Great Ad - vo - cate, al - might - y Friend! On him our hum - ble hopes de - pend;

And now, be - fore his Fa - ther, God, He pleads the mer - its of his blood.
But in the Sav - iour's love - ly face Sweet mer - cy smiles, and all is peace.
Let this dear hope re - pel the dart, That Je - sus bears us on his heart.
Our cause can nev - er, nev - er fail, For Je - sus pleads, and must pre - vail.

516

C. WESLEY, 1741

J. ZUNDEL, 1870

1. Love di - vine, all loves ex - cel - ling, Joy of heav'n, to earth come down,
2. Breathe, oh, breathe thy lov - ing Spir - it In - to ev - 'ry troub - led breast;
3. Come, Al-might - y to de - liv - er! Let us all thy life re - ceive;
4. Fin - ish, then, thy new cre - a - tion; Pure, un - spot - ted let us be;

Fix in us thy hum - ble dwell-ing, All thy faith - ful mer - cies crown.
Let us all in thee in - her - it, Let us find thy prom - ised rest;
Sud - den - ly re - turn, and nev - er, Nev - er-more thy temp - les leave.
Let us see our whole sal - va - tion Per - fect - ly se - cured by thee,

Je - sus, thou art all com - pas - sion, Pure, un-bound-ed love thou art;
Take a - way the love of sin - ning, Al - pha and O - me - ga be;
Thee we would be al - ways bless-ing; Serve thee as thy hosts a - bove;
Changed from glo - ry in - to glo - ry Till in heav'n we take our place—

Vis - it us with thy sal - va - tion, En - ter ev - 'ry trem - bling heart.
End of faith, as its be - gin - ning, Set our hearts at lib - er - ty.
Pray, and praise thee with - out ceas - ing; Glo - ry in thy per - fect love.
Till we cast our crowns be - fore thee, Lost in won - der, love, and praise.

517 Sweet is the Story

Rev. E. A. Hoffman   W. T. Giffe

1. Oh, wondrously sweet is the sto - ry, That Je - sus came down from a- bove,
2. Oh, wondrously sweet is his mer - cy, And wondrous-ly free is his grace,
3. Oh, beau- ti - ful sto - ry of Je - sus, The sweet-est that ev - er was told,

To make an a-tone-ment for sin - ners, And bless this poor world with his love.
And wondrously rich his com- pas - sion, For did he not die in our place?
The ho - li- est, pur- est, most pre - cious, That God could to mor-tals un - fold !

REFRAIN.

The sto-ry grows sweeter and sweet - er, And cheers me a - long the way;

The Saviour grows sweeter and dear - er; His love is more precious each day.

Used by permission of THE HOME MUSIC Co., Logansport, Ind.

518 Church of God, Awake

Mrs. EMILY BUGBEE

T. C. O'KANE, by per.

1. Church of God, whose con-quer-ing banners, Float a-long the glo-rious years,
2. In your cost-ly tem-ples pray-ing, "Let thy kingdom come, we pray,"
3. Shake the earth and rend the heav-en, Wake thy sleep-ing chil-dren, Lord,

Gath'ring har-vest rich and gold-en, Sowed in pov-er-ty and tears,
Are but words of i-dle mean-ing If with these we turn a-way.
Till the meas-ure full and e-ven Has been ren-dered at thy word.

On-ward press, the cross is bend-ing Far to-ward the morn-ing skies,
Bound-less wealth to you is giv-en From his hand who owns it all,
Then from out her chrism of sor-row Shall the earth redeemed a-rise,

Speed-y dawn of light por-tend-ing: Church of God a-wake! a-rise!
And his eye be-holds in heav-en What ye ren-der back for all.
And the fair mil-len-nial mor-row Dawn with o-pal tint-ed skies.

REFRAIN.

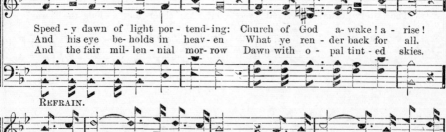

Church of God,........ a-wake! a-rise! Christ, your Head...... and Mas-ter,
Church of God, a-wake! a-rise! Christ, your Head and

520 Something to Do

Words Arr.   W. H. RUEBUSH

1. There's work for the hand and there's work for the heart, Something to do,
2. The sick must be sooth'd and the hun-gry be fed, Something to do,
3. The Mas-ter says "Work," and has shown us the way, Something to do,

some-thing to do; And each should be bus-y per-form-ing his part,
some-thing to do; The nak-ed be cloth'd and the er-ring be led,
some-thing to do; He says "Not to-mor-row, the time is to-day,"

REFRAIN.

There's some-thing for all to do. There's work for the a-ged and
work for the young; There's work for us all and ex-cus-es for none; There's
work for the fee-ble and work for the strong; There's something for all to do.

521 Tell Me the Old, Old Story

"Tell them how great things the Lord hath done." MARK. 5: 19.

Miss KATE HANKEY   W. H. DOANE

1. Tell me the old, old sto - ry, Of un - seen things a - bove, Of Je - sus
2. Tell me the sto - ry slow - ly, That I may take it in— That won - der-
3. Tell me the sto - ry soft - ly, With earn - est tones, and grave; Re - mem - ber!
4. Tell me the same old sto - ry, When you have cause to fear That this world's

and his glo - ry, Of Je - sus and his love. Tell me the sto - ry sim - ply, As
ful re - demption, God's rem - e - dy for sin. Tell me the sto - ry oft - en, For
I'm the sin - ner Whom Je - sus came to save; Tell me the sto - ry al - ways, If
emp - ty glo - ry Is cost - ing me too dear. Yes, and when that world's glory Is

to a lit - tle child, For I am weak and wea - ry, And help-less and de - filed.
I for - get so soon, The "ear-ly dew" of morn-ing Has passed a - way at noon.
you would really be, In an - y time of trou - ble, A com-fort - er to me.
dawn-ing on my soul, Tell me the old, old sto - ry: "Christ Jesus makes thee whole."

REFRAIN.

Tell me the old, old sto - ry, Tell me the old, old sto - ry,

Tell me the old, old sto - ry Of Je - sus and his love.

522 It Must be Told

ALMEDA E. WIGHT

ROBT. C. MARQUIS

1. 'Tis a sweet and ten- der sto - ry, How the Fa- ther from a-bove Looked down
2. 'Tis the ver - y same old sto - ry That has warm'd the cold world's heart Thro' the
3. Say you not that un - a- vail- ing Seem the words you try to speak; Trust the

on his err - ing chil-dren With the pity- ing eyes of love; How he sent his
centuries that have vanished, But its charm can ne'er de-part; There are souls that
Ho - ly Spir - it's unc- tion, It shall strengthen what is weak. Go forth to

Well - Be - lov - ed, For - give- ness to un- fold; That sweet and ten - der
have not heard it, Some hearts so strange- ly cold; To these, O fal - t'ring
do his bid- ding; The truth shall make you bold; Tho' few shall heed your

REFRAIN.

sto - ry, O Christain, must be told.)
Chris - tian, The sto - ry must be told. } It must be told, It
sto - ry, That sto - ry must be told.) It must be told, it must be told, It

must be told, The sto - ry must be told.
must be told, it must be told, The sto - ry must be sweetly told, be oft- en sweet-ly told;

It Must Be Told

That sweet and ten-der sto - ry,
wondrous story.
O Christian, must be told.
be oft-en sweetly told.

523 Rescue the Perishing

F. J. CROSBY
W. H. DOANE

1. Res - cue the per - ish - ing, Care for the dy - ing, Snatch them in pi - ty from
2. Tho' they are slight-ing him, Still he is wait - ing, Wait-ing the pen - i - tent
3. Down in the hu - man heart, Crush'd by the temp-ter, Feel-ings lie bur - ied that
4. Res - cue the per - ish - ing, Du - ty de-mands it; Strength for thy la - bor the

sin and the grave; Weep o'er the err - ing one, Lift up the fall - en,
child to re - ceive. Plead with them earn - est - ly, Plead with them gen - tly;
grace can re - store: Touched by a lov - ing heart, Wak - ened by kind - ness,
Lord will pro - vide: Back to the nar - row way Pa - tient - ly win them;

REFRAIN.

Tell them of Je - sus the might - y to save.
He will for - give if they on - ly be - lieve.
Chords that were brok - en will vi - brate once more.
Tell the poor wan-d'rer a Sav - iour has died.
} Res - cue the per - ish - ing,

Care for the dy - ing; Je - sus is mer - ci - ful, Je - sus will save.

Serving the Lord in Song

Rev. H. H. SHERMAN

E. T. HILDEBRAND

Con spirito.

1. Serv- ing the Lord with glad-ness, Waft-ing the strain a- long; Serv-ing the Lord with
2. Tell- ing the world his good-ness, Ye who his peo- ple are, Tell of the lov - ing
3. Sing of the bless- ed Sav - iour, Praising his wondrous love; Tell how he came to

glad - ness, Prais-ing the Lord in song. Make to him joy - ful mu - sic,
Shep - herd, Tho' ye have wan- dered far. En - ter his gates with prais - es,
save us, Leav- ing his home a - bove. Ye who are now his chil - dren,

In - to his presence sing; All ye his lands and peo-ple, Letting your voices ring.
Blessing his ho - ly name, Speaking his lov - ing kindness, Spreading abroad his fame.
Lift-ing your voic-es high, Sing of the God of mer-cy,—Laud him and magnify.

REFRAIN.

Serv- ing the Lord with gladness, Waft- ing the strain a- long; Serv-ing the Lord with

glad - ness, Prais- ing the Lord in song. En - ter his gates with prais - es,

Serving the Lord in Song

Bless-ing his ho - ly name, Speaking his lov-ing kindness, Spreading a-broad his fame.

525 Let the Lower Lights Be Burning

P. P. B.

P. P. BLISS

1. Bright - ly beams our Fa-ther's mer - cy From his light-house ev - er - more,
2. Dark the night of sin has set - tled, Loud the an - gry bil-lows roar;
3. Trim your fee - ble lamp, my broth - er: Some poor sail - or tem-pest-toss'd,

But to us he gives a keep - ing Of the lights a - long the shore.
Ea - ger eyes are watch-ing, long-ing, For the lights a - long the shore.
Try - ing now to make the har - bor, In the dark-ness may be lost.

REFRAIN.

Let the low - er lights be burn - ing! Send a gleam a - cross the wave!

Some poor faint - ing struggling sea - man You may res - cue, you may save.

526

Have You Sought

"My sheep wandered through all the mountains. EZE. 34 : 6.

F. J. C.

IRA D. SANKEY

1. Have you sought for the sheep that have wandered, Far a - way on the
2. Have you been to the sad and the lone - ly Whose bur - dens are
3. Have you knelt by the sick and the dy - ing, The mes - sage of
4. If to Je - sus you an - swer these ques - tions, And to him have been

dark mount-ains cold? Have you gone, like the ten - der Shep-herd, To
heav - y to bear? Have you car - ried the name of Je - sus, And
mer - cy to tell? Have you stood by the trem-b'ling cap - tive A
faith - ful and true, Then be - hold, in the man- sions yon - der Are

bring them a - gain to the fold? Have you fol - lowed their wea - ry
ten - der - ly breathed it in prayer? Have you told of the great sal -
lone in his dark pris - on cell? Have you point - ed the lost to
crowns of re - joic - ing for you; And there from the King e -

foot - steps? And the wild des - ert waste have you crossed, Nor lin - gered till
va - tion He died on the cross to se - cure? Have you asked them to
Je - sus, And urged them on him to be - lieve? Have you told of the
ter - nal Your wel - come and greet-ing shall be, "In - as- much" as 'twas

Have You Sought?

safe home re - turn - ing, You have gath - ered the sheep that were lost?
trust in the Sav - iour Whose love shall for - ev - er en - dure?
life ev - er - last - ing That all, if they will, may re - ceive?
done for "my breth - ren," E - ven so it was done "un - to me."

527 Must I Go and Empty Handed?

After a month only of Christian life, nearly all of it upon a sick bed, a young man of nearly thirty years lay dying. Suddenly a look of sadness crossed his face, and to the query of a friend he exclaimed : " No, I am not afraid, Jesus saves me now ; but oh, *must I go and empty handed?*"

C. C. LUTHER   DAN. 12 : 3   GEO. C. STEBBINS, by per.

DUET.

1. "Must I go and emp - ty hand - ed," Thus my dear Re - deem - er meet?
2. Not at death I shrink nor fal - ter, For my Sav - iour saves me now;
3. Oh, the years of sin - ning wast - ed, Could I but re - call them now,
4. Oh, ye saints, a - rouse, be earn - est, Up and work while yet 'tis day,

Not one day of ser - vice give him, Lay no tro - phy at his feet.
But to meet him emp - ty hand - ed, Tho't of that now clouds my brow.
I would give them to my Sav - iour, To his will I'd glad - ly bow.
Ere the night of death o'er-takes thee, Strive for souls while still you may.

CHORUS.

"Must I go and emp - ty hand- ed," Must I meet my Sav - iour so?

Not one soul with which to greet him, Must I emp - ty hand - ed go?

Labor On

"The harvest truly is plenteous; but the laborers are few." MATT. 9: 37.

C. R. BLACKALL

Spirited.

W. H. DOANE

1. In the har-vest field there is work to do, For the grain is ripe,
2. Crowd the gar-ner well with its sheaves all bright. Let the song be glad,
3. In the glean-er's path may be rich re-ward, Tho' the time seems long,
4. Lo! the Har-vest Home in the realms a-bove Shall be gained by each

and the reap-ers few; And the Mas-ter's voice bids the work-ers true
and the heart be light; Fill the pre-cious hours, ere the shades of night
and the la-bor hard; For the Mas-ter's joy, with his cho-sen shared,
who has toiled and strove, When the Mas-ter's voice, in its tones of love,

REFRAIN.

Heed the call that he gives to-day.
Take the place of the gold-en day.
Drives the gloom from the dark-est day.
Calls a-way to e-ter-nal day.

La-bor on! la-bor
La-bor on!

on! Keep the bright re-ward in view; For the Mas-ter has
la-bor on!

said, he will strength re-new; La-bor on till the close of day!

Winning Souls for Jesus
"He that winneth souls is wise." Pr. 11 : 30.

J. B. M.   J. B. Mackay

1. Rouse, ye Chris-tian work-ers, be ye up and do-ing; Shall the
2. Wait no lon-ger for some more con-ven-ient sea-son; Souls are
3. Do your spir-its fal-ter at the un-der-tak-ing, Lest one
4. Ev-'ry soul you win shall add a star of beau-ty To the

Mas-ter's king-dom suf-fer at your hands? There are pre-cious souls just
dy-ing 'round you, let them not be lost; Talk or sing of Je-sus,
might re-pay you with a cru-el sneer? Do not let them per-ish;
crown of glo-ry Je-sus has for you; Al-ways thus be work-ing,

:S: Fine.

wait-ing for your woo-ing; Go ye forth and win them, Christ your Lord commands.
they will yield to rea-son; Tell of their re-demp-tion, what a price it cost.
stand no lon-ger quak-ing; Win them for the Mas-ter, tell them he is near.
do-ing all your du-ty, Win-ning souls for Je-sus; they will bless you too.

D.S.—seek-ing to re-claim them, O be up and win-ning souls, While 'tis call'd to-day.

Refrain.

Winning souls, winning souls, win-ning souls for Je-sus, O what joy in

D.S.

win-ning souls from the down-ward way; Out up-on the high-ways,

530 Only Remembered

HORATIUS BONAR, alt.
IRA D. SANKEY

1. Fad - ing a - way like the stars of the morn-ing, Los - ing their
2. Shall we be miss'd though by oth - ers suc-ceed - ed, Reap-ing the
3. On - ly the truth that in life we have spok - en, On - ly the
4. Oh, when the Sav - iour shall make up his jew - els, When the bright

light in the glo - ri - ous sun— Thus would we pass from the
fields we in spring - time have sown? No, for the sow - ers may
seed that on earth we have sown; These shall pass on - ward when
crowns of re - joic - ing are won, Then shall his wea - ry and

earth and its toil - ing, On - ly re - mem - bered by what we have done.
pass from their la - bors, On - ly re - mem - bered by what they have done.
we are for - got - ten, Fruits of the har - vest and what we have done.
faith - ful dis - ci - ples, All be re - mem - bered by what they have done.

REFRAIN.

On - ly re - mem - bered, on - ly re - mem - bered, On - ly re -

mem - bered by what we have done. Thus would we pass from the

Only Remembered

earth and its toil-ing, On - ly re-mem-bered by what we have done.

531 Where Will You Spend Eternity?

Rev. E. A. Hoffman   J. H. Tenney

1. Where will you spend e - ter - ni - ty? This question comes to you and me!
2. Ma - ny are choos-ing Christ to-day, Turn-ing from all their sins a - way,
3. Leav-ing the strait and nar - row way, Go - ing the downward road to - day,
4. Re - pent, believe, this ver - y hour, Trust in the Sav-iour's grace and pow'r,

Tell me, what shall your an - swer be? Where will you spend e - ter - ni - ty?
Heav'n shall their hap-py por - tion be, Where will you spend e - ter - ni - ty?
Sad will their fin - al end - ing be,— Lost thro' a long e - ter - ni - ty!
Then will your joy - ous an - swer be, Saved thro' a long e - ter - ni - ty!

REFRAIN.

E - ter - ni - ty! e - ter - ni - ty! Where will you spend e - ter - ni - ty?
3d v. E - ter - ni - ty! e - ter - ni - ty! Lost thro' a long e - ter - ni - ty!
4th v. E - ter - ni - ty! e - ter - ni - ty! Saved thro' a long e - ter - ni - ty!

532 Christ the Lord Cometh?

"The coming of the Lord draweth nigh" JAMES 5:8.

Rev. E. G. WESLEY

WILLIAM W. BENTLEY

With vigor.

1. Christ the Lord com-eth? per-chance at the dawn, Where earth a-wak-eth to
2. Christ the Lord com-eth? earth's evening may bring Back to his vineyard our
3. Christ the Lord com-eth? man know-eth not when, But when ye think not he

welcome the morn; Hath he not told us the hour draweth near; Watch-ing and
Sav-iour and King; Death shall be conquered and sin o-ver-thrown, When he re-
com-eth a-gain; To all found watching he bringeth no fear, Nev-er a

REFRAIN.

read-y, his summons to hear.)
turn-eth to gath-er his own. } Je-sus is com-ing! we know not how soon,
shad-ow, a part-ing, a tear.)

Com-ing at mid-night, at morn-ing or noon; Even-ing may bring him to

rit.

bear us a-way; For him I'm watching and wait-ing each day.

SUBJECT INDEX

GENERAL INDEX

Titles in Roman, First Lines in Italics, When Titles and First Lines are alike, Capitals.

GENERAL INDEX

GENERAL INDEX

Deutscher Anhang.

Vor der Predigt.

Mel.: " Monmouth."

1

8, 7, 8, 7, 8, 8, 7.

1 O Gott Vater, wir loben dich,
Und deine Güte preisen;
Daß du dich, o Herr! gnädiglich,
An uns neu hast bewiesen.
Und hast uns, Herr, zusammen g'führt,
Uns zu ermahnen durch dein Wort,
Gieb uns Genad zu diesem.

2 Oeffne den Mund, Herr, deiner Knecht,
Gib ihn'n Weisheit darneben,
Daß sie dein Wort mög'n sprechen recht,
Was dient zum frommen Leben,
Und nützlich ist zu deinem Preis,
Gib uns Hunger nach solcher Speis',
Das ist unser Begehren.

3 Gib unserm Herzen auch Verstand,
Erleuchtung hie auf Erden,
Daß dein Wort in uns werd bekannt,
Daß wir fromm mögen werden,
Und leben in Gerechtigkeit,
Achten auf dein Wort allezeit,
So bleibt man unbetrogen.

4 Dein, o Herr! ist das Reich allein,
Und auch die Macht zusammen,
Wir loben dich in der Gemein
Und danken deinem Namen,
Und bitten dich aus Herzensgrund,
Wollst bei uns sein zu dieser Stund,
Durch Jesum Christum, Amen.

Mel.: " Hebron."

2

L. M. 8, 8, 8, 8.

1 Herr Jesu Christ, dich zu uns wend',
Den heiligen Geist du zu uns send',
Der uns mit seiner Gnad' regier',
Und uns den Weg zur Wahrheit führ'.

2 Thu' auf den Mund zum Lobe dein,
Bereit das Herz zur Andacht fein,
Den Glauben mehr, stärk den Verstand,
Daß uns dein Nam' werd wohl bekannt.

3 Bis wir singen mit Gottes Heer:
Heilig, heilig ist Gott der Herr,
Und schauen dich von Angesicht,
In ew'ger Freud und sel'gem Licht.

4 Ehr' sei dem Vater und dem Sohn,
Sammt heil'gem Geist in einem Thron,
Der heiligen Dreieinigkeit
Sei Lob und Preis in Ewigkeit.

Mel.: "Sessions."

3

L. M. 8, 8, 8, 8.

1 O Jesu Christi, wahres Licht;
Erleuchte die dich kennen nicht,
Und bringe sie zu deiner Herd',
Daß ihre Seel' auch selig werd'.

2 Erfüll' mit deinem Gnadenschein,
Die in Irrthum verführet sein;
Auch die, so heimlich fichtet an
In ihrem Sinn ein falscher Wahn.

3 Und was sich sonst verlaufen hat
Von dir, das suche du in Gnad',
Und sein verwund't Gewissen heil',
Laß sie am Himmel haben Theil.

4 Den Tauben öffne das Gehör,
Die Stummen richtig reden lehr,
Die, so bekennen wollen frei,
Was ihres Herzens Glaube sei.

5 Erleuchte, die da sind verblend't,
Bring her, die sich von dir gewend't,
Versammle, die zerstreuet gehn,
Mach feste die im Zweifel stehn.

6 So werden sie mit uns zugleich
Auf Erden und im Himmelreich,
Hier zeitlich, und dort ewiglich,
Für solche Gnade preisen dich.

Mel. : "Greenville."

4

8, 7, 8, 7.

1 Jeſu, Jeſu, Brunn des Lebens!
Stell, ach ſtell dich bei uns ein!
Daß wir jetzund nicht vergebens
Wirken und beiſammen ſein.

2 Du verheißeſt ja den Deinen,
Daß du willeſt Wunder thun,
Und in ihnen willſt erſcheinen,
Ach! erfülls, erfülls auch nun.

3 Herr! wir tragen deinen Namen,
Herr! wir ſind auf dich getauft,
Und du haſt zu deinem Samen
Uns mit deinem Blut erkauft.

4 O! ſo laß uns dich erkennen,
Komm, erkläre ſelbſt dein Wort,
Daß wir dich recht Meiſter nennen,
Und dir dienen immer fort.

5 Biſt du mitten unter denen,
Welche ſich nach deinem Heil
Mit vereintem Seufzen ſehnen,
O! ſo ſei auch unſer Theil.

6 Lehr uns ſingen, lehr uns beten,
Hauch uns an mit deinem Geiſt,
Daß wir vor den Vater treten,
Wie es kindlich iſt und heißt.

7 Sammle die zerſtreuten Sinnen,
Stör' die Flatterhaftigkeit,
Laß uns Licht und Kraft gewinnen,
Zu der Chriſten Weſenheit.

8 O du Haupt der rechten Glieder!
Nimm uns auch zu ſolchen an;
Bring das Abgewich'ne wieder
Auf die frohe Himmels=Bahn.

Nach der Predigt.

Mel. : "Mear."

5

C. M. 8, 6, 8, 6.

1 O Gott, du großer Herr der Welt,
Den Niemand ſehen kann;
Du ſiehſt auf uns vom Himmelszelt,
Hör unſer Seufzen an.

2 Schreib alles was man heut gelehrt,
In unſre Herzen ein,
Und laſſe die ſo es gehört,
Dir auch gehorſam ſein.

3 Erhalt uns fernerhin dein Wort,
Und thu' uns immer wohl,
Damit man ſtets an dieſem Ort,
Gott diene wie man ſoll.

4 Gib Allen eine gute Nacht,
Die chriſtlich heut gelebt,
Und beſſre d e n der unbedacht,
Der Gnade widerſtrebt.

5 Und endlich führe, wenn es Zeit,
Uns in den Himmel ein,
Da wird in deiner Herrlichkeit,
Es ewig Sabbath ſein.

Mel. : "Monmouth."

6

8, 7, 8, 7, 8, 8, 7.

Der Herr uns ſegne und behüt,
Und laß ſein Antlitz leuchten
Ueber uns, und mit ſeiner Güt
Uns Gnade woll' erzeigen;
Der Herr erheb' ſein Angeſicht
Und ſchenk uns ſeines Friedens Licht,
Durch Jeſum Chriſtum, Amen.

Von der Nachfolge Chriſti.

Mel. : "Memphis."

7

C. M. 8, 6, 8, 6.

1 Geh, Seele friſch im Glauben fort,
Und ſei nur unverzagt,
Und dring hier durch die enge Pfort,
Nur Jeſu zugeſagt.

2 Dein Heiland gehet ſelbſt vorher,
Durch Kreuz und Trübſal hin;
So folg du auch durch's rothe Meer,
Es bringt dir viel Gewinn.

3 O Jeſu, Heiland meiner Seel,
Ich komm getroſt zu dir!
Waſch ab mein' Sünd', Emanuel,
Ach komm doch ſelbſt zu mir!

4 Vergib mir meine Missethat
Und was mein Herze nagt,
Und schenk mir, Jesu, deine Gnad,
Daß ich sei unverzagt.

5 Gib, daß ich dir mit Wort und That,
Stets treulich dienen mag;
Und all mein Sorgen deinem Rath
Ganz kindlich übertrag.

6 Die Glieder alle der Gemein',
Laß sie nur eine Seel'
Und deiner Treu empfohlen sein,
Du Wächter Israel.

Mel.: "Balerma."

8 C. M. 8, 6, 8, 6.

1 Was mich auf dieser Welt betrübt,
Das währet kurze Zeit:
Was aber meine Seele liebt,
Das bleibt in Ewigkeit.

2 Drum fahr, o Welt, mit Ehr und Geld,
Und deiner Wollust hin!
Im Kreuz und Spott kann mir mein Gott
Erquicken Herz und Sinn.

3 Die Thorenfreude dieser Welt,
Wie süß sie immer lacht,
Hat schleunig ihr Gesicht verstellt,
Schon Viel' in Leid gebracht.

4 Wer ihr nicht traut, und gläubig baut
Allein auf Gottes Treu,
Der siehet schon die Himmelskron
Und freut sich ohne Reu.

5 Mein Jesus bleibet meine Freud,
Was frag ich nach der Welt!
Welt ist nur Furcht und Traurigkeit,
Die endlich selbst zerfällt.

6 Ich bin ja schon mit Gottes Sohn
Im Glauben hier vertraut,
Der droben sitzt, und hier beschützt
Sein' auserwählte Braut.

7 Ach, Jesu, töbt' in mir die Welt,
Und meinen alten Sinn
Der sich so gerne zu ihr hält, —
Herr, nimm mich selbst nur hin.

8 Und binde mich ganz festiglich
An dich, o Herr, mein Hort!
So irr' dich nicht in deinem Licht,
Bis in die Himmelspfort.

Trost in Kreuz und Trübsal.

Mel.: "Windham."

9 L. M. 8, 8, 8, 8.

1 Ach Gott, ein manches Herzeleid
Begegnet mir in dieser Zeit!
Der schmale Weg ist Trübsal voll,
Den ich zum Himmel wandeln soll.

2 Wie schwerlich läßt sich Fleisch und Blut
Doch zwingen zu dem ew'gen Gut!
Wo soll ich mich denn wenden hin?
Zu dir, Herr Jesu, steht mein Sinn!

3 Bei dir mein Herz Trost, Hülf' und Rath
Allzeit gewiß gefunden hat;
Niemand jemals verlassen ist,
Der sich gegründ't auf Jesum Christ.

4 Drum will ich, weil ich lebe noch,
Das Kreuz dir willig tragen nach.
Mein Gott mach mich dazu bereit,
Es dient zum Besten allezeit.

5 Hilf mir mein Sach' recht greifen an,
Daß ich mein Lauf vollenden kann;
Hilf mir auch zwingen Fleisch und Blut
Für Sünd' und Schanden mich behüt.

6 Erhalt mein Herz im Glauben rein,
So leb' und sterb' ich dir allein.
Ja, Heiland, höre mein' Begier,
Und bring mich endlich heim zu dir!

Vom geistlichen Kampf und Sieg.

Mel.: "Nettleton."

10 8, 7, 8, 7.

1 Ringe recht, wenn Gottes Gnade
Dich nun ziehet und bekehrt,
Daß dein Geist sich recht entlade
Von der Last die ihn beschwert.

2 Ringe, denn die Pfort ist enge,
Und der Lebensweg ist schmal;
Hier bleibt alles im Gedränge,
Was nicht zielt zum Himmelssaal.

3 Kämpfe bis aufs Blut und Leben,
　Dring hinein in Gottes Reich;
　Will der Satan widerstreben,
　Werde weder matt noch weich.

4 Ringe, daß dein Eifer glühe,
　Und die erste Liebe dich
　Von der ganzen Welt abziehe:
　Halbe Liebe hält nicht Stich.

5 Ringe mit Gebet und Schreien,
　Halte damit eifrig an;
　Laß dich keine Zeit gereuen,
　Wärs auch Tag und Nacht gethan.

6 Hast du dann die Perl errungen,
　Denke ja nicht, daß du nun
　Alles Böse hast bezwungen,
　Das uns Schaden pflegt zu thun.

7 Nimm mit Furcht ja deiner Seele,
　Deines Heils mit Zittern wahr:
　Hier in dieser Leibeshöhle
　Schwebst du täglich in Gefahr.

8 Halt ja deine Krone feste,
　Halte männlich was du hast:
　Recht beharren ist das Beste;
　Rückfall ist ein böser Gast.

9 Dies bedenket wohl ihr Streiter,
　Streitet recht und fürchtet euch;
　Geht doch alle Tage weiter,
　Bis ihr kommt ins Himmelreich.

10 Denkt bei jedem Augenblicke,
　Obs vielleicht der letzte sei;
　Bringt die Lampen ins Geschicke,
　Holt stets neues Oel herbei.

Mel.: "What a friend we have in Jesus."
11　　　　8, 7, 8, 7.

1 Wo ist Jesus, mein Verlangen,
　Mein Geliebter und mein Freund?
　Wo ist er denn hingegangen!
　Wo mag er zu finden sein?

2 Ach, ich ruf vor Pein und Schmerzen!
　Wo ist denn mein Jesus hin?
　Keine Ruh hab ich im Herzen,
　Bis ich um und bei ihm bin.

3 Meine Seel ist sehr betrübet,
　Mit viel Sünd und Ungemach!
　Wo ist Jesus, den sie liebet
　Und begehret Tag und Nacht?

4 Ach, wer gibt mir Taubenflügel,
　Daß ich könnt zu jeder Frist
　Fliegen über Berg und Hügel
　Suchen wo mein Jesus ist?

5 Er vertreibt mir Sünd und Hölle;
　Er vertreibt mir Angst und Noth;
　Er erquicket meine Seele,
　Und hilft mir aus aller Noth.

6 Nunmehr will ich nicht mehr lassen,
　Will ihn suchen mehr und mehr;
　In den Wäldern, in den Straßen,
　Will ihn suchen hin und her.

7 Liebster Jesu, laß dich finden,
　Meine Seele schreit zu dir;
　Thu' mir mit den Augen winken,
　Eilend laß mich sein bei dir.

Klag= und Bittlieder.
Mel.: "Hursley."
12　　　L. M.　8, 8, 8, 8.

1 Du unbegreiflich höchstes Gut,
　An welchem klebt mein Herz und Muth
　Ich dürst, o Lebensquell, nach dir!
　Ach hilf, ach lauf, ach komm zu mir!

2 Gleichwie ein Hirsch, der durstig ist,
　Schrei ich zu dir, Herr Jesu Christ!
　Sei du für mich ein Seelentrank;
　Erquicke mich, denn ich bin krank.

3 Ich rufe zu dir mit der Stimm,
　Ich seufze auch, o Herr, vernimm,
　Vernimm es doch, du Gnadenquell,
　Und labe meine dürre Seel!

4 Ein frisches Wasser fehlet mir,
　Herr Jesu, ziehe mich nach dir:
　Nach dir ein großer Durst mich treibt,
　Ach, wär ich dir doch einverleibt!

5 Wo bist du denn, o Bräutigam?
　Wo weidest du, o Gotteslamm?
　An welchem Brünnlein ruhest du?
　Mich dürst, ach laß mich auch dazu!

Mel. : "Ortonville."

13 C. M. 8, 6, 8, 6.

1 Mein Gott! das Herz ich bringe dir,
Zur Gabe und Geschenk;
Du forderst dieses ja von mir,
Deß bin ich eingedenk.

2 Gib mir, mein Kind, dein Herz, sprichst du,
Das ist mir lieb und werth;
Du findest anders doch nicht Ruh
Im Himmel und auf Erd.

3 Nun du, mein Vater, nimm es an,
Mein Herz, veracht es nicht,
Ich geb's so gut ich's geben kann,
Kehr zu mir dein Gesicht.

4 Zwar ist es voller Sündenwust,
Und voller Eitelkeit,
Des Guten aber unbewußt,
Der wahren Frömmigkeit.

5 Doch aber steht es nun in Reu,
Erkennt sein'n Uebelstand,
Und träget jetztund vor dem Scheu,
Woran's zuvor Lust fand.

6 Schenk mir, nach deiner Jesushuld
Gerechtigkeit und Heil;
Erlaß mir auch mein Sündenschuld
Und meiner Strafe Theil.

7 Hilf, daß ich sei von Herzen klein,
Demuth und Sanftmuth üb',
Daß ich von aller Weltlieb rein,
Stets wachs in deiner Lieb.

8 Hilf, daß ich sei von Herzen fromm,
Ohn alle Heuchelei,
Damit mein ganzes Christenthum
Dir wohlgefällig sei.

9 Weg Welt, weg Sünd, dir geb ich nicht
Mein Herz; nur, Jesu, dir
Ist dies Geschenke zugericht,
Behalt es für und für!

Sterb= und Begräbnißlieder.

Mel. : "Monmouth."

14 8, 7, 8, 7, 8, 8, 7.

1 Nun gute Nacht, ihr Liebsten mein,
Ich muß nun von euch scheiden;

Mein' ganze Hoffnung steht allein
In Jesu Tod und Leiden:
Das ist mein Trost in meiner Noth,
Daß er für mich geschmeckt den Tod,
Dadurch er mich erlöset.

2 Ach herzgeliebte Gattin mein,
Laß es dich ja nicht kränken,
Weil Gott mich von der Seite dein
Ins kühle Grab läßt senken!
Ich werde nun befreiet sein
Von allem Elend, Noth und Pein,—
Mein Jesus wird mich trösten.

3 Mein Jesus wird auch trösten dich,
Dein Gatte will er werden;
Halt dich nur an ihm festiglich,
Weil du hier lebst auf Erden.
Bald wird er dich auch holen heim,
Auf daß wir da beisammen sein,
Wo wir uns ewig freuen.

4 Ach allerliebste Kinder mein,
Gott woll auch euch begleiten!
Er selbst woll euer Vater sein,
Weil ich von euch thu scheiden!
Laßt Jesus und sein Wort allein
Doch eures Lebens Richtschnur sein,
So wird der Herr euch segnen.

5 Weil mich der Herr geschenket euch,
Drum werdet seine Glieder,
Und laßt euch führen in sein Reich,
Dann sehen wir uns wieder
In lauter Freud und Herrlichkeit,
Von Ewigkeit zu Ewigkeit,
In Jesu Christo, Amen.

Mel. : "Old Hundred."

15 L. M. 8, 8, 8, 8.

1 Nun bringen wir den Leib zur Ruh,
Und decken ihn mit Erde zu;
Den Leib, der nach des Schöpfers Schluß
Zu Staub und Erde werden muß.

2 Er bleibt nicht immer Asch und Staub,
Nicht immer der Verwesung Raub;
Er wird, wenn Christus einst erscheint,
Mit seiner Seele neu vereint.

3 Hier, Mensch, hier lerne was du bist;
Lern hier was unser Leben ist.
Nach Sorge, Furcht und mancher Noth,
Kommt endlich noch zuletzt der Tod.

4 Schnell schwindet unsre Lebenszeit,
Auf's Sterben folgt die Ewigkeit;
Wie wir die Zeit hier angewandt,
So folgt der Lohn aus Gottes Hand.

5 O sichrer Mensch, besinne dich!
Tod, Grab und Richter nahen sich;
In Allem was du denkst und thust,
Bedenke, daß du sterben mußt.

6 Hier, wo wir bei den Gräbern stehn,
Soll Jeder zu dem Vater flehn:
Ich bitt, o Gott, durch Christi Blut,
Mach's einst mit meinem Ende gut!

7 Laß alle Sünden uns bereun,
Vor unserm Gott uns kindlich scheun!
Wir sind hier immer in Gefahr:
Nehm Jeder seine Seele wahr.

———

Mel.: "Varina."

16
C. M.   8, 6, 8, 6.

1 Es gibt ein wunderschönes Land,
Wo reine Freude wohnt,
Wo Haß und Hader sind verbannt,
Weil dort die Liebe thront.

2 Da schleicht sich auch kein Kummer ein,
Kein Unmuth nagt das Herz;
Die Nacht weicht stets des Lichtes Schein,
Dem Jubel aller Schmerz.

3 Die Herrlichkeit des Herrn durchglüht
Das Ganze nah und fern;
Ein ew'ger Frühlingsmorgen blüht,
Und feiert Lob dem Herrn.

4 Der müde Pilger gehet da,
In Gottes Ruhe ein;
Im ewigen Hallelujah
Verstummt der Erden Pein.

5 O wunderschönes Gottesland,
Ach, wenn erreich ich dich?
Wie lang bin ich von dir verbannt,
Wie lang verbirgst du dich?

6 Gern leg ich ab die schwere Last,
Gern allen Erdentand;
In dir nur such ich meine Rast
Du schönes Gottesland.

———

Mel.: "Webb."

17
7, 6, 7, 6, 7, 6, 7, 6.

1 Bedenke, Mensch, das Ende,
Bedenke deinen Tod;
Der Tod kommt oft behende:
Der heute frisch und roth
Kann morgen und geschwinde
Hinweg gestorben sein;
Drum bilde dir, o Sünder,
Ein täglich Sterben ein!

2 Bedenke, Mensch, das Ende,
Bedenke das Gericht;
Es müssen alle Stände
Vor Jesus Angesicht:
Kein Mensch ist ausgenommen,
Hier muß ein Jeder dran,
Und Jerd den Lohn bekommen
Nachdem er hat gethan.

3 Bedenke, Mensch, das Ende,
Der Höllen Angst und Leid,
Daß dich nicht Satan blende
Mit seiner Eitelkeit!
Hier ist ein kurzes Freuen,
Dort aber ewiglich
Ein kläglich Schmerzenschreien
Ach, Sünder! hüte dich.

4 Bedenke, Mensch, dein Ende,
Bedenke stets die Zeit,
Daß dich ja nichts abwende
Von jener Herrlichkeit,
Damit vor Gottes Throne
Die Seele wird verpflegt:
Dort ist die Lebenskrone
Den Frommen beigelegt.

5 Herr, lehre mich bedenken
Der Zeiten letzte Zeit,
Daß sich nach dir zu lenken
Mein Herze sei bereit:
Laß mich den Tod betrachten,
Und deinen Richterstuhl;
Laß mich auch nicht verachten
Der Höllen Feuerpfuhl.

6 Hilf, Gott, daß ich in Zeiten
Auf meinen letzten Tag
Mit Buße mich bereiten,
Und täglich sterben mag.

Im Tod und vor Gerichte
Steh mir, o Jesu bei,
Daß ich im Himmelslichte
Zu wohnen würdig sei!

Gute Nacht.

18

Pf. 4, 9.: Ich liege und schlafe ganz mit Frieden.

1. Gu = te Nacht, ihr mei = ne Lie = ben, Gu = te Nacht, ihr Her = zens = freund',
Gu = te Nacht, die sich be = trü = ben, Und aus Lieb für mich jetzt weint!

Scheid ich gleich wohl von euch ab, Und ihr legt mein'n Leib ins Grab

Wird er wie = der auf = er = ste = hen Und ich werd euch e = wig se = hen.

2 O, wie wird ich euch umfassen
Und euch herzen mit Begier!
Muß ich euch ein' Zeit verlassen,
Welches zwar betrübet hier,
Bringts ein Tag doch wieder ein,
Wenn wir werden selig sein;
Ewig wird kein' Müh uns reuen,
Tausend, tausend Mal mehr freuen.

3 Meiner zarten Jugend Jahren
Und vergnügte Tage mein
Sind so schnell dahin gefahren,
Daß man meint, es könnt nicht sein;
Wenn man lebt ohn Klag und Noth,
Hat in kurzer Zeit der Tod
Schon die Seel vom Leib getrennet,
Daß man mich im Sarg kaum kennet.

4 Weil mein Jammer ist zu Ende,
Mein' herzliebste Eltern werth,
Dankt es Gottes Liebeshände,
Seid nicht mehr um mich beschwert.
Brüder, Schwestern, habt gut' Nacht,
Denkt: Gott hat es wohl gemacht;
Thut Er zwar eu'r Herz betrüben,
Thut Er mich und euch doch lieben.

Von der Liebe Gottes.

Mel.: "Merrick."

19   8, 7, 8, 7, 8, 7.

1 Ich will lieben und mich üben,
Daß ich meinem Bräutigam
Nun in allem mag gefallen,
Welcher an des Kreuzesstamm
Hat sein Leben für mich geben
Ganz geduldig als ein Lamm.

2 Ich will lieben, und mich üben
Im Gebet zu Tag und Nacht,
Daß nun balde, alles Alte
In mir werd zum Grab gebracht,
Und hingegen allerwegen
Alles werde neu gemacht.

3 Ich will lieben, und mich üben
Daß ich rein und heilig werd,
Und mein Leben führe eben,
Wie es Gott von mir begehrt;
Ja, im Wandel, Thun und Handel
Sei unsträflich auf der Erd.

4 Ich will lieben, und mich üben
Meine ganze Lebenszeit,
Mich zu schicken und zu schmücken
Mit dem reinen Hochzeitkleid,
Zu erscheinen, mit den Reinen,
Auf des Lammes Hochzeitfreud.

Morgenlied.

Mel.: "Arlington."

20   C. M.   8, 6, 8, 6.

1 Nun sich die Nacht geendet hat,
Die Finsterniß zertheilt,
Wacht Alles, was am Abend spat
Zu seiner Ruh' geeilt.

2 Hab Dank, o Jesu, habe Dank
Für deine Lieb' und Treu!
Hilf, daß ich dir mein Lebenlang
Von Herzen dankbar sei!

3 Gedenke, Herr, auch heut an mich,
An diesem ganzen Tag,
Und wende von mir gnädiglich,
Was dir mißfallen mag!

4 Erhör, o Jesu, meine Bitt,
Nimm meine Seufzer an,
Und laß all meine Tritt und Schritt
Gehn auf der rechten Bahn!

5 Gib deinen Segen diesen Tag
Zu meinem Werk und That,
Damit ich fröhlich sagen mag:
Wohl dem, der Jesum hat!

6 Wohl dem, der Jesum bei sich führt,
Schließt ihn ins Herz hinein;
So ist sein ganzes Thun geziert,
Und er kann selig sein!

Abendlieder.

Mel.: "Ortonvile."

21   C. M.   8, 6, 8, 6.

1 Nun sich der Tag geendet hat,
Und keine Sonn' mehr scheint,
Ruht alles was sich abgematt't,
Und was zuvor geweint.

2 Der du den Schlaf nicht nöthig hast,
Mein Gott, du schlummerst nicht,
Die Finsterniß ist dir verhaßt,
Weil du bist selbst das Licht.

3 Gedenke, Herr, doch auch an mich
In dieser finstern Nacht,
Und schenke mir gnädiglich,
Den Schirm von deiner Macht.

4 Wend ab des Satans Wütherei,
Durch deiner Engel Schaar,
So bin ich aller Sorgen frei,
Und bringt mir nichts Gefahr.

5 Drauf thu' ich meine Augen zu,
Und schlafe fröhlich ein;
Mein Gott wacht jetzt in meiner Ruh,
Wer wollte traurig sein?

6 Soll diese Nacht die letzte sein
In diesem Jammerthal,
So führ mich in den Himmel ein,
Zur auserwählten Zahl.

7 Und also leb und sterb ich dir,
O Herr Gott Zebaoth!
Im Tod und Leben hilf du mir,
Aus aller Angst und Noth.

———

Mel.: "Hebron."

22 L. M. 8, 8, 8, 8.

1 Ach bleib bei uns, Herr Jesu Christ,
Weil es nun Abend worden ist;
Dein göttlich Wort das helle Licht,
Laß ja bei uns auslöschen nicht.

2 In dieser letzt betrübten Zeit,
Verleih uns, Herr, Beständigkeit,
Daß wir dein Wort in Einigkeit,
Beleben recht in dieser Zeit.

3 Daß wir in guter stiller Ruh
Dies zeitlich Leben bringen zu;
Und wenn das Leben neiget sich,
Laß uns einschlafen seliglich.

———

Christtags-Lieder.

Mel.: "Arlington."

23 C. M. 8, 6, 8, 6.

1 Auf, Seele, auf und säume nicht!
Es bricht das Licht hervor;
Der Wunderstern gibt dir Bericht,
Der Held sei vor dem Thor.

2 Geh' weg aus deinem Vaterland,
Zu suchen solchen Herrn;
Laß deine Augen sein gewandt
Auf diesen Morgenstern.

3 Gib Acht auf diesen hellen Schein,
Der dir aufgangen ist;
Er führet dich zum Kindelein,
Das heißet Jesus Christ.

4 Er ist der Held aus Davids Stamm,
Die theure Saronsblum,
Und auch das wahre Gotteslamm,
Israels Preis und Ruhm.

5 Drum höre, merke, sei bereit,
Verlaß des Vaters Haus,
Die Freundschaft, deine Eigenheit,
Geh von dir selbsten aus.

6 Und mache dich behende auf,
Befreit von aller Last;
Ja laß nicht ab von deinem Lauf,
Bis du dies Kindlein hast.

7 Du, du bist selbst das Bethlehem,
Die rechte Davids Stadt;
Wenn du dein Herze machst bequem
Zu solcher großen Gnad.

8 Da findest du das Lebensbrod,
Das dich erlaben kann,
Für deiner Seelen Hungersnoth
Das allerbeste Mann'.

———

Mel.: "Wells."

24 L. M. 8, 8, 8, 8.

1 Vom Himmel hoch da komm ich her,
Ich bring euch Heil und Gnadenlehr;
Der guten Lehr bring ich so viel,
Davon ich singend sagen will.

2 Euch ist ein Kindlein heut gebor'n,
Von einer Jungfrau auserkor'n;
Ein Kindelein so zart und fein,
Soll eure Freud und Wonne sein.

3 Es ist der Herr Christ, unser Gott,
Der will euch führ'n aus aller Noth;
Er will der Heiland selber sein, —
Von allen Sünden machen rein.

4 Er bringt euch alle Seligkeit,
Die Gott der Vater hat bereit,
Daß ihr mit uns im Himmelreich
Sollt leben nun und ewiglich.

5 Deß laßt uns alle fröhlich sein,
Und mit den Hirten gehn hinein,
Zu sehen, was Gott hat beschert,
Und uns mit seinem Sohn verehrt.

6 Das hat also gefallen dir,
Die Wahrheit anzuzeigen mir,
So tröste selbst damit mein Herz:
Es kommt ein beff'res Leben.

Neujahrs-Lied.

Mel. : "Woodland."

25   C. M. 8, 6, 8, 6.

1 Heut fänget an das neue Jahr,
Mit neuem Gnadenschein;
Wir loben alle unsern Gott,
Und singen insgemein.

2 Seh, wie sich Gottes Vaterhuld
Erzeiget euch aufs neu;
Wir merken seine Wundergüt,
Und spüren seine Treu.

3 Was suchet doch der fromme Gott
Durchs Gute, so er thut?
Ach, wer uns das recht lehren wollt,
Erweckte Herz und Muth!

4 Der Geist der spricht es deutlich aus,
Er leitet euch zur Buß'!
Wir bücken uns von Herzensgrund,
Und fallen ihm zu Fuß.

5 Wohl euch, wenn dieses recht geschieht
Und geht von Herzensgrund;
Ja, ja, es schreiet Seel und Geist,
Und nicht allein der Mund.

6 Thut das, und haltet brünstig an,
Bis Gott geholfen hat;
Wir senken uns in seine Huld,
Und hoffen blos auf Gnad.

7 Das ist gewiß der rechte Weg,
Der euch nicht trügen kann;
Ach Jesu, Jesu, seufzen wir,
Nimm du dich unser an!

8 Den hat euch Gott zum Gnadenstuhl
Und Mittler vorgestellt;
Drum nehmen wir ihn willig auf,
Er ist das Heil der Welt.

Vom Leiden und Sterben Jesu Christi.

Mel. : "Happy Zion."

26   8, 7, 8, 7, 8, 7.

1 Setze dich, mein Geist, ein wenig,
Und beschau dies Wunder groß,
Wie dein Herr und Ehrenkönig
Hängt am Kreuze nackt und bloß!
Schau die Liebe, die ihn triebe
Zu dir, aus des Vaters Schooß!

2 Ob dich Jesus liebt von Herzen,
Kannst du hier am Kreuze sehn:
Schau, wie alle Höllenschmerzen
Ihm bis in die Seele gehn!
Fluch und Schrecken Ihn bedecken;
Höre doch sein Klaggetön!

3 Seine Seel', von Gott verlassen,
Ist betrübt bis in den Tod,
Und sein Leib hängt gleichermaßen
Voller Wunden, Blut und Koth;
Alle Kräfte, alle Säfte,
Sind erschöpft in höchster Noth.

4 Dies sind meiner Sünden Früchte,
Die, mein Heiland! ängsten dich;
Dieser Leiden schwer Gewichte
Sollt zum Abgrund drücken mich;
Diese Nöthen, die dich tödten,
Sollt ich fühlen ewiglich.

5 Doch, du hast für mich besieget
Sünde, Tod und Höllenmacht;
Du hast Gottes Recht vergnüget,
Seinen Willen ganz vollbracht,
Und mir eben zu dem Leben,
Durch dein Sterben Bahn gemacht.

6 Ach, ich Sündenwurm der Erden!
Jesu, stirbst du mir zu gut?
Soll dein Feind erlöset werden
Durch dein eigen Herzensblut?
Ich muß schweigen und mich beugen
Für dies unverdiente Gut.

7 Seel' und Leben, Leib und Glieder,
Gibst du alle für mich hin;
Sollt ich dir nicht schenken wieder
Alles, was ich hab und bin!
Ich bin deine, ganz alleine,
Dir verschreib ich Herz und Sinn.

8 Dir will ich, durch deine Gnade,
Bleiben bis in Tod getreu;
Alle Leiden, Schand und Schade,
Sollen mich nicht machen scheu;
Deinen Willen zu erfüllen,
Meiner Seele Speise sei.

9 Tränk mit deinem Blut mich Armen,
Es zerbricht der Sünden Kraft;

Es kann bald mein Herz erwärmen,
Und ein neues Leben schafft.
Ach, durchfließe! Ach durchsüße
Mich mit diesem Lebensaft!

Mel.: "Brown."

27   C. M.   8, 6, 8, 6.

1 Wie bist du mir so innig gut,
Mein Hoherpriester du!
Wie theu'r und kräftig ist dein Blut!
Es setzt mich stets in Ruh.

2 Wenn mein Gewissen zagen will
Vor meiner Sündenschuld,
So macht dein Blut mich wieder still,
Setzt mich bei Gott in Huld.

3 Es gebet dem gedrängten Sinn
Freimüthigkeit zu dir,
Daß ich in dir zufrieden bin,
Wie arm ich bin in mir.

4 Hab ich gestrauchelt hier und da,
Und will verzagen fast,
So spür ich dein Versöhnblut nah,
Das nimmt mir meine Last.

5 So sänftigt meinen tiefen Schmerz
Durch deine Balsamskraft;
Es stillet mein gestörtes Herz,
Und neuen Glauben schafft.

6 Zieh mich in dein versöhnend Herz,
Mein Jesu, tief hinein;
Laß es in aller Noth und Schmerz
Mein Schloß und Zuflucht sein.

7 Kommt groß' und kleine Sünder doch,
Die ihr mühselig seid!
Das liebend Herz steht offen noch,
Das euch von Sünd befreit.

Einladung an die Jugend.

Mel.: "Hebron."

28   L. M.   8, 8, 8, 8.

1 Ihr jungen Helden, aufgewacht!
Die ganze Welt muß sein veracht't;
Drum eilt, daß ihr in kurzer Zeit
Macht eure Seelen wohl bereit.

2 Was ist die Welt mit allem Thun!
Den Bund gemacht mit Gottes Sohn;

Das bleibt der Seel in Ewigkeit
Ein Zuckersüße Lust und Freud.

3 Ja nimmermehr geliebt die Welt,
Vielmehr sich Jesu zugesellt,
So überkommt man Glaubenskraft,
Daß man auch bald ihr Thun bestraft.

4 Nun weg hiemit, du Eitelkeit!
Es ist mir nun zu lieb die Zeit,
Daß ich sie nicht mehr so anwend,
Daß ich den Namen Gottes schänd.

5 Ich hab es nun bei mir bedacht,
Und diesen Schluß gar fest gemacht,
Daß es mir nur soll Jesus sein,
Und wollt mein Fleisch nicht ganz darein.

6 Zur falschen Welt und ihrem Trug
Spricht meine Seel: es ist genug!
Zu lang hab ich die Lust geliebt,
Und damit meinen Gott betrübt.

Mel.: "Mt. Vernon."

29   8, 7, 8, 7.

1 Kinder, lernt die Ordnung fassen,
Die zum selig werden führt.
Dem muß man sich überlassen,
Der die ganze Welt regiert.

2 Höret auf zu widerstreben,
Gebt euch eurem Heiland hin,
So gibt er euch Geist und Leben,
Und verändert euren Sinn.

3 Selber könnt ihr gar nichts machen,
Denn ihr seid zum Guten todt;
Jesus führt die Seelensachen,
Er allein hilft aus der Noth.

4 Bittet ihn um wahre Reue;
Bittet ihn um Glaubenskraft;
So geschieht's, daß seine Treue
Neue Herzen in euch schafft.

5 Sucht Erkenntniß eurer Sünden;
Forscht des bösen Herzensgrund;
Lernt die Gräuel in euch finden;
Da ist alles ungesund.

6 Und als solche kranke Sünder
Sucht der Gnade Licht und Spur;
Werdet rechte Glaubenskinder,
Denn der Glaube rettet nur.

7 Glauben heißt die Gnad erkennen
  Die den Sünder selig macht;
  Jesum meinen Heiland nennen,
  Der auch mir das Heil gebracht.

Mel. : "Nettleton."

30   8, 7, 8, 7.

1 Kinder, eilt euch zu bekehren;
  Jesus stehet vor der Thür.
  Seine Stimme läßt er hören:
  Gib, mein Sohn, dein Herze mir.

2 Ihm müßt ihr das Jawort geben,
  Da er euch so freundlich lockt;
  Wahrlich, länger widerstreben
  Macht euch endlich ganz verstockt.

3 Ist nicht das schon großer Schade,
  Daß ihr so, die Jugendzeit,
  Ohne Gott und seine Gnade
  Zugebracht in Sicherheit?

4 Nun, die ihr noch todt in Sünden
  Und entfernt von Jesu seid,
  Hört, ihr könnt noch Gnade finden—
  Kommet, alles ist bereit.

5 Jesu Herz ist voll Erbarmen
  Jetzt noch wie es immer war;
  Ach, er reichet zu euch Armen
  Seine beiden Hände dar!

6 Kinder, gebet mir die Herzen;
  Sagt, was hab' ich euch gethan?
  Seht ich suche euch mit Schmerzen:
  Eure Rettung liegt mir an.

7 Kinder, schauet meine Wunden,
  Die ihr mir geschlagen habt!
  Denket, was ich hab empfunden,
  Wegen eurer Missethat!

Nun begehr ich nichts zu haben
  Als daß euer Herz mich liebt,
  Und ich geb euch beßf're Gaben,
  Als euch diese Welt je gibt.

9 Ich will alle Schuld vergeben,
  Meinen Frieden schenk ich euch,
  Kraft und Freude, Trost und Leben,
  Und ein ewig Himmelreich.

10 Kinder, seid doch nicht so träge!
  Seht doch Jesu Liebe an!
  Wird dabei das Herz nicht rege.
  Was ist denn, das rühren kann?

Kommt, Brüder.

31

Röm. 12, 11: Seid nicht träge was ihr thun sollt.

1. Kommt, Brü = der, steht nicht still = le, O laßt uns vor = wärts zieh'n,
Den Leib wird bald um = fan = gen Der Er = de dun = kles Grab,

Seht nur, wie un = ser Le = ben So rast = los eilt da = hin!
D'rum weil's noch "Heu = te" hei = ßet, Er = greift den Pil = ger = stab!

Chor.

In dem Him = mel ist Ruh', in dem Him = mel ist Ruh', in dem
Him = mel, in dem Him = mel, in dem Him = mel ist Ruh'.

2 Schon sind viel unf'rer Lieben
   Im ober'n Canaan;
  Sie haben überwunden
   Und ruhen nun fortan.
  Wir haben noch zu kämpfen,
   Wie's uns verordnet ist;
  Doch werden wir auch siegen
   Wie sie durch Jesum Christ.
              Chor.

3 Der große Herr und König
   Geht uns voran im Streit
  Er führt durch's Kreuz zur Krone,
   Durch Nacht zur Herrlichkeit.
  O laß uns auf Ihn sehen
   Mit Wachsamkeit und Fleh'n
  Bis wir als Ueberwinder
   In Zion auch eingeh'n.
              Chor.

Mel.: "Marlow."

32   C. M. 8, 6, 3, 6.

1 Wer will mit uns nach Zion gehn,
  Wo Christus selbst uns weid't,
  Wo wir um seinen Thron her stehn
  In höchst verklärter Freud?

2 Wo der Märtyrer große Zahl
  In lauter Prangen gehn,
  Und die Propheten allzumal,
  Auch die Aposteln stehn.

3 Wo wir so manche schöne Schaar
  Dort werden treffen an;
  Wo sie erzählen wunderbar,
  Was Gott für sie gethan.

4 Ach Gott, was wird für Freude sein
  In jenem Land und Ort,
  Da wo kein Tod, noch Schmach, noch Pein
  Wird herrschen fort und fort.

5 Dort wird die kleine Zionsschaar,
  Die hier nicht war erkannt,
  Gott für sich selbsten stellen dar
  In ihrem Vaterland.

6 Ach Gott! wann wird das frohe Jahr
  Doch endlich brechen ein,
  Daß Zions vielgeliebte Schaar
  Im Triumph ziehet heim?

Abendmahl.

Mel.: "Webb."

33   7, 6, 7, 6, 7, 6, 7, 6.

1 Wir werfen uns danieder
  Vor dir, Herr Zebaoth!
  Und singen Dankeslieder,
  Und feiern Jesu Tod;

Er war in seinem Leben
Der Tugend stets getreu;
O gib, daß unser Leben
Dem seinen ähnlich sei!

2 Den Tag vor Christi Leiden,
Beim letzten Abendmahl,
Indem er wollte scheiden
Aus diesem Jammerthal,
Hat er das Brod gebrochen,
Und ausgetheilt den Wein,
Gesegnet und gesprochen:
Dies thut und denket mein!

3 Er sprach: nehmt hin und esset,
Dies ist mein Leib und Blut,
Damit ihr nicht vergesset
Was meine Liebe thut;
Freiwillig will ich sterben
Am Kreuz, zum Heil für euch:
Wer an mich glaubt soll erben
Mit mir das Himmelreich.

4 Aus Gottes Munde gehet
Das Evangelium;
Auf diesem Grund bestehet
Das wahre Christenthum;
Gott selbst hat es gelehret,
Der nicht betrügen kann;
Wohl dem der's gerne höret,
Und es nimmt willig an.

Mel.: " Sessions."

34   8, 8, 8, 8.

1 Der Heiland rufet mir und dir:
Wen dürstet, der komm her zu mir!
Ich selber bin die Lebensquell,
Ich labe deine dürre Seel.

2 Ach, komm und kaufe ohne Geld,
Auch Milch und Wein, wie dir's gefällt!
Wer arm und dürftig, und nichts hat,
Der ess' und trink' umsonst sich satt.

3 Nun ist die schöne Gnadenzeit,
Die Gnadentafel ist bereit;
Ach, komm nur bald zu mir mit Dank,
Ich geb mich dir zur Speis und Trank!

4 Ich will, ich will, ich komme jetzt
Zum Gnadentisch, der mir gesetzt,

Zu laben mich an Jesu Brust,
Zu haben reine Himmelslust!

5 Ganz rein ist diese Himmelsgluth,
Sie schmeckt dem Herzen süß und gut.
Ach, sucht und schmeckt, wie gut er ist,
Und komm zu ihm wer durstig ist.

6 Laß nimmer, nimmer, niemals ab,
Bleib Gott getreu bis in das Grab!
Im Himmel folgt der große Lohn,
Das Hochzeitskleid, die Ehrenkron.

Vom Fußwaschen.

Mel.: " Webb."

35   7, 6, 7, 6, 7, 6, 7, 6.

1 Von Herzen woll'n wir singen
In Fried' und Einigkeit,
Mit Fleiß und Ernste dringen
Zu der Vollkommenheit,
Daß wir Gott mögen g'fallen,
Wozu er uns will hon,
Das merkt ihr Frommen alle,
Laßt euchs zu Herzen gohn.

2 O Gott! du wollst uns geben,
Jetzt und zu aller Stund,
In deinem Wort zu leben,
Zu halten deinen Bund;
Wollst uns vollkommen machen,
In Fried und Einigkeit,
Daß du uns findest wachen,
Und allezeit bereit.

3 So thut zu Herzen fassen
Die Tugend Jesu Christ,
Wie er ihn nicht hat lassen
Dienen zu jeder Frist.
Er spricht: ich bin nicht kommen,
Daß man mir dienen soll,
Sondern für alle Frommen
Mein Leben lassen woll.

4 Damit thut er anzeigen
Demuth und Niedrigkeit,
Dazu die große Liebe,
Die er beweisen thät,
Da er auf Erd' gewesen
Bei seinen Jüngern schon,
Die Füß' thät ihnen wäschen,
Zeigt ihn'n die Liebe an.

5 Also thät er ihn'n sagen:
Laßt euch zu Herzen gohn,
Was ich euch jetzt than habe,
Sollt ihr zum Vorbildhan.
Also sollt ihr's erfüllen,
Einander lieben thun,
Das ist mein's Vaters Willen,
Kein'r soll den andern lahn.

6 O ihr geliebte Brüder,
Und Schwestern allgemein!
Dieweil wir alle Glieder
In einem Leibe sein,
Sa laß uns treu beweisen,
Einander lieben thun,
Dadurch wird Gott gepreiset
In seinem höchsten Thron.

Scheidelied.

Mel.: "Brown."

36 C. M. 8, 6, 8, 6.

1 Nun scheiden wir, ihr Herzensfreund
Von diesem Orte fort;
Ob wir zwar jetzt betrübet sein,
Wir sehn uns wieder dort.

2 Ach wachet, liebste Brüder mein,
Auf allem eurem Weg!
Laßt Gottes Wort die Richtschnur sein,
Das zeigt den Lebenssteg.

3 Ihr Schwestern mein, es geht nun fort
Zum eignen Kampfplatz hin;
Da wacht und betet immerfort,
Es bringet viel Gewinn.

4 Nun laßt uns alle munter sein
In unserm Pilgerstand,
Bis wir zur Ruhe gehen ein,
Im rechten Vaterland!

Ehestandslied.

Mel.: "Hebron."

37 L. M. 8, 8, 8, 8.

1 Gott, der du alles wohl bedacht,
Die gute Ordnung auch gemacht,

Daß in der Ehe Mann und Weib,
Vereinigt sein, Ein Fleisch, Ein Leib.

2 Wend ab des Satans Macht und List,
Als der ein Feind der Ehe ist,
Daß der unreine Geist ja nicht
Bei ihnen Haß und Zank anricht!

3 Hilf, daß von ihnen stets mit Fleiß,
In ihres Angesichtes Schweiß,
Die Nahrung werde rortgesetzt,
Und das Gewissen nicht verletzt!

4 Gib, daß sie oft einmüthiglich,
Mit Beten kommen, Herr, vor dich,
Und rufen dich um Segen an,
Auf daß ihr Werk sei wohl gethan!

5 Wenn sie auch drückt des Kreuzes Last,
So laß sie denken, daß du hast
Zur Hülf' und Trost durch deine Hand,
Selbst eingesetzet diesen Stand.

6 Laß diese Ehelente nun,
Nach solchem deinen Willen thun,
Und haben ein' erwünschte Eh',
Ohn' Herzeleid und alles Weh.

7 Das bitten wir, o Vater, dich!
Regiere sie selbst gnädiglich,
Daß sie in wahrer Heiligkeit,
Zubringen ihre Lebenszeit.

Verschiedene Lieder.

Mel.: "Bethany."

38

1 Näher, mein Gott zu Dir,
Näher zu Dir!
Wenn auch des Kreuzes Last
Lieget auf mir,
Doch will ich singen hier:
Näher, mein Gott, zu Dir, :,:
Näher zu Dir!

2 Sinkt auch die Sonne hin,
Bin ich allein,
Legt sich sein müdes Haupt
Hin auf den Stein;
O, daß ein Traum mich führ
Näher, mein Gott zu Dir, :,:
Näher zu Dir!

3 Zeig mir die Stufen, die
Himmelan gehn;
Laß mich in Allem nur
Deine Huld sehn.
Boten zuwinken mir:
Näher, mein Gott, zu Dir, :,:
Näher zu Dir!

4 Dann wird nach Schlaf und Nacht
Lichthell es sein,
Und mit verjüngtem Muth
Salb ich den Stein.
So hilft auch Trübsal mir,
Näher, mein Gott, zu Dir, :,:
Näher zu Dir!

5 Und wenn auf Flügeln einst
Auffährt mein Geist,
Weit übers Sternenheer
Aufwärts sich reißt,
Dann bleibt das Höchste mir:
Näher, mein Gott, zu Dir, :,:
Näher zu Dir!

———

39 Mel.: "Oh Happy Day."

1 Glücksel'ger Tag, da ich erkor
Dich, Jesum, meinen Gott und Herrn!
Wie wallt mein Herz voll Freud' empor,
Die Gnad zu rühmen nah und fern!

Chor: Sel'ger Tag, sel'ger Tag,
Da Jesus mich von Schuld freisprach;
Er lehrt mich Sein Gebot versteh'n,
Und fröhlich meines Weges geh'n.

2 O sel'ges Band, das mich vereint
Mit Ihm, der einzig liebenswerth;
Lobsinge, Seele, diesem Freund,
Der nichts als Lieb und Lob begehrt!
Chor.

3 Nun ist das große Werk gescheh'n;
Der Herr ist mein, ich bin des Herrn;
Er zog mich, daß ich konnte geh'n,
Er rief mich, und ich folgte gern.
Chor.

4 Nun ruh, mein lang getheiltes Herz,
Auf diesem Felsen kannst du ruh'n;
Hier bleibe, bleib in Freud und Schmerz,
Denn, was du suchtest, hast du nun.
Chor.

5 Ihr Himmel höret diesen Bund,
Und täglich will ich ihn erneu'n,
Bis in des Lebens letzter Stund
Ich mich des sel'gen Tags werd freu'n,
Chor.

———

40 Mel.: "Oh How Happy are They."

1 O wie selig sind die,
Schon in Jesu allhie,
Die des Erbtheils im Himmel gewiß!
Welch ein seliger Stand,
Da zuerst Er mich fand,
O des Himmels Genuß, wie so süß!

2 Ja, der Trost, der war mein,
Da in Jesu allein
Die Vergebung der Sünden ich fand;
Da mein Herz an Ihm hing,
Welche Freud' ich empfing!
O mein Gott, welch ein seliger Stand!

3 Ja, der Himmel war nah,
Mein Erlöser war da,
Und die Engel, die lobten mit mir;
Und ich fiel Ihm zu Fuß
In der Liebe Genuß,
Die mein Jesus bewiesen an mir.

4 Und den ganzen Tag lang
War mein Freudengesang
Nur von Jesu, dem Heiland der Welt!
Ach, ich rief: Er liebt mich,
Denn Er opferte Sich
An dem Kreuz für die Sünden der Welt!

5 O begeisterte Zeit,
Welche heilige Freud'
Durch das Blut des Erlösers schon hier!
Von dem Heiland bewohnt,
Bin ich reichlich belohnt
Und erfüllet mit göttlicher Zier.

6 O wie tröstlich im Schmerz
Ist der Glaub', der mein Herz
Von den Schulden und Sünden befreit!
Was ich leb, leb ich Gott
In der Heiligung fort,
Bis der Glaube durch Schauen erfreut!

Nach dem Englischen von Carl Wesley, † 1788.

41 Mel. : " We'll work till Jesus comes.''

1 Wir zieh'n nach dem verheiß'nen Land,
Ein Land so wunderschön,
Die Sünde ist dort ganz verbannt,
Man hört blos Lobgetön.

Chor: Ich wart' bis Jesus kommt,
Ich wart' bis Jesus kommt,
Ich wart' bis Jesus kommt,
Und er mich holet heim.

2 Kommt, laßt uns Alle Hand in Hand
Nach diesem Lande zieh'n,

Das Vaterland ist es genannt,
Die Kinder kommen hin.
Chor.

3 Dort ist der Heiland Jesus Christ,
Der gute Lämmerhirt,
Der einst für uns gestorben ist,
Und uns annehmen wird.
Chor.

4 Es sind schon viele Kinder dort,
Und Eng'lein sind auch da,
Mit welchen wir am sel'gen Ort,
Singen Hallelujah.
Chor.

---

42   Gott ist die Liebe.

1. Gott ist die Lie be, läßt mich er = lö = sen; Gott ist die Lie = be, Er liebt auch mich.
2. Er sand = te Je = sum, den treu = en Hei = land; Er sand = te Je = sum und macht' mich los.
3. Er ließ mich lad - en durch's Wort der Gnaden; Er ließ mich la = den durch Sei = nen Geist.
4. Du heilst, o Lie = be, all - mei=nen Jam mer; Du stillst, o Lie = be, mein tief = stes Weh!
5. Dich will ich prei = sen, du ew' = ge Lie = be; Dich will ich lo = ben, so lang ich bin.

CHOR.

D'rum sag' ich noch ein = mal: Gott ist die Lie = be, Gott ist die Lie = be, Er liebt auch mich.

---

43   Mel. : " Elkhart.''

1 Aus Gnaden wird der Mensch gerecht,
Aus Gnaden nur allein ;
Des Menschen Thun ist viel zu schlecht,
Vor Gott gerecht zu sein.

2 Gerechtigkeit, die droben gilt,
Erwirbt der Sünder nicht ;

Wer das Gesetz nicht ganz erfüllt,
Besteht nicht im Gericht.

---

44   Ein reines Herz.

Mel. : " Help me, dear Saviour, Thee to own.''

1 Schenk mir ein sanft, zerbrochnes Herz,
Das gläubig sei und rein,

Auch demuthsvoll in allem Schmerz,
Geduldig laß mich sein.
Chor:
Schaff' in mir, Gott! zu deinem Dienst
Ein Herz von Sünden frei,
Das Jesum ganz zu haben wünscht,
Sein Blut stets fühlt aufs Neu'.

2 Ein Herz, ergeben dir allein,
Als meines Heilands Thron;
Da Keiner soll regierend sein
Als Christus, Gottes Sohn.
Chor.

3 Ein Herz, das sich nicht von dir trennt
Im Leben, Noth und Tod,
Sondern in deiner Liebe brennt,
Ein solches schenk' mir, Gott!
Chor.

Die wahre Religion.

45　　8, 7, 8, 7.

1 Wenn's doch alle Seelen wüßten,
Jesu! daß du freundlich bist,
Und der Zustand wahrer Christen
Unaussprechlich herrlich ist!

Chor: O, wie köstlich und wie edel,
Ist die wahre Rel'gion,
Ja, sie tröstet mich im Leiden
Und führt mich zur Himmelswonn'.

2 Ach, sie würden bald mit Freuden
Aus der Welt Gemeinschaft gehn,
Und bei Jesu Blut und Leiden
Fest und unbeweglich stehn!
Chor.

3 Denn es ist ein Freudenleben,
Eine große Seligkeit,
Wenn man Gott ist ganz ergeben
Hier, und dort in Ewigkeit.
Chor.

Müde bin ich, geh' zur Ruh'.

46　Mel.: "I am coming to the cross."

1 Müde bin ich, geh' zur Ruh',
Schließe meine Augen zu;

Vater, laß die Augen dein
Ueber meinem Bette sein.

2 Hab' ich Unrecht heut' gethan,
Sieh' es, lieber Gott, nicht an;
Deine Gnad' und Christi Blut
Macht ja allen Schaden gut.

3 Alle, die mir sind verwandt,
Gott, laß ruh'n in deiner Hand;
Alle Menschen, groß und klein,
Sollen dir befohlen sein.

4 Kranken Herzen sende Ruh',
Nasse Augen schließe zu;
Laß den Mond am Himmel steh'n
Und die stille Welt beseh'n.

47　　10's.

1 Freudenvoll, freudenvoll walle ich fort,
Hin zu dem Lande der Seligen dort;
Land der Verheißung, wie lieblich bist du,
End meiner Pilgerschaft, selige Ruh'.
Chöre der Engel mit fröhlichem Reim
Singen entgegen mir, holen mich heim.
Freudenvoll zieh ich mein Pilgerkleid aus,
Freudenvoll, freudenvoll eilend nach Haus!

2 Herzlich Geliebte, schon drüben ich weiß,
Fröhlich und selig im himmlischen Kreis
Glücklich vollendet, sie zogen voran,
Warten am Ufer, auch mich zu empfah'n.
Höret! Sie singen so süß in mein Ohr,
Winken mir freundlich zu ihnen empor.
Werfe ich Anker am himmlischen Strand,
Freudenvoll jauchzend: O seliges Land!

3 Streckst du, o Tod mich in's düstere
　　　Grab,
König der Schrecken, mich schreckt nicht
　　　dein Stab!
Jesus, der Held, hat die Macht dir ge-
　　　raubt,
Selig, o selig ist, wer an ihn glaubt!
Hell wird der Morgen der Ewigkeit
　　　grau'n,
Hell wird mein Auge die Krone einst
　　　schau'n;
Schmiegend an Jesu Brust ruhe ich aus,
Freudenvoll, freudenvoll, selig zu Haus.

48 Mel.: "Love at Home."

1 Wonne lächelt überall,
Wo die Liebe wohnt;
Freude jauchzt in jedem Schall,
Wo die Liebe wohnt;
Da wohnt die Zufriedenheit,
Still versüßend alles Leid,
Wonnevoll entflieht die Zeit,
Wo die Liebe wohnt.
Wonnevoll entflieht die Zeit,
Wo die Liebe wohnt.

2 In der Hütte lacht die Lust,
Wo die Liebe wohnt;
Haß und Neid füllt nie die Brust,
Wo die Liebe wohnt;
Uns umblüht ein Rosenfeld,
Macht das Haus zum Wonnezelt
Und zum Paradies die Welt,
Wo die Liebe wohnt.
Und zum Paradies die Welt,
Wo die Liebe wohnt.

3 Freundlich strahlt des Himmels Blau,
Wo die Liebe wohnt;
Friede lächelt auf der Au',
Wo die Liebe wohnt;
Munter rauscht des Bächleins Tanz,
Holder flammt der Sonne Glanz,
Engel freuen sich mit uns,
Wo die Liebe wohnt.
Engel freuen sich mit uns,
Wo die Liebe wohnt.

49 Mel.: "God be with you."

1 Gott mit euch, bis wir uns wiederseh'n:
Sein Erbarmen, Seine Güte
Euch begleite, euch behüte;
Gott mit euch, bis wir uns wiederseh'n!
Wiederseh'n, wiederseh'n.
Ja, bis wir uns wiederseh'n!
Wiederseh'n, wiederseh'n,
Gott mit euch, bis wir uns wiederseh'n!

2 Gott mit euch, bis wir uns wiederseh'n:
Sein Erkenntniß, Seine Fülle
Euren Durst und Hunger stille;
Gott mit euch, bis wir uns wiederseh'n:

3 Gott mit euch, bis wir uns wiederseh'n:
Seine Allmacht, Sein Beschirmen
Tröste euch in allen Stürmen;
Gott mit euch, bis wir uns wiederseh'n:

4 Gott mit euch, bis wir uns wiederseh'n:
Seiner Nähe, Licht und Wonne
Sei im Dunkeln eure Sonne;
Gott mit euch, bis wir uns wiederseh'n:

Aus dem Englischen.

Mel.: "Old Hundred."

50 L. M. 8, 8, 8, 8.

1 Preist Gott, der allen Segen gibt!
Preist ihn ihr Menschen, die er liebt!
Ihr Himmelschöre alle preist
Den Vater, Sohn und heil'gen Geist.

Register.